The NEUTER COMPUTER:

COMPUTERS
FOR GIRLS AND BOYS

Jo Shuchat Sanders and Antonia Stone
for the Women's Action Alliance

Neal-Schuman Publishers, Inc.
New York　　　London

This book was developed by the staff of the Computer Equity Training Project at Women's Action Alliance under Grant No. G008302954 from the Women's Educational Equity Act Program, U.S. Department of Education.

The activity which is the subject of this report was supported in whole or in part by the U.S. Department of Education. However, the opinions expressed herein do not necessarily reflect the position or policy of the Department of Education, and no official endorsement by the Department of Education should be inferred.

Illustrations by Bekka Lindstrom.

Published by Neal-Schuman Publishers, Inc.
23 Leonard Street
New York, NY 10013

Copyright © 1986 by Women's Action Alliance

All rights reserved. Reproduction of this book, in whole or in part, without written permission of the publisher is prohibited.

Printed and bound in the United States of America.

Library of Congress Cataloging-in-Publication Data

Sanders, Jo Shuchat.
   The neuter computer.

   Bibliography: p.
   Includes index.
   Summary: Activities for learning what can be done with a computer, for all ages, and guidelines and strategies for planning and evaluating a computer equity program in school.
    1. Computers—Juvenile literature. [1. Computers]
I. Stone, Antonia. II. Women's Action Alliance.
III. Title.
QA76.23.S26 1986   004   86-8516
ISBN 1-55570-006-3

Contents

About This Book   vii
Acknowledgments   xiii
Introduction   Is Your Computer Neuter?   1
   The Computer Neutrality Self-Test   2
   Evidence of the Computer Gender Gap   4
      Consequences of the Computer Gender Gap   8
      Causes of the Computer Gender Gap   13
      The Link with Math Avoidance   16
      The Great Software Debate   18

PART ONE   What Kids Can Do with Computers

Pencils and Computers   25
1   Graphics   30
      Subject Areas   31
      Computer Activities 1–7   31
      Hardware and Software   33
      Graphics Resources   34
2   Word Processing   36
      Subject Areas   37
      Computer Activities 1–11   37
      Hardware and Software   41
      Preparation Requirements   42
      Word Processing Resources   43
3   Database Programs   45
      Subject Areas   46
      Computer Activities 1–6   47
      Hardware and Software   49
      Preparation Requirements   51
      Database Resources   51
4   Number Crunchers   52
      Subject Areas   53
      Computer Activities 1–7   55

        Hardware and Software   57
        Preparation Requirements for Using
        Software   58
        Number-Cruncher Resources   58
5   Programming Languages   60
        Subject Areas   61
        Choosing a Programming
        Language   61
        Computer Activities 1–7   62
        Hardware and Software   66
        Preparation Requirements   67
        Programming Resources   67
6   Computer-Based Instructional
    Software   69
        Subject Areas   70
        Computer Activities 1–8   71
        Evaluating Software   75
        Hardware and Software   78
        Preparation Requirements   78
        Instructional Software Resources   78
7   Telecommunications
    By Joy Wallace and Raymond M. Rose   80
        Subject Areas   81
        Computer Activities 1–10   82
        Hardware and Software   85
        Preparation Requirements   87
        Telecommunications Resources   89

PART TWO   Strategies for Computer Equity

The Basics of Equity   93
8   Computer Equity Strategies for Teachers
    and Staff   97
        Introduction   100
        Classroom Strategies 1–12   100
        Schoolwide Strategies 13–27   108
        Community Strategies 28–38   120
9   Computer Equity Strategies for
    Administrators   131
        Introduction   133
        Building-Level Strategies 1–7   133

Contents v

            District-Level Strategies 8–10   141
            State and National Strategies 11–12   144
 10   Computer Equity Strategies for
      Parents   146
            Introduction   148
            Home Strategies 1–9   149
            School Strategies 10–19   153
            Community Strategies 20–28   156
 11   Computer Equity Strategies for
      Students   160
            Introduction   162
            School Strategies 1–8   162
            Home Strategies 9–12   170
            Community Strategies 13–18   173

PART THREE   The Computer Equity Program

Putting It All Together   181
 12   Planning a Computer Equity
      Program   183
            Introduction   184
            Team Membership   185
            Preparation for the Planning
            Session   187
            Conducting the Planning
            Session   187
            Followup Meetings   190
 13   Evaluating a Computer Equity
      Program   191
            Introduction   192
            Program Evaluation   192
            Accountability Evaluation   195
            And for Next Year . . .   197

APPENDIXES
 A   Copyables   199
            Forms   201
            Questionnaires   211
 B   Resources   238
            Computer Equity   239
            Computer Education   248

		Sex Equity 251
		Other Resources 253
	C	About the Computer Equity Training Project 256
		Introduction 257
		Background and Goal 257
		Advisory Committee 257
		Literature Review 258
		Pilot Test 258
		Development of *The Neuter Computer* 262
		Field Test 262
		Public Education Component 266

Index 269

About This Book

The Neuter Computer: Computers for Girls and Boys was written for everyone who wants to increase or improve computer use by children, especially girls. This would include:

- Educators working in high school, middle and junior high school, and elementary school
- Parents
- Students
- Teacher trainers working in college and university education departments and teacher resource centers, and working as in-service training providers
- Educational policy makers, such as school district and state department of education officials

To be successful, *The Neuter Computer* doesn't require roomsful of computer hardware and software. Among the fifty-six computer activities and the ninety-six computer equity strategies in this book are a good number that don't require a computer at all. These are marked with a

THE COMPUTER GENDER GAP

Starting usually at the middle school age, girls are a distinct minority when it comes to computer use. Except for required computer classes (which all children take) and word processing classes (which future secretaries take), most optional computer users are male. During school, the kids who dash to the computer room at lunchtime are usually boys. Many after-school computer clubs are nearly 100 percent male. Programming electives have overwhelmingly male enrollments. A young boy's parents are more likely to buy him a home computer than a young girl's parents are, and their fathers and brothers are more likely to use it than their mothers and sisters. A young boy's parents are also more likely to send him to computer camp in the summer, especially if the camp is expensive.

The computer gender gap is evident in American schools, homes, and camps. It can be experienced in computer stores and computer trade fairs: we recently attended a computer show where about nine out of ten of the visitors and vendors were men and teenage boys. Identify the majority of computer magazine subscribers and purchasers of computer hardware and software, and the sex of people appearing in computer advertisements on television and in magazines, and you will have additional evidence of the computer gender gap.

The computer gender gap is also pronounced in the workplace, where women are outnumbered two to one as programmers and even more so at higher-level computer jobs. The one computer job in which women are well represented is that of word processing secretary, a relatively low-status and low-paying occupation.

All this is not a conspiracy on the part of American males to deprive females of their computer rights. Indeed, many girls decline the computer opportunities that are available to them. Nevertheless, a girl who says "No, thank you" to the computer in junior high or high school may also be saying "No, thank you" to a better education now and a better job later. We who are able to foresee the adult consequences of adolescent decisions have to get girls to change their attitude about computers quickly, before valuable educational and occupational options are closed to them.

Some teachers and parents of preschool and elementary school-age girls are seeing to it that they use and enjoy computers from early childhood. Unfortunately, it's quite possible that these same girls won't continue to use and enjoy computers when they get to junior high. It is the rare adolescent who can withstand the pressure of her friends, most of whom won't have had a history of familiarity with the computer, about what is—and is not—appropriate behavior for a girl, particularly when the grown-up world remains male when it comes to computers.

Equity means a fair shake. This is a book about computer equity for girls—and boys.

HOW THIS BOOK WAS DEVELOPED

The authors of *The Neuter Computer* conducted the twenty-seven-month Computer Equity Training Project at the Women's Action Alliance, a nonprofit organization that carries out research and development projects to improve educational equity for girls and women. We were funded by a grant from the Women's Educational Equity Act Program, United States Department of Education.

Working with teams of teachers, administrators, and parents at three middle and junior high schools in New Jersey, Oregon, and Wisconsin, we developed a number of strategies for increasing girls' computer use. They worked well; as a result, we wrote the first draft of this work. This preliminary version of *The Neuter Computer* was field tested with teacher/administrator/parent teams at five additional schools in California, Nebraska, Rhode Island, Texas, and Vermont.

The project was resoundingly successful. Using many of the strategies in this book, girls at the field test schools increased their computer use 144 percent in one term. Girls went from being a quarter of the optional-time computer users at the beginning of the term to half of them at the end. Teachers reported benefits to boys as well, observing that the computer equity program in their schools encouraged some boys to become interested in the computer for the first time. The computer equity field test programs gave teachers an occasion to focus on and improve the quality of computer education they offered to all students, boys and girls alike. (More about the development of this book is in Appendix C.)

WHAT THIS BOOK CONTAINS

In *The Neuter Computer* you will find what you need to know about computer equity. It provides an overview of the computer gender gap, fifty-six computer activities for kids, ninety-six strategies for increasing girls' computer use, guidelines for planning and evaluating a computer equity program in a school, forms and questionnaires (copyables), and resources. The Introduction contains a Computer Neutrality Self-Test and describes the evidence, consequences, and causes of the computer gender gap. There is also a discussion of the relationship of math avoidance and software to computer equity.

The seven chapters in Part One present fifty-six things kids can do with computers, as well as a number of introductory suggestions on how you can provide computer education if you have few or no computers. The chapters have identical formats and cover: subject areas in which each type of computer application can be used, enjoyable and educational computer activities for girls and boys, hardware and software needed, teacher (or parent) preparation requirements, and resources for each computer application. Although the fifty-six computer activities were chosen for their appeal to girls, we have observed their attractiveness to boys as well.

The computer activity chapters are Chapter 1: Graphics, Chapter 2: Word Processing, Chapter 3: Database Programs, Chapter 4: Number Crunchers (spreadsheets and graph-drawing programs), Chapter 5: Programming Languages, Chapter 6: Computer-Based Instructional Software, and Chapter 7: Telecommunications.

Following a discussion of the six basic principles underlying the computer equity strategies are the four chapters in Part Two which describe ninety-six ways to increase girls' computer use. The strategies in Chapters 8 through 11 are appropriate for teachers and staff, administrators, parents, and students who want to increase girls' computer involvement. They range in effort level from "a piece of cake" to "a martyr to the cause"; they range in hardware requirements from none to a lot; they range in locations from the home and school to the nation; and they range in interest areas from the ordinary to budding poets, physicists, and tycoons—something for everybody.

The computer equity strategy chapters are Chapter 8: Strategies for Teachers and Staff, Chapter 9: Strategies for Administrators, Chapter 10: Strategies for Parents, and Chapter 11: Strategies for Students.

In Part Three we explain how to plan and evaluate a computer equity program. The introduction makes our case for a team approach to planning and evaluating a computer equity program in a school. Then, in Chapter 12: Planning a Computer Equity Program, we cover team membership, how to prepare and conduct the planning session for the program, and follow-up meetings. Chapter 13: Evaluating a Computer Equity Program, discusses why and how to do two necessary kinds of evaluation—private program evaluation and public accountability evaluation, and what to do next year.

Three appendixes include a variety of useful materials and information. In Appendix A: Copyables, are a number of forms and questionnaires about computer use, behavior, and attitudes to be filled out by students, faculty, and parents in your computer equity program. You can copy them directly or adapt them to your needs. Appendix B: Resources, lists and describes print, audiovisual, and organizational resources in the areas of computer equity, computer education, sex equity, technology careers, and teacher training. Appendix C: About the Computer Equity Training Project, is a detailed description of the project that produced *The Neuter Computer*.

We warmly wish you the same success and pleasure in your computer equity program that we enjoyed in ours.

Acknowledgments

This book may have two authors, but many more people than we two have brought it into being. With warmest thanks and gratitude, we salute them.

THE GIRLS WHO BECAME INTERESTED IN COMPUTERS

At the pilot- and field-test schools, hundreds of girls responded to the efforts of their teachers and got "hooked" on computers. We are delighted for their sake, and are grateful to them for teaching us what we needed to know.

NATIONAL ADVISORY COMMITTEE

In two meetings and countless individual telephone conversations and letters, the members of our Advisory Committee helped us make hard decisions, served as a first-rate sounding board, and provided needed information and much common sense. We are grateful to Beryle Banfield, Bonnie Brownstein, Pat Campbell, Walteen Grady, Mario Guzman, Herb Kohl, Ann Lewin, Marlaine Lockheed, Becky Lubetkin, Carole Morning, Adeline Naiman, Linda Roberts, Guy Watson, and Mary Alice White. Their affiliations are listed in Appendix C, About the Computer Equity Training Project.

PILOT-TEST PARTICIPANTS

As computer equity pioneers, these people were among the first in the country to grapple with solutions to the computer gender gap. They built the foundation on which this book rests. At *Franklin Junior High School* in Whitewater, Wisconsin: Anne Zarinnia, Reid

Jorgeson, Mary Marion, Terri Staples, Pat Jacobson, and the principal, Jim Jacobson. At *Mount Hebron Middle School* in Upper Montclair, New Jersey: Terry Trigg Scales, Bettie Simon, Lou D'Argenzio, Sheila Allen, Kathy Stroming, Paul Koch, and the principal, Agnes Bulmer. And at *Waldport Junior High School* in Waldport, Oregon: Craig Brummett, Ginia Strickland, Sue Miller, Linda Likwarz, Kathy Ille, Gail Cape, Dee Waldo, Jill Bucy, Barbara Crandall, Kathy Kollasch, and Stan Miller; the principal, Ron Corbell; and the superintendent, John Rogers.

FIELD-TEST PARTICIPANTS

Field-test participants taught us enormously valuable lessons about how computer equity is really done in a school, and graciously contributed scarce time and enthusiastic effort to a newly discovered cause. They were wonderful partners to have.

At *Alfred Nobel Junior High School* in Northridge (Los Angeles), California: Marilyn Rehwald, Margo Pepe, Pat Stahoski, Judy Gordon, Mary Olson, Gracie Iwamasa, Ernie Scarcelli, Wayne Keith, and Sandy Stuart; the principal, George Tabain; the Director of Secondary Instruction, Dora Ballard; the superintendent, Tony Rivas; and the Los Angeles Title IX coordinator, Benita Chaum. We are especially grateful to Margo Pepe for her skills as a photographer and for her boundless and creative enthusiasm. At *Gering Junior High School* in Gering, Nebraska: Junior Alvarez, Pat Broderick, Bob Kraft, and Debby Thomas; the principal, Frank Craft; and a member of the Nebraska Department of Education vocational equity staff, Sharon Katt.

At *Camel's Hump Middle School* in Richmond, Vermont: the principal, Bob Goudreau; Steve Koenemaan, Marianne Worden, Willa Hotte, and Jim Leach; and the Vermont Department of Education sex equity consultant, Judy Stephany. At *Cumberland Middle School* in Cumberland, Rhode Island: the assistant principal, Joe Nasif, and the entire faculty for participating in our computer equity in-service session, fulfilling all the data collection requirements, and becoming aware of the computer equity issue.

In McAllen, Texas, our thanks go to the McAllen district computer coordinator, Lou Allison, for her kindness and support in offering us a control site, and to the faculty at *Lamar at Trenton Middle School*, who administered questionnaires and maintained student computer-use records without knowing exactly why they were doing so. We apologize now for keeping you in the dark.

OTHERS WHO HELPED

We are grateful to Donald del Seni, principal of Shallow Junior High School in Brooklyn, New York, and to his faculty, who were the first to show us how a principal's active leadership, commitment to sex equity, and enthusiasm for computers can inspire a faculty to eliminate the computer gender gap in their school.

We thank the following people who took time to teach us what they had learned about computer equity: Jamieson McKenzie, assistant superintendent, Princeton Regional Schools; Markita Price, Stephens College, Columbia, Missouri; Geneva Bowlin, Conway Middle School, Conway, Arkansas; David Wooley, Alma School District, Alma, Arkansas; Beth Lowd, Computer Specialist, Lexington (Massachusetts) Public Schools; Bobby Goodson, Cupertino (California) Union School District; Cliff Eberhardt, Education Specialist, Oregon Department of Education; Susan Norin, Minooka High School, Minooka, Illinois; Joan Targ, Jordan Middle School, Palo Alto, California; and Jeanne Daniel, Sex Equity Consultant, Ohio Department of Education.

We are grateful to Marian Fish and Alan Gross, our evaluation consultants for the field test. Their common sense, clarity, helpfulness, and commitment to the substance and process of the project were of enormous help to us. We thank Joy Wallace and Ray Rose, who contributed the chapter on telecommunications in record time and in fine shape.

We express our appreciation to Sharon Franklin, former editor, and Anita Best, current editor, of *The Computing Teacher*, for stretching our article deadlines and space limitations because they cared about computer equity.

We are very grateful to Nikki Persley, our administrative assistant. Although joining the staff toward the end of the project, she immediately became a full member of the team and made this project hers. Her energy and follow-through at a difficult and detailed time of the project contributed significantly to the success of this book.

Most of all, we are grateful to Sylvia Kramer, the Executive Director of Women's Action Alliance, who originated the wonderful title of this book. Her alertness to the computer gender gap at a time when no one else seemed to know about it brought the Computer Equity Training Project into being. Her uncompromising insistence on the highest standards, and the help and moral support she gave us for attaining them, have been a comfort and an inspiration to us throughout the Computer Equity Training Project.

Jo Sanders, Women's Action Alliance
Antonia Stone, Playing to Win
New York City

Introduction   Is Your Computer Neuter?

Menu

	GOTO PAGE
The Computer Neutrality Self-Test	2
Evidence of the Computer Gender Gap	4
In School	4
At Home	5
In Summer Camp	6
In the Media	7
In the Workplace	8
Consequences of the Computer Gender Gap	8
Educational Consequences	8
Occupational Consequences	9
Societal Consequences	12
Objections You Might Have	12
Causes of the Computer Gender Gap	13
The Fundamental Cause	13
Factors That Affect Girls' Computer Use	14
The Link with Math Avoidance	16
The Great Software Debate	18

The Computer Neutrality Self-Test

Is your computer neuter? Find out by means of a short diagnostic self-test.

DIRECTIONS: Answer the questions, then choose A or B for each one.

1. Does your school make the computers available to students on a free-time basis before, during, or after school? If so, make a quick count of the students you see taking advantage of the opportunity:

    _____ Number of girls   _____ Number of boys

        A. _____ Number of girls is higher.
        B. _____ Number of boys is higher.

2. Who is the computer coordinator in your school district?

        A. _____ A woman.
        B. _____ A man.

3. Does your school have a computer elective course? (If it has several, find out about the most advanced programming course.) If so, ask the person who teaches it for these figures:

    _____ Total enrollment   _____ Number of girls   _____ Number of boys

        A. _____ Number of girls is higher.
        B. _____ Number of boys is higher.

4. Ask your students for a show of hands about how many of them have ever used a computer when they didn't have to for a class:

    _____ Number of girls   _____ Number of boys

        A. _____ Number of girls is higher.
        B. _____ Number of boys is higher.

5. Ask your students for a show of hands about how many of their mothers and fathers know how to use a computer:

   ____ Number of mothers   ____ Number of fathers

       A. ____ Number of mothers is higher.
       B. ____ Number of fathers is higher.

6. Ask for a show of hands about how many of your students have a computer at home:

   ____ Number of girls   ____ Number of boys

       A. ____ Number of girls is higher.
       B. ____ Number of boys is higher.

7. Ask the computer owners for a show of hands about who uses it most at home:

   ____ Number saying girls or women use it most.
   ____ Number saying boys or men use it most.

       A. ____ Number of girls or women is higher.
       B. ____ Number of boys or men is higher.

8. Who do you see in the video arcades?

       A. ____ Mostly girls.
       B. ____ Mostly boys.

9. Who do you see in computer ads on TV and in newspapers and magazines?

       A. ____ Mostly women or girls.
       B. ____ Mostly men or boys.

SCORING: Give yourself one point for each B answer, and 0 points for each A answer.

SCORE: ____   (Maximum score: 9)

Unless your score was five, your computer isn't neuter. Most people taking this test score between six and nine. If you do too, this book was written especially for you.

4   THE NEUTER COMPUTER

EVIDENCE OF THE COMPUTER GENDER GAP

Now that computers are becoming commonplace, evidence of the gender gap in computer use is cropping up everywhere: in schools, homes, computer camps, the media, and the workplace.

The Computer Gender Gap in Schools

There is a great deal of evidence that boys are using school computers much more than girls are, especially on an optional basis such as computer electives and drop-in computer time after school.

- At the junior high and middle schools we worked with in 1984–85 in the Computer Equity Training Project, girls were one-fourth of the students who used computers on an optional basis. (See Appendix C for a full description of the project.)
- Researcher Marlaine Lockheed found in 1982 that while 40 percent of the boys at Princeton High School said they used the school computers during their free periods, only 8 percent of the girls said they did.[1]
- EQUALS, a program that promotes math, science, and computers for girls, reports that girls made up 29 percent of the students enrolled in computer electives in a 1980–81 survey.[2]
- The 1981–82 National Assessment of Educational Progress in Science found that the computer gender gap widened slightly between 1978 and 1982 for 17-year-olds who enrolled in programming courses.[3]
- The Project on Equal Education Rights tells of surveys conducted in California, Maryland, and Michigan on high school computer course enrollments. The results were remarkably similar: 38 percent, 36 percent, and 36 percent of the students in these states respectively were female, nearly a two-to-one ratio.[4]
- Albuquerque Public Schools found in 1984 that among K-12 students surveyed, 46 percent of the boys but only 32 percent of the girls said they had written a computer program. Thirty-seven percent of the boys but only 20 percent of the girls said they had taught themselves how to use a computer.[5]
- The pattern in higher education is similar.[6] In 1982, women earned 33 percent of the bachelor's, 23 percent of the master's, and 10 percent of the Ph.D.'s degrees in computer science. This is the greatest relative decline for women from bachelors to doctorate for any field except law—including mathematics.

There isn't much evidence of a computer gender gap in the elementary grades. We have heard some anecdotal evidence of little boys pushing little girls off the computer chairs, but most elementary school teachers report that children of this age are equally enthusiastic about the computer. Girls who avoid the computer generally start doing so in the middle-school years. The gap between boys' and girls' computer participation widens in high school, then widens further still through college and graduate school.

Types of Computer Use. It's important to distinguish among different types of computer use when thinking about computer equity. Learning about the computer, the first type, is generally done in computer literacy courses which, being required of all students, don't show a gender gap. Second, computer applications courses (spreadsheets, word processing, etc.) are often electives, and some observers are saying that girls are taking the word processing courses while boys are taking the math-related spreadsheet courses. If this pattern is widespread it is not a good sign occupationally.

Third, programming courses (COBOL, advanced BASIC, Pascal, and other languages), clearly exhibit a large gender gap: a ratio of 15 boys to 0 girls is far from rare. Such figures lead to the continuation of professional computer occupations (e.g., programmer, systems analyst) as mostly male. Finally, there is drop-in computer use, when students can use available computers before, during, or after school for purposes of their own choosing. At these times, the computer room is usually frequented by boys. Since computer competence is in part a result of accumulated contact hours, this is not a good development.

The Computer Gender Gap at Home

There has been less published on this subject than in the school arena, but what there is echoes the school results.

- In a survey we conducted in 1984, 459 seventh and eighth graders responded to questions about home computer use. Thirty-seven percent of the boys reported having a computer at home, as opposed to 28 percent of the girls. Of the children who had computers at home, 11 percent of the girls but only 3.5 percent of the boys said they did not use them at all. When we asked who used the computer most at home, the computer-owners replied as shown in Table 1.

Table 1 Who Uses the Home Computer the Most?

	Boys Say	Girls Say
Brother	7%	24%
Father	6%	11%
Misc. others or no one	5%	13%
Mother	4%	9%
Self	67%	21%
Self and father or brother	9%	9%
Self and mother or sister	1%	—
Sister	1%	13%

- Researchers Irene Miura and Robert Hess reported in a 1983 paper that twice as many boys as girls used their home computers, and that boys used them for longer periods of time than girls.[7]

The Computer Gender Gap in Summer Computer Camps

There is evidence that the sex discrepancy in computer use can even be seen in summer camps. In their 1983 paper,[8] Miura and Hess surveyed the directors of twenty-three computer camps (with private, public school, or university sponsorship) about their enrollments by sex and grade level. They learned that girls were 30 percent of the primary grade computer campers, 26 percent of the middle school campers, and 24 percent of the high school campers.

They also found that female enrollment declined as the difficulty of the computer curriculum increased—from 27 percent female for beginning and intermediate programming courses, to 5 percent female for assembly language courses. It also declined as the camps became more expensive—from 32 percent female for camps costing under one hundred dollars, to 15 percent female for those costing over $1,000. While the home and camp figures reflect children's personal interests and preferences, they may also reflect parents' willingness to pay for computer enrichment experiences for their sons as opposed to their daughters.

The Computer Gender Gap in the Media

The public media are often useful in showing us what we're like, so looking at computer magazines is instructive. We examined four issues of large-circulation computer magazines published in 1984: *Compute!*, *Personal Computing*, *Info World*, and *Popular Computing*. In one analysis, we counted photographs of people who were directly involved with computers, either passively—watching other people use computers or demonstrate computer products, or actively—using computers or demonstrating computer products oneself. We analyzed the photographs we found according to sex and active vs. passive computer roles:

PHOTOGRAPHS OF PEOPLE IN COMPUTER MAGAZINES

	Total no. of Photos	Percent photos of females
Passive role	28	36%
Active role	144	17%

We also looked at articles on prominent individuals in the computer industry. Only one of the four feature articles was about a woman, and it focused on her views as a woman in a male-intensive industry rather than on her experience as the executive of a software company. In addition, there were two columns of briefer profiles. One of the seven people described was Gloria Steinem. Ms. Steinem had been asked by a software developer for her opinion on the marketing strategy of a new line of software intended for a female market. The software was to be sold on hangers and feature such topics as houseplant care and shopping mall games.

Finally, we counted the authorship of all signed articles in the four issues. Of the total of ninety-one articles, 76 percent were written by men, 12 percent by women, and the rest by people with ambiguous first names. (On a related subject, we were fascinated to read in the July 1984 issue of *Concerns* that an executive of a major computer company was quoted as saying, "The buyers of [our] computers are 98 percent male. We do not feel that women represent any great untapped market.")

The advertisers and magazine publishers are showing us a world in which it is primarily men who use, sell, and write about computers. It is hard to distinguish cause from effect, though. Are the computer magazines serving a male audience because the audience is in fact male? Or are they helping to create a male audience by giving women the message that computers are not for them?

The Computer Gender Gap in the Workplace

As you are probably expecting, women are indeed underrepresented in professional computer jobs. These are 1984 figures[9]:

WOMEN IN COMPUTER-RELATED OCCUPATIONS[9]

Occupation	Percent Female
Programmers	35%
Operations and systems research analysts	31%
Systems analysts	30%

Women are even more underrepresented in computer management jobs. According to the National Alliance of Women in Communications Industries, women hold only 11 percent of the upper- and middle-management high technology positions. They are, however, well-represented in clerical computer jobs: 91 percent of data-entry keyers, the lowest-paid computer job, and 65 percent of computer and peripheral equipment operators were women in 1984.

As this review of the computer gender gap in school, at home, at camp, in the media, and in the workplace has shown, women and girls are significantly underrepresented as computer users. While it would be silly to insist on fifty-fifty parity, these figures are far more imbalanced than that. These are the facts. What are the consequences?

CONSEQUENCES OF THE COMPUTER GENDER GAP

Computers are valuable in school, for recreation, at work, and in our society at large. Girls without computer skills will experience some degree of loss in all these areas.

Educational Consequences

The next seven chapters detail dozens of ways computers can be used by children for educational purposes. Graphics, word processing, database programs, number crunchers, programming languages, computer-based instructional software, and telecommunications all have uses that extend children's knowledge, enable them to do some things in a more efficient and better way, and provide constructive enjoyment in their leisure time.

Being deprived of these advantages obviously isn't fatal, but it's not good, either, especially when it comes to school. Knowledgeable teachers feel that using a computer enables many children to learn more and better. All students deserve the opportunity to do their work better with computers. We assume you agree.

Occupational Consequences

Girls who don't have computer skills won't be able to get jobs that involve computers. About 2.5 percent of the workforce today is in a computer-related occupation, such as programmer or computer-equipment operator; in the computer industry itself; and in other industries such as communications, manufacturing, transportation. But much more than 2.5 percent of the work force uses computers in their jobs. More and more people in advertising, wholesale and retail trade, business services, banking, medicine, and administration can't believe they ever managed to do their work before the advent of word processing, database programs, spreadsheets, and graphics programs. The computer enables them to work more efficiently, and in many cases to accomplish tasks they could not accomplish without a computer.

A "computers are not for me" mind set will spell bad news for anyone planning to work for a living. All indications point to computer skills as a strong advantage or a requirement in an increasing number of occupations.

Computer Job Projections. The U.S. Department of Labor estimates that 50 to 75 percent of the jobs available to the next generation will involve computers in some way. Although many will only involve simple button pushing, others will require higher-level skills for jobs in sales and service, development of computer applications in many fields, operation of computer equipment, design of hardware and software, and especially manipulation of information in their jobs.

Fields that are now just beginning, such as laser technology, genetic engineering, and robotics all have the computer as their common denominator. They are expected to expand greatly within the next decade. In the old familiar standbys of manufacturing and business, the workplace has changed more in the last ten years than in the previous hundred. This change is due to computers.

10   THE NEUTER COMPUTER

In a recent article on the job outlook through 1995,[10] Valerie Personick, an economist with the U.S. Department of Labor, writes: "Most industry forecasts indicate that there will be more than ten times as many computers in use during the next decade than exist today." Another way to grasp the magnitude of the computer revolution is her projection that "purchases of computer equipment will represent about one-fifth of all capital expenditures by businesses, by far their largest item of durable equipment spending."

According to Personick, the occupations of computer systems analysts, computer programmers, and computer equipment operators are expected to have larger growth ratios from 1982 to 1995 than any other occupation: 85.3 percent, 76.9 percent, and 75.8 percent respectively. These three occupations alone will create over half a million new jobs by 1995, while related high technology occupations will create a million more.

Computer Careers Pay Well. Most computer occupations compare favorably to many other professional jobs in terms of salary. In U.S. Department of Labor statistics for 1981 we find that three of the top twenty jobs ranked by salary were directly computer-related: electrical/electronic engineers, computer systems analysts, and operations and systems researchers.[11] This is twice the proportion of computer occupations present in the list of all professional jobs. Moreover, computers are widely used in most of the other occupations on the top-twenty list as well.

A computer career does not guarantee a high salary, of course. A systems analyst, the top professional computer job, earned $31,158 on the average in 1984, while a data-entry keyer, the lowest job, earned $13,291.[12] However, women in the computer field—as in every other job field in our economy without exception—earn less than men in the same job classifications. In fact, there is an unfortunate but very reliable rule of thumb to occupational salary levels: the more women working in a particular job, the lower the salary.

Nevertheless, the computer field promises high pay to women in comparison with other occupations. As a computer industry researcher observes, "Relative to what professional women earn in other occupations requiring similar years of educational attainment, computer programming and systems analyst positions enable women to earn at the top of the female earnings hierarchy."[13] For example, a bachelor's degree in computer science tends to lead to a beginning salary in the mid-twenties, while the same four years spent getting a bachelor's degree in elementary education will only yield a salary in the upper teens. And since raises are usually percentages of base salaries, the gap widens with time.

Money is obviously not the only consideration in the choice of a career, but it ranks way up there with job satisfaction at the top of most people's list of factors to consider when we choose careers. This is as true of women as of men.

But how important are careers for women? The answers to the following questions may surprise you.[14]

1. What percentage of American women are in the civilian labor force?
    ANSWER: Fifty-five percent in 1985. The others are in school, retired, disabled, or full-time homemakers.
2. How many years will girls now in school spend in the work force?
    ANSWER: Twenty-nine years. Men will spend thirty-nine years.
3. How many of today's high school girls will work for a living?
    ANSWER: Nine out of ten.
4. What percent of mothers with children under age 18 are working for pay now?
    ANSWER: 62 percent in 1985.
5. How many families are supported solely by women?
    ANSWER: Ten and a half million families in 1985, or 17 percent of all families. The women supporting them had average incomes of about $9,000 a year.
7. What percent of American households today consist of a wage-earning father, a homemaker mother, and two children?
    ANSWER: Only 5 percent resembled the traditional American family in 1985. (Think about single-parent families, including those who are separated or divorced, the widows and widowers, the never-married, the families with fewer or more than two children, and especially the working wives.)

Women are working, and will continue to work, for the same reason men work: to support themselves and their families. The Women's Bureau of the Department of Labor estimates that two-thirds of working women are in the labor force because of economic need: they are the sole support of their families, or their husbands earn less than $15,000 per year. The salary element of a career choice—other job considerations such as working conditions and advancement potential notwithstanding—is an important one for the average girl or woman to think about.

12 THE NEUTER COMPUTER

In this light, computer skills take on new meaning. Girls who choose to avoid the computer now may close off job options and advancement possibilities later on.

Societal Consequences

Computer equity also matters in terms of our role as citizens. Our society is changing rapidly under the impact of computers, lasers, robotics, and other high-technology developments. Many people are concerned about what these developments will do to employment patterns, national security, privacy rights, crime, and our sense of ourselves as independent beings with control over our lives. While these are in part real issues that deserve all the attention and intelligence we can devote to them, they are also in part exaggerated fears, fed by ignorance of the technology and our relation to it.

Students who are uncomfortable with the computer and avoid it are likely to continue to feel threatened by computers as adults. They are likely to see technology not as a tool we elect to use, but a force against which we are helpless. Refusing to deal with technology or becoming obsessed with its power are products of this fear. Both are dangerous ways for citizens to make decisions about the role of technology in our government and our lives. Since women are half of our citizens we need to make sure that girls have enough contact with computers so that they can make informed decisions when they grow up.

Objections You Might Have

Perhaps you feel that these dire consequences are exaggerated. You might object that when today's girls grow up and see for themselves the need for computer skills they will obtain the training they need then. This is not necessarily true for two reasons. For one, it is much more difficult to attend school as an adult than as an adolescent. The time and energy demands of maintaining a home, caring for children, being a wife, and often working to support the family can make school an unattainable luxury. Second, as you will see later in this chapter, there is an emotional component to computer avoidance. A woman without computer skills may not respond to help-wanted ads requiring computer know-how by saying to herself, "Well, I guess I'll learn computers now." Instead, she might eliminate them from consideration.

Another objection you might make is that if girls choose not to study computers, that's their business. In answer to that objection we offer the following analogy. We know that most children would choose recess over reading if they could. We don't give them the choice because they're too young to make it wisely since they don't realize they're going to need reading skills far more than ball-playing skills when they grow up.

In the same way, we need to exert strong pressure on girls who don't realize the implications of computer avoidance. This is not to say that we insist that every girl become a computer professional, but rather that we must do what we can to counteract their tendency to say "No, thank you" to the computer.

CAUSES OF THE COMPUTER GENDER GAP

So why are girls avoiding the computer? With all the educational, occupational, and societal advantages of computer skills, why do we see a computer gender gap? We are only beginning to find out what causes it. Computers have been widely used in school and at home for at most five years, and the observation that they seem to appeal particularly to males is even more recent. Nevertheless, some explanations have surfaced.

The Fundamental Cause

The gender gap usually begins to show up at the middle-school level because this is the age of puberty. Adolescents are figuring out what it means to be men and women in this society, and their conclusions are naturally not yet very subtle. Behavior that seems especially characteristic of the opposite sex becomes forbidden at this age. To fit in with the all-powerful peer group, adolescents adopt the accepted sex role norms with almost fanatic fidelity.

To adolescent eyes, one of the many characteristics that distinguish males from females is that males use computers. Young girls see boys in the video arcade and men in the TV computer ads. If a parent uses a computer, it's probably the father. Computer "hackers" are almost always male. In school, girls see boys flocking to the computer room whenever they have time, and they hear boys using esoteric computer language very much like the esoteric language boys use to talk about sports or cars.

Most of us would agree that crossing the sex-role line can make us more or less uncomfortable. As we get older, we cross it nevertheless—men diaper babies, women do home repairs—because our sense of ourselves as masculine or feminine is no longer dependent on such superficial indications. For teenagers, however, outward manifestations such as style of dress or how one spends free time are perhaps the major element of their fledgling sex-role definition. It is threatening to ignore the rules that dictate proper behavior for each sex; teenagers run the risk of alienating their friends, all of whom appear to obey the rules scrupulously.

This is why simply making the computer equally available to each sex doesn't work. Girls do a sort of mental and emotional arithmetic. The minus of accepting the invitation—entering what they perceive as a male domain and therefore throwing their sex-role development into confusion and running the risk of losing their friends—can easily outweigh the plus of learning a valuable and enjoyable new skill. Moreover, since girls have had little experience with computers, the plus is abstract; it pales compared to the immediacy of the minus.

Factors that Affect Girls' Computer Use

To come down a bit from the rarefied atmosphere of this analysis, let's see how the computer gender gap translates into the reality of school and home. Please remember that even though we are referring to "girls" for the sake of brevity, these factors are not true for all girls—and they are true for some boys. Do you recognize your school in any of these?

Discouraging Factors in General. There are a number of reasons why, in general, girls are discouraged from using computers.

- *Computer Users.* Girls observe that computer users are mostly men and boys. More precisely, girls observe that their girlfriends don't use computers and are reluctant to enter the computer room.
- *Math.* Computers are associated with math because of their history as number-crunchers, the fact that they are used in math classes more than any other subject, and the frequency with which computer teachers are math teachers. We already know that math is male-identified; see below for more on math.
- *Machines.* Computers are seen as machines. Not socialized as children to be comfortable with machines, many girls are uncomfortable around computer-machines.

- *Software.* Much recreational and even some educational software has a definite male slant, featuring war, sports, and other typically male interests. When a program has an identifiable central character, it is nearly always male. See below for more on software.
- *Classes.* Computers are more often used in classes that particularly interest boys and usually have male teachers: math, science, business management, etc. They are less often used in classes that especially appeal to girls and usually have female teachers: language arts, music, art, etc.
- *Teachers' assumption.* Verbally or behaviorally, teachers express an assumption that computers are more appropriate for boys or that boys are more interested in them. This becomes a self-fulfilling prophecy.
- *Parents' assumption.* Ditto, and parents' assumption can also be expressed financially.

Factors that Discourage Active Interest. There are other factors that operate to discourage girls who are interested in computers from using them. Among these factors are:

- *Boys capture computer time.* When there are few computers and many children, boys in their enthusiasm for the computer tend to capture the available time slots. This is especially true when computer use is on a first-come, first-served basis.
- *Nonassertiveness.* Socialized to believe that assertiveness is unfeminine, girls tend to be more reluctant than boys to claim their right to a fair share of computer time.
- *Competing interests.* Some adolescent boys get involved with computers to the exclusion of other interests. Adolescent girls, because of their desire for social contact that is developmentally strong at this age, tend to have many other interests that compete for their free time.
- *Home responsibilities.* Some parents require more home responsibilities after school from girls than boys—for babysitting, housework, cooking, or other chores—thus reducing the amount of free time girls could spend at the computer.
- *Overprotectiveness.* Some parents respond to their daughters' puberty by limiting unstructured time away from home, even if it's to take place at school.
- *Unorganized computer time.* Unorganized free-time computer use can be a solitary and fragmented activity; many girls prefer sustained projects and group activities with their friends.

- *Computers without instruction.* Computer use without instruction encourages the use of video games and similar software that require no preparation. Many girls prefer applications such as graphics or spreadsheets, which they are not likely to pick up on their own. (Many teachers have observed that girls seem to be interested in the computer as a practical, purposeful tool—the means to an end, while boys seem to be intrigued by what it can do for its own sake—the end itself.)

The Sex of the Teacher Doesn't Matter. One factor commonly thought to be at the root of the computer gender gap is the sex of the computer teacher. If there were more women in this job, the thinking goes, the role model influence would close the gap. The best evidence indicates this is barely true. Asked if "seeing female teachers use computers" would encourage them to use computers more, only 11 percent of the girls we asked in our pilot test said yes. This compares with 7 percent for "seeing male teachers use computers," and 62 percent for "seeing girls you like use computers."[15]

A recent study has confirmed our own observation that women are in fact quite well represented among computer teachers. In a national survey conducted in early 1983, it was found that 67 percent of the computer teachers in grades one through six and 44 percent of those in grades seven through twelve were female.[16]

The most convincing evidence to our mind that the sex of the computer teacher is relatively unimportant arises from our own experience. Of the eight schools that participated in the Computer Equity Training Project, three had male teachers, four had female teachers, and one had both a male and a female teacher. Nevertheless, all eight schools had computer gender gaps ranging from three-to-one to four-to-one.

We have even heard of schools whose programs were helped by having a male computer teacher. (We call this our "Gorgeous George" strategy of computer equity.) When the teacher is a teenage heartthrob type, the computer room is invariably jammed with girls. This book, however, is for the rest of us—male and female—who have to make up in other ways for our lack of the natural endowments Gorgeous George possesses.

THE LINK WITH MATH AVOIDANCE

Because of the history and primary use of computers in math classes, the association of computers and math is important to understand. During the last ten years or so, much attention has been paid to math avoidance among women. It surfaced first as an employment issue. In 1976, Lucy Sells published a paper[17] in which she reported on a survey of high school students admitted to the University of California at Berkeley in 1972. Forty-three percent of the young men and an astounding 92 percent of the young women had taken so little high school math that they were effectively limited to five majors: humanities, music, social work, elementary education, and guidance and counseling. These career fields, while surely satisfying, pay significantly less than many others. Sells called mathematics "the critical filter," a memorable phrase that called public attention to the high price paid by women and the society at large when girls are not encouraged to take—or are discouraged from taking—math.

Two years later, Sheila Tobias wrote *Overcoming Math Anxiety*, a book that widened the debate.[18] Emphasizing the emotional and attitudinal component of math avoidance, Tobias pointed out that many women believe themselves incapable of doing mathematics having been told that they are since childhood. Society considers mathematical ability a male characteristic, much as we might consider nurturing ability a female characteristic.

As a result, girls learn early to equate mathematical achievement with masculinity. It is easy to see how this becomes a self-fulfilling prophecy, with the results Lucy Sells observed. Since then, many other researchers and educators have documented and tried to overcome math avoidance among girls and women. There is much to support the contention that math avoidance is learned. Standardized tests for mathematical ability and achievement show no difference between the sexes until adolescence, when girls begin to fall behind boys. The gap widens through high school. It is not a coincidence that this is the age when girls begin to conform to society's norms of "appropriate" female behavior in preparation for their lives as adult women.

Since the tests taken by younger children show no difference in mathematical ability, it must be that adolescent girls find it necessary to deny their mathematical ability in favor of their femininity. As a result, many women agree that "women are no good at math" and shy away from courses and jobs that require math. And on the whole, math-related careers pay better than those that involve no math.

To the extent that girls' feelings about computers are similar to their feelings about math, we should be concerned about the emotional basis of computer avoidance. We can't at all be sure that they will learn computers later, when they see the value of computer skills in the job market.

THE GREAT SOFTWARE DEBATE

There are really two great software debates. One concerns violence in children's software and the other addresses software that is "appropriate" for girls.

Does Violent Software Turn Girls Off?

Writers of articles about the computer gender gap usually blame violent, macho software. Children who use recreational programs and a good number of educational programs engage in search-and-destroy missions, laser and missile attacks, combat with bad guys or hostile aliens, and other acts of aggression and war. There is even a program called GLOBAL THERMONUCLEAR WAR in which players develop strategies for destroying the world. The program provides complete figures on human and economic casualties; presumably, the higher the figures, the better a player one is.

Naturally, the writers say, this kind of environment is not hospitable to girls. Naturally, they say, girls avoid computers. But to our knowledge neither these writers nor anyone else has conducted a really reliable test of the assumption that shoot-'em-ups turn girls off. In fact, we found in one of our surveys that both girls and boys like arcade games, although boys were far more likely to say they "loved" them than girls, who merely "liked" them.

So the debate rages on. Recognizing that neither we nor anyone else knows enough about the effect of violent software on girls, we think we know how to resolve the debate. We have to throw out the question.

A far more important question to answer is whether violent software is good for children of either sex. We can't possibly want to teach children antisocial values, to solve problems by annihilating whatever gets in their way, or to have a win-survive/lose-die attitude in the face of difficulty. The best evidence indicates that children learn from and are shaped by everything they do in their formative years, although not necessarily in equally influential ways. Even though we cannot say for sure that a child who plays a violent computer game will become a violent adult, it makes no sense to believe it has no effect at all on him or her. And that effect, however small it may be, cannot be good.

Recently, some software designed especially for girls has come on the market. These programs stress cooperation rather than conflict. Are we supposed to conclude that girls cooperate while boys fight? If we have "good" software for girls, are we supposed to leave the violent software in place for the boys? And if we have girl software and boy software, shouldn't we have girl readers and boy readers, girl math books and boy math books?

Few teachers would permit children to read magazines on sadism or pornography in school, because such material is harmful to the emotional and social development of young people. If that is so, then we should not permit them to play computer games that convey equally harmful messages. Asking whether violent software turns girls off begs the question. If it's not good for girls, it's bad for boys, too. It should have no place in our schools.

Is Some Software "Appropriate" for Girls?

In their well-meaning and laudable efforts to make girls as enthusiastic about the computer as boys are, some people are pushing "appropriate" software. Translated, this means software with subjects that are supposedly attractive to female people. For instance, programs that feature interior decoration, recipe records, and shopping mall games.

One database program specifically aimed at the female market reveals its manufacturer's notion of what computer-using females need and like. The package comes on a hanger and pictures a woman's carefully manicured and nail-polished hand resting delicately on a computer keyboard. The instruction booklet introduces the use of a database (essentially a computerized card file used to record and cross-reference information) with a situation every woman is presumed to identify with:

> It's Saturday morning and it's time to take out my [name of software]. I just vacuumed the living room and you should see the mess I had to clean up under my Boston Fern! Dead leaves all over the floor! And the African Violet hasn't had flowers in months.
> It's so hard to remember which plants like to be moist; which should dry out between waterings. And feeding all my plants! Who can remember when I did and when I should? I really feel like my plants represent the most disorganized part of my life! So [name of software]—here I come!

"I forgot to tell you," Marie of the instruction guide continues, "Sam is my husband and while he means well, he's forgetful about holidays." So she prints out the information on roses "so I can leave it where Sam will find it." Then she discards the roses entry "because I really don't want it in with all my plant entries—I just want the roses for Valentine's Day."

As you can see, software developed especially for girls or women tends to play to the lowest common denominator: female as wifey at best, and as sneaky manipulator or dumb bunny at worst. These programs are sexist and insulting to girls and women with normal intelligence and interests. So pushing this kind of software (or "fluffware" as Brady and Slesnick call it in their article; see the computer equity bibliography) is hardly to be recommended as a way to introduce girls to the advantages of computers.

There is another version of the "appropriate software" theme: pushing word processing and graphics and music software because girls allegedly love writing and art and music. There's certainly nothing wrong with these applications—indeed, we devote whole chapters to them in this book—and we have seen the power of PRINT SHOP, for example, to attract girls in droves to the computer. But there's plenty wrong with assuming that girls won't go on to develop an interest in spreadsheets or telecommunications or programming. This is a sexist assumption.

So by all means use any software that works (and that isn't insulting) to get the girls to the computer, but then introduce them to all the other challenging and rewarding ways in which people use computers.

NOTES

1. Gina Kolata, "Equal Time for Women," *Discover* (January 1984), pp. 24–27.
2. Kay Gilliland, "EQUALS—Computers in Education," *Math/Science Network Broadcast* 2 (Fall 1981). EQUALS is at the Lawrence Hall of Science, University of California, Berkeley.
3. Ronald E. Anderson, Wayne W. Welch, and Linda J. Harris, "Inequities in Opportunities for Computer Literacy," *The Computing Teacher* (April 1984), pp. 10–12.
4. J. Lipkin and L. Martin-McCormick, "Microcomputers in the Classroom: Are Girls Getting an Even Break?" Project on Equal Education Rights (PEER), Washington, D.C.
5. "A. P. S. Computer Education Pilot Project Evaluation. Report #2: Implementation." Albuquerque Public Schools, Division of Instructional Research, Testing, and Evaluation. December 1984, pp. 39–40.

6. National Center for Education Statistics, *Digest of Education Statistics 1983–84*. Government Printing Office, 1984, p. 114.
7. Miura, Irene and Hess, Robert D., "Sex Differences in Computer Access, Interest, and Usage." Paper presented at the American Psychological Association meeting, Anaheim, Calif., August 1983. Miura and Hess are at Stanford University, Palo Alto, Calif.
8. Ibid.
9. Gloria P. Green, and Rosalie K. Epstein, *Employment and Earnings* 32 (January 1985), pp. 176–80.
10. Valerie A. Personick, "The Job Outlook Through 1995: Industry Output and Employment Projections," *Monthly Labor Review* (November 1983), pp. 24–49.
11. Peter Ward, "Occupational Earnings from Top to Bottom," *Occupational Outlook Quarterly* (Winter 1982), pp. 21–25. The OOQ is published by the Bureau of Labor Statistics, U.S. Department of Labor.
12. Bureau of Labor Statistics, U.S. Department of Labor. "Usual Weekly Earnings of Employed Wage and Salary Workers," 1984 Annual Averages, unpublished tabulations from The Current Population Survey.
13. Myra H. Strober and Carolyn L. Arnold, "Integrated Circuits/Segregated Labor: Women in Three Computer-Related Occupations." Institute for Research on Educational Finance and Governance, School of Education, Stanford University, November 1984, p. 15. Project Report No. 84-A27.
14. "Facts on U.S. Women Working." Women's Bureau, U.S. Department of Labor, 1986. Also "Working Mothers and Their Families: A Fact Sheet." National Commission on Working Women, Washington, D.C., March 1985.
15. Jo Shuchat Sanders, "Making the Computer Neuter," *The Computing Teacher* (April 1985), pp. 23–27.
16. Henry Jay Becker, "Man and Women as Computer-Using Teachers," *Sex Roles* (August 1985), pp. 137–48.
17. Lucy Sells, "The Mathematics Filter and the Education of Women and Minorities." ERIC Reports, 1976.
18. Sheila Tobias, *Overcoming Math Anxiety*. (Boston: Houghton Mifflin Company, 1978.)

PART ONE: WHAT KIDS CAN DO WITH COMPUTERS

Pencils and Computers

Think about pencils. Does the use of pencils create a sex equity problem? So it could be with computers. School computer use by girls and boys becomes more equal as the computer becomes a routine piece of classroom equipment in virtually every kind of classroom and class projects routinely involve the computer. Because they are just starting to use computers, most schools don't yet have this pervasive, multidisciplinary approach to the use of computers in education. Many are concentrating on providing students with computer literacy courses and on teaching beginning programming.

While this emphasis can be valuable for students who have never worked with computers before, those who have already learned something about computers are asking what they can do with the skills they have acquired. More often than not, teachers don't have enough answers. In the near future, more and more students at all grade levels will be asking that question. This is a good time to start stockpiling the answers.

Interestingly, girls may be more concerned about these answers than boys. While boys often seem to be interested in the computer for its own sake, just to see what it can do, girls are often more interested in the useful things the computer can do for them. Those of us, therefore, who see the importance of maintaining and strengthening girls' interest in computers need to identify and have at the ready a number of computer skills applications which will serve the interests of girls. Not coincidentally, these applications are good for boys, too.

The seven chapters in Part One present an overview of ways in which schools can use computers throughout grade levels and across subject areas. We have tried to make our suggestions comprehensive. Although the hardware and software of computer technology are constantly changing, the activities we offer will remain educationally sound, stimulating, and especially attractive to girls.

Some computer activities presented in these chapters can be implemented in the classroom to enrich existing curriculum. Others are more appropriate as student projects in optional computer time such as during lunch, before or after school, or at home. Some of the activities can be carried out by individual teachers, while others call for team planning. Most involve at least some preparation on the part of the teacher. But learning to use new and powerful tools always requires some training, and usually practice as well. Fortunately, in the case of computers the rewards for time spent are enormous.

You will notice a few recurrent themes in the next seven chapters. First, we emphasize the computer as a tool as opposed to an object of study. This isn't just because we think tool applications such as spreadsheets or database programs are versatile and cost-effective, but because we believe they promote creative teaching and learning by doing. Since the applications in this book reflect adult uses of computers, learning them gives students skills they will need when they enter the adult world.

Another theme is group learning, social interaction, and cooperative problem solving. Adults recognize that many life and career problems, to say nothing of national or world problems, are most productively tackled in group situations: think of brainstorming sessions and think tanks. Nevertheless, the traditional school emphasis on individual work and achievement does little to prepare students for a group approach to problem solving. The computer activities in Chapters 1 through 7 enable students to experience more interdependent problem-solving techniques.

Finally, since this is a book about raising girls' computer participation to the level of boys', our computer activities appeal especially to girls. But we don't suggest catering to some stereotypical idea of what girls want; don't buy recipe and interior decorating software—unless you also plan to use it with boys. And we most emphatically do not recommend excluding boys from the computer. In fact, our experience is that the computer activities in this book tend to increase boys' computer participation as well as that of girls. There certainly isn't anything wrong with that.

When You Don't Have Enough Computers

Schools that have many computers in their classrooms, or can move them around the building according to need, are already set up to use the computer in classroom activities. But most schools don't have a lot of computers, and some don't have any.

If yours is a school with none or too few, there are still ways to integrate computer activities in your classroom work. You'll have to do some homework of your own, though, to find ways for your students to get access to computers outside of class time. Some suggestions:

- *Using the school computers.* If your school has any computers at all, talk to the person in charge of them and try to arrange a schedule of times when your students can use them. In one of our test sites, the first school computer was in the front office. A social studies teacher made arrangements with the school secretary for some of his students to use that machine. The secretary even offered to teach them word processing.
- *Using another school's computers.* Another school nearby may have computers that your students could use. A local college or university might have a teacher-training computer laboratory with time that could be made available to your students.
- *Using a community organization's computers.* Does a community center—YMCA, YWCA, YMHA, YWHA—library, science museum, or other community-based organization where you live have computers available to the public?
- *Using home computers.* Some of your students probably have computers at home. Perhaps you can arrange with their parents to invite a few classmates over.
- *Using a computer store's computers.* If there is a local computer store (or a business that has many computers), try to schedule after-school time when your students can go there to do their computer assignments. These arrangements can result in some useful publicity when the local paper prints a story about it: publicity for your work in promoting equity of computer access, and free publicity for the computer store.

If none of these methods pans out, all is not lost. In Chapters 1 through 7 you will recognize computer-related activities that don't require any computers at all by

Choosing and Using Software

Choosing what software to use is perhaps the most important part as well as the most difficult part of using computers well. In Chapter 6 we suggest criteria to apply when selecting software. A list of application-specific resources is found at the end of Chapters 1 through 7, and among the copyables in Appendix A are several software evaluation forms.

Whether you are selecting software from an existing school supply or evaluating it for possible purchase, it is important to keep in mind how it is going to be used. If you have only one computer in your classroom, choosing a program that requires one student to a computer and sixteen hours to work through it simply isn't practical, no matter how wonderful the program is.

If students can use school computers during their free time—study periods, lunch, or before or after school—the available software should be suitable to that kind of use. One school stocked their software library with applications programs such as spreadsheets and word processing, but didn't teach students how to use them. As you can imagine, there wasn't much free-time computer use by students in this school. With instruction, however, these programs would have been excellent for the students' free time, along with good educational games that generally don't require instruction beforehand.

We recommend excluding arcade games from school software libraries. There is nothing educational about them, they glorify violence and destruction, and their near-exclusive appeal to boys increases the computer gender gap.

From Technophobe to Technophile

Whatever your resources, introducing computer projects that are useful in the subjects girls and boys are studying will enhance the value of computers in girls' eyes, and give them a chance to exercise their creativity. You don't have to become a computer buff yourself. You may not even have to learn how to operate a computer, although we urge you to try. You might like it.

In fact, as a way to build a comprehensive and equitable computer program in any school, it's important for all the teachers to have an opportunity to learn how to use a computer. This can be done by in-service training (see Chapter 9, Administrator Strategies), or you can plunge ahead and learn on your own. If your school has the software and you decide to go ahead and teach yourself, don't be discouraged by manuals. Reading manuals can give the impression that they are written in cahoots with the people who advertise "Learn D-Base II in a weekend—only $300." Use the manuals as a resource instead of a training course.

If you can't find the answer to a question in the manual, call the store that sold the software to the school, or call the 800 (toll-free) number of the software publisher and ask. Almost every serious applications program has such a number and lists it in the manual, so use it. The folks on the other end are usually bored and happy to hear from you. Make a friend. On the other hand, be wary about giving your students these 800 numbers. You could lose your friend.

If you are a dyed-in-the-wool technophobe, there is probably another teacher in your school, or even a student, who can help your students learn how to use computers. What you do need, however, if you are going to integrate computer activities into your class planning or homework assignments, are ideas. There's nothing more discouraging than staring at a computer and having no idea of what to use it for.

We think the ideas presented in the next seven chapters will breed more and better ideas in you, and eventually your students. Seeing their enthusiasm and joy in learning may be what is needed to transform you into a technophile.

1 Graphics

Menu

	GOTO PAGE
Subject Areas	31
Computer Activities 1–7	31
Activities 2, 5, and 6	
Hardware and Software	33
Graphics Resources	34

SUBJECT AREAS

ART	SCIENCE	SOCIAL STUDIES
LANGUAGE ARTS	MATH	PHYSICAL EDUCATION
BUSINESS EDUCATION	HOME ECONOMICS	HEALTH EDUCATION
SPECIAL EDUCATION		

Creating graphics on the computer engages students' imaginations and their analytical abilities. It's also fun. Schools have found graphics one of the best ways to integrate the computer across the curriculum, and it's a nearly foolproof way to get girls involved with computers. When you visit a school, you can tell right away if graphics software is being used: there are computer-generated banners, signs, and posters all over the place.

Computer graphics has found widespread use in art and design occupations as well as in business. By incorporating this computer application in a class, you are introducing students to a valuable employment skill, one that has special appeal for many girls.

Graphics activities that don't require hands-on use of a computer are indicated below by 🚫💻.

COMPUTER ACTIVITIES 1–7

Activity 1: Illustrate Student Writing

Students can illustrate their creative writing or reports in any of their subjects, including social studies, geometry, science, and physical education (that's right: students can illustrate plays in team sports). The illustrations can range in sophistication from stick figures to the design of a stamp or a diagram of parts of the heart.

Activity 2: Compare Different Art Media 🚫💻

Compare the treatment of a subject in clay, pencil or charcoal, paint, collage, and computer graphics. This can be an individual or a class art project.

Activity 3: Cards or Invitations

Girls especially love to create greeting cards or party invitations to send to family and friends, and it's very easy to do. See the next activity, which involves the same software.

Activity 4: Posters and Library Displays

Fanfold computer paper is used to make banners for school events. Remember that banners will be displayed horizontally but come out of the printer vertically. It's an intriguing problem for students to solve. This is an activity for which inexpensive commercial software is widely available, such as PRINT SHOP. The software makes it easy for students to create banners, signs, and posters by providing ready-made graphics or allowing students to create their own. It makes a great after-school activity, particularly around holidays.

Since the software can combine text and graphics, students can use it to announce new library books or software as a school service project. Their presentations, recorded on disk, can be preserved for continued use. The printouts make a nice display in the library, the computer room, or on a main hall bulletin board.

Activity 5: Computer Graphics Audiovisuals

"TRON" was not particularly stimulating as a motion picture, but its computer graphics design was terrific. Showing professionally developed computer graphics is best after students have tried it themselves, so they can appreciate what they are seeing. On the other hand, this is a way of exposing students to computer graphics even if your school doesn't have any computers. (See Graphics Resources at the end of this chapter for a list of such movies.)

Activity 6: Field Trips

Field trips to businesses or organizations that use computer graphics can be fascinating. Consider print shops where type is set electronically, commercial art studios that use computers for layout and design, businesses that use computer graphics for sales presentations and/or company reports, and many others.

You don't even have to visit if you can get a copy of some of the computer-generated visuals. Ask a company representative to come in and explain them to your students. You can display them on a bulletin board and discuss the way computers have made this kind of artwork possible.

Activity 7: Computer Art Show

Show students' computer graphics work either on the computer monitor or in printout form. If you charge admission to parents and friends you can raise money to buy another computer. Ask the owner of a local silk screening shop to contribute the silk screening of student designs onto T-shirts or plain fabric. Show and sell those, too. Someone who's a demon for extra work could really have a good time with this one. (There's more on computer art shows in Teacher Strategy 20 in Chapter 8.)

HARDWARE AND SOFTWARE

A *color monitor* for the microcomputer is desirable, although much can be done with a monochrome (black and white) monitor. A *color printer/plotter* would also be a plus, but this is still a fairly expensive piece of hardware. An ordinary dot matrix printer with a graphics interface enables students to print out black and white versions of their graphics work.

A *graphics tablet*, such as the currently popular KOALA PAD, and the software that accompanies it are easy to learn how to use. It takes about twenty minutes for a novice to find out what a graphics tablet can do. This hardware/software combination offers a wide range of applications, from simple line drawing and framing with circles and rectangles to multicolored pictorial representations.

There are other programs that enable students to do almost the same things, but use a *lightpen, mouse,* or *joystick* to draw on the screen instead of a tablet. A program like PAINT, for example, or one of its spinoffs such as MacPAINT for the Macintosh computer, are simple enough for a first grader to use. As with the graphics tablet, learning to use this software takes only a few minutes, but achieving skill in its use can take considerably longer. Young or disabled children usually find the tablet easier to handle than a joystick or lightpen, which respond more slowly and less accurately to user direction.

Graphics utility programs are used commercially and can be used in schools as well. They require more study and practice before one becomes adept. Because they have greater versatility and can produce more sophisticated results, graphics utility programs can be just right for older or more advanced students. You will need considerably more preparation time for learning the program yourself than if you use programs like KOALA PAD or PAINT.

Programming languages can be used for graphics activities. Some, such as Logo, Commodore 64 BASIC, or True BASIC, let students create multicharacter animated graphics as well as more static designs. Logo is particularly good for graphics work by students who have had little or no programming experience. Beginners can create simple but interesting shapes and designs with Logo, and advanced students can make a whole animated world. Tablets and graphics utilities afford a more direct route to the end result, but using a programming language for computer graphics provides programming experience as well. If your school doesn't have graphics software, you might want to consider this alternative. Logo and other programming languages are discussed in greater detail in Chapter 5.

GRAPHICS RESOURCES

Articles and Books

1. The October 1985 issue of *The Computing Teacher* contains a two-page spread of computer art done by junior high students, including a cross-section of an active volcano. Two other pictures shown were award winners in a computer art contest.
2. The same issue of *The Computing Teacher* contains two articles describing integration of graphics into classroom learning activities:
   "Learning Opportunities with Delta Drawing," by Cynthia Burt, pp. 42–43."Computers and the Language Arts: Koala Pad Pictures Have a Place in Your Classroom," by Scott Greer, pp. 45–48. See also People Resources, below.

3. "Hardware Hits Hollywood," by Kathy Chin, *Infoworld*, vol. 5, no. 25, pp. 33–36. Describes the role of computer graphics in making movies.
4. "Easy Sources of AV Materials for Computer Literacy," by Jerry Johnson, *The Computing Teacher*, October 1984, pp. 56–57. Lists types of sources Johnson found in his community and gives suggestions for locating similar sources in yours; bibliography. Jerry Johnson is a regular contributor to *The Computing Teacher* and you can write to him for an update on this article.
5. "Creating Poster Art," by Shirley Torgerson, *The Computing Teacher*, November 1985, pp. 16–18. Good ideas for teaching communications skills via poster-making.
6. The November 1985 issue of *Byte* is a special issue on graphics hardware. While the equipment described is perhaps too sophisticated (and expensive) for school use, these articles give a good idea of how the hardware is being used professionally.
7. *Preparing for High Technology: CAD/CAM Programs*, by A. Abram, W. Ashley, R. Hofmann, and J. Thompson. National Center for Research in Vocational Education, Ohio State University, Columbus, OH 43210. Of practical interest to design and drafting teachers in high school, this book describes the current state of computer-assisted design (CAD) and computer-assisted manufacturing (CAM), and may be of general interest to other teachers.

Films with Computer Graphics

Many of the movies that follow deal with intergalactic war or space violence in one form or another, unfortunately. Our list is a list, not a recommendation.

Tron   *Star Trek II*
The Wrath of Khan   *Blade Runner*
The Last Starfighter *Star Wars*
Looker   *"V"*
2001   *Raiders of the Lost Ark*
2010

People Resources

SCOTT GREER
8525 N.E. Wygant
Portland, OR 97220

"Koala Pictures Idea Disk with Booklet." Send $10 for a booklet of project ideas, references, a bibliography, and examples of student work accompanied by a utility disk. Specify the make and model of your computer. Don't send for this unless you have a Koala Pad.

2 Word Processing

Menu

	GOTO PAGE
Subject Areas	37
Computer Activities 1–11	37
Activities 10 and 11	
Hardware and Software	41
Preparation Requirements	42
Word Processing Resources	43

SUBJECT AREAS

ALL SUBJECT AREAS THAT INVOLVE WRITING, INCLUDING SPECIAL EDUCATION

It's pretty safe to say that no one who has become comfortable with word processing wants to write without a word processor ever again. Among the most widely known of computer applications, word processing has uses that extend way beyond the production of business letters and reports. Journalists use a word processor to file stories; authors use it to write books; ordinary people use it to write letters.

Any kind of writing at work or at home can be done more easily with a word processor. Electronic editing capabilities remove the drudgery of rewriting, thus freeing the writer to focus on content and pay attention to thought sequence, sentence structure, grammar, spelling, punctuation, proofreading, and other components of good writing. Students, like the rest of us, hate to rewrite by hand.

Teachers have told us that special education students in particular make impressive progress in their writing and reading skills when they use word processors. Not having to form letters laboriously by hand encourages a freedom of expression they haven't had before. They write, and what they write, they read.

If you're concerned about introducing word processors because your students lack typing skills (called "keyboarding" in computerese), you can take heart from our special education teachers. Their students are certainly not alone in feeling rewarded for their hunt-and-peck typing with perfectly formed and printed characters. They and other students may even become motivated to learn touch-typing when they realize how it speeds up progress at the keyboard. The main thing is that no matter which typing method they use, students do more writing, do better writing, and enjoy it more with a word processor.

COMPUTER ACTIVITIES 1–11

Activity 1: Creative Writing

Encourage your students to use word processors for their creative writing assignments. In addition to the benefits described above, students can achieve wonderful special effects with a word processor, such as:

>   Although
>   formatting com-
>   mands can be seen as
>   "troublesome," they can enable
>   students to give visual shape to their
>   written work. Imagine a poem or story
>   about the Earth where the words form
>   a ball in the middle of the page.
>   Most of the work can be
>   accomplished with a
>   centering format
>   command.

Or how about this?

```
The
    snake
        slithered
            through
                the                        under
                  tall      disappeared       a
                    grass, and                 – –
                                              –   –
                                             –
                                            –    rock.–
```

Activity 2: Group Writing

Encourage your students to work together on stories and poems. Two or three or even more kids around the computer can share ideas, change words, and experiment with format using each other as sounding boards and editors. Or they can take turns contributing sentences or paragraphs. Group writing stimulates cooperation and expands vocabulary and writing skills.

Activity 3: Essays and Reports

Almost everything we said about creative writing applies equally well to student essays and reports in any subject area. If you'd like students to include graphs and charts in their work, look at the suggestions in Chapters 3 and 4 on databases and number crunchers.

Activity 4: Letters

Letter writing is fun, perhaps because it implies a response. It's even more fun with a word processor because of the special functions that make formatting a business or formal letter so easy. Your students will learn these formats almost by osmosis as they express their opinions to members of Congress and newspaper editors, write to organizations and businesses for information, or respond to items they've read about in computer magazines. Friendly letters are good, too. The informal style can be learned in the process of writing to relatives, acquaintances, and pen-pals. Word-processed letters can even be illustrated if you have the graphics software (see Chapter 1).

Activity 5: Drill-and-Practice Exercises

You or your students can use the word processor to construct drill-and-practice exercises to be done on the computer:

- *Reading comprehension drills:* students answer the questions that follow the paragraphs.
- *Spelling drills:* students correct misspellings or fill in missing letters.
- *Punctuation drills:* students insert punctuation that fits the needs of the sentence.
- *Style exercises:* Students rewrite a paragraph in narrative style into conversational style.
- *Grammar:* students highlight all the adverbial phrases or construct "silly sentences" from supplied lists of nouns, adjectives, verbs, adverbs, etc.
- *Word problems in arithmetic or algebra:* if students do the inventing and entering, you'll never again have to resort to those boring boats getting rowed upstream.

Activity 6: Individualized Instruction

All these drill-and-practice exercises can be individualized, either by printing them out selectively or by using the word processor as the medium for communication between you and the student. A drill or a test can be saved under the student's name and contain individualized comments and instructions. Similarly, the student can leave messages for you.

Activity 7: Class Notes

When class note-taking is encouraged or required you can plan a rotation so that each student has the opportunity to take the notes directly on the word processor or to enter them later. Having the sequence of notes available on disk is helpful to students who have been absent, or others who simply want to check their notes against the class record. You can review these notes at leisure, insert comments, or add information.

This procedure is also helpful in teaching note-taking techniques and saves you time in looking through each student's notebook.

Activity 8: Literary Magazine

A classwide or schoolwide literary magazine can be put together by a group of students, each of whom enters his or her own work. If you're the advisor to such a magazine or interested in starting one, you'll be delighted that all editing can be done on the word processor and the final product can be printed out immediately. With a graphics program, students can also include illustrations of their work. (See Teacher Strategy 22, Chapter 8.)

Activity 9: School Newspaper

A school newspaper or a club newsletter can be organized in the same way. (See Teacher Strategy 23, Chapter 8.)

Activity 10: Field Trip

Visit a local business where word processing is used. Your local newspaper's use of word processing might be interesting for students to see. (See Teacher Strategy 29, Chapter 8.)

Activity 11: Guest Speaker

If there is an author among the parents who uses a word processor, ask her or him to come and talk to the class. Was it hard to learn? Has using it changed thinking, writing, or work habits? (See Teacher Strategy 28, Chapter 8.)

HARDWARE AND SOFTWARE

A *monochrome (black and white) screen* or *monitor* is preferable for word processing. Ordinary television sets or lower-priced color monitors give poor print resolution, particularly if the word processor you are using adjusts the screen to eighty columns across. Eyestrain is never enjoyable. A color monitor that corrects this problem costs about a hundred dollars more than those usually used in schools.

Word processing requires a *printer*. An ordinary dot matrix printer will do, but get one that prints the full width of the page. Most teachers prefer the dot matrix for student use, since type style and special character generation can be controlled with computer commands rather than by changing parts of the printer. A letter-quality (or daisy wheel) printer is usually more expensive than a dot matrix and is needed only when the text is intended for formal or professional presentation.

There are hundreds of *word processing programs* available for virtually every model of microcomputer and new arrivals on the market appear weekly. No one word processing program does everything, so it's vital to try out the program that you intend to buy before committing to purchase. Find a store that will let you do this.

Beware of the trap set by the program that is easy to learn but cumbersome and limited in day-to-day use: you and your students will be using it for much longer than you'll be learning it. We can't recommend a particular word processing program, but we can offer some criteria for choosing one:

- *Screen display*. It's important to see the text on the screen as it will appear in the printed copy. This seems like a simple condition, but most standard computer screens accommodate only forty characters per line of type. The standard paper size accommodates eighty typewritten characters. Some computers (we're talking about hardware now) come with adapters that permit either a forty-column or

an eighty-column screen display. If you have an eighty-column adaptor, look for a word processing program that takes advantage of the capability. If your computer can't create a screen display of eighty columns, be sure the program you buy has a command to make the text appear on the screen exactly the way it will be printed.
- *Preformatted text.* Try to get a word processing program that has built-in formatting commands. The most troublesome commands to master in learning word processing are those that format, for example, set margins, justify text, center, and set tabs. If the program is preformatted students don't have to learn the commands until they're needed for some special purpose.
- *Special features.* Investigate the capabilities of the program for underlining, boldface, and sub- and super-scripts. Perhaps you'll need accent marks for foreign languages or Greek letters for math. Be sure that both the software and the printer have these capabilities.
- *Spelling Checker.* Many teachers like to use word processors that can be integrated with spelling checkers. We're not about to start debating the pedagogical virtues of spelling checkers here, but if this is important to you look for a program that has a compatible and easy-to-use checker.
- *Other questions* you may wish to ask are:

    Is the "search and replace" function easy to use?

    How many lines of text can be stored before you have to start a new disk?

    Is it possible to join one disk-stored file to another?

    Can you choose single, double, or triple spacing? Can you see your text this way on screen?

    Are instructions for returning to the main menu printed on the screen?

    Is there a "help" screen available to jog your memory if you forget a command or if something happens that you don't understand?

    What other software can be integrated with this word processor?

PREPARATION REQUIREMENTS FOR SOFTWARE USE

Plan to spend anywhere from two to ten hours learning how to use the word processing software, depending on its degree of complexity and how you expect to use it. Three cautions: students tend to learn faster than adults, so don't eliminate a program that meets all your other requirements just because it's hard for you to master. You'll be surprised how easily students can learn the key-stroke sequences.

Second, don't wait until you know everything about the program before you start using it, either for yourself or with your students. The best way to learn how to use a word processor is to set yourself a task that needs doing and then do it. Use the manual to look up answers, not as a step-by-step guide. Finally, don't expect word processing to save you time the first time you work with it. That will come later.

WORD PROCESSING RESOURCES

Articles and Books

1. *Using Computers in the Teaching of Writing,* edited by James L. Collins and Elizabeth A. Sommers, Upper Montclair, N.J.: Boynton Cook, 1985. Reports from teachers who use word processing to teach writing, all of whom were initially opposed to the method. Their experiences are provocative, honest, and perhaps inspirational.
2. *Writing with a Word Processor,* by William Zinszer, New York: Harper & Row, 1983. The author relates his journey from technophobe to technophile with all the gory details.
3. *Without Me You're Nothing,* by Frank Herbert, New York: Simon & Schuster, 1980. The author of the *Dune* series relates his experiences with personal computing, including word processing.
4. *Every Teacher's Guide to Word Processing,* by Michael N. Milone, Jr., Englewood Cliffs, N.J.: Prentice-Hall, 1985. One hundred and one computer activities using a word processor for classroom teachers in all grades.
5. The February and October 1984 issues of *Consumer Reports* contain unbiased reports on word processing, especially software.
6. "Can Word Processing Help the Writing Process?" by Fay Wheeler, *Learning Magazine,* March 1985. Frank discussion of the pros and cons of word processing in the classroom. Emphasizes that without good teaching students will not learn no matter what the tool.
7. "Classroom Publishing with Micros" by Peter Anderson, *The Computing Teacher,* October 1985. A how-to guide for producing a literary publication with a computer. (See People Resources, below.)
8. "Free or Inexpensive Software for Teaching the Language Arts" by Dorothy Starshine, *The Computing Teacher,* November 1985. Free or cheap

public domain sources of adequate-to-good word processing and other language arts-oriented software.

People Resources

STEPHEN MARCUS
South Coast Writing Project
Graduate School of Education
University of California
Santa Barbara, CA 93106

Dr. Marcus offers low-cost (about $3.50) books, curriculum ideas, and reprint articles on word processing to increase entry-level writing skills of college students. Many suggestions are appropriate for junior and senior high classrooms.

PETER ANDERSON
Marion W. Cross School
Norwich, VT 05055
(Or via CompuServe: 72437,2251)

Peter Anderson has set up Book/net, an international exchange of books and other publications produced by students on microcomputers. The project contains suggestions for all curriculum areas.

3 Database Programs

Menu

	GOTO PAGE
Subject Areas	46
Computer Activities 1–6	47
Activity 5	
Hardware and Software	49
Preparation Requirements	51
Database Resources	51

SUBJECT AREAS

ART	SCIENCE	MATH
MUSIC	SOCIAL STUDIES	PHYSICAL EDUCATION
HOME ECONOMICS	HEALTH	LITERATURE
		SPECIAL EDUCATION

This is the information age, and its downside is information overload. Teaching students the new skill of information management with a database shows them how information—facts, figures, notes, etc.—can be organized and made easily retrievable.

A database program is simply a computerized, cross-referenceable file cabinet holding many individual file cards. Databases assist doctors in diagnosis, provide access to legal history and precedent for lawyers, send catalogs in ever-increasing volume to homes and businesses, and aid researchers and students in all fields. They are used whenever cataloged or listed information needs to be cross referenced.

The total information contained on the computer version of a file card is called a "record." Any heading for information on the record (the category used for cross referencing) is called a "field." Different programs have different limits on the number of characters that can be used in a single field, from as few as twelve to thousands. The collection of all records with a single field design is called a "file."

Unlike paper file cards, one database record can contain many pages of information; the computer equivalent of a page is what can be seen on the screen at one time. Depending on the program, records vary from one page to a hundred pages of data. Some permit unlimited amounts of data. You probably don't need a program with this unlimited capability, which is costly, but unless you're using the software only with first or second graders you shouldn't limit yourself to the one-page kind.

Using database software in school introduces students to this very practical computer application. Some of the computer activities listed below can provide valuable resources to your school.

The major part of the student's learning takes place from the research done to obtain the information for the database, and from the process of organizing this information into usable form. There are at least three other benefits gained from using the computer to record information: the process of entering the information reinforces the student's learning, the records being made may have long-term usefulness, and finally, the student is learning a practical computer skill.

We know of one student who got a fine lesson in the logical difference between the words "and" and "or" when he tried to do a search for all the United States presidents born in Massachusetts *and* Vermont.

COMPUTER ACTIVITIES 1-6

Activity 1: Personal Interest Files

We're convinced that no girl (or boy, either) of middle or high school age exists who doesn't have a personal interest that involves cataloging information of all types: stamps, stars, coins, recording artists and groups, birds or butterflies, cosmetics, astrology, friends, sports, biorhythms, movies, computers, books, opera—you name it. All can be cataloged and cross-referenced with a database program. This makes a good after-school project.

Activity 2: School Files

Ask students to use a database for the school library, class lists, team lists, and win/lose records. They can develop a system for evaluating teachers. Don't be nervous—most students are too scared of you not to be generous. They can catalog the school's software collection and include student comments. Make these files available for students to search so they can have the experience of using a database as well as making it.

Activity 3: Curriculum Applications

If you plan carefully, the database work done by your students can be used by your class next year, by other classes, or it can become part of the school's reference library.

- *Science:* Important scientists in world history; major technological inventions; records of lab experiments detailing equipment and procedures used, expected results, observed results, and conclusions; classifications of animals, plants, minerals; bibliographies or written sources of information; listing of student projects; parts of the body, the earth, the sky, or the sea, with appropriate detail.
- *Health:* Foods with caloric content, vitamin content, recommendations for daily consumption, sample menus; accidents with common hazards, appropriate action to be taken, and safety precautions; illnesses with symptoms, action to be taken, possible after effects, and treatment; and exercise—its purpose, posture, description.
- *Geography:* States of the Union or countries of the world, with population, land area, climate, principal products, government leaders.
- *Career Education:* Jobs with educational requirements, average starting salary, work environments, career ladders, growth projections, locations of availability.
- *Reports (all subjects):* Research tools, bibliographies, statistical information.
- *Art:* Cataloging artists by era or school, listing works of art and museums where they can be seen.
- *Mathematics:* Word problems by application and process.
- *Literature:* Summer and winter reading lists, with authors, titles, capsule summaries, and student evaluations; authors in literature, with dates, countries, works, style, personality quirks, prizes won, special interest areas, student recommendations for reading.

This list is only a sample. We're sure you will think of many more applications in your particular subject area.

Activity 4: Field Trip

Visit a local legal office that uses LEXIS or another legal database. This is a fine field trip for a computer science class, but it might also be appropriate to social studies when the class is studying the judicial system. If your community's library or hospital is computerized a visit to see how they use a database could be equally valuable. Find out what other businesses or service agencies use databases and pay them a call.

Activity 5: Public Information Database

A commercial online database is accessed via telecommunications. It costs real dollars, but if your school subscribes to an online network such as CompuServe or The Source have the class log in and explore the vastness and complexity of a main-frame computer database. Before using one, discuss with students the considerable differences between these commercial database systems, which have to process enormous amounts of information for many users simultaneously, and the school database students have learned to use that processes information one piece at a time.

If your school doesn't belong to an online service, find out if a parent or one of your friends does and is willing to demonstrate it to the class. Bear in mind that the host will get a bill for fifty dollars or more for an hour of online time. Meet with her or him ahead of time to learn thoroughly what information is available and prepare your class on what they will be doing and what questions they want answered. Afterward, be sure the class sends its host a special thank-you for the opportunity.

For more about telecommunications, see Chapter 7.

Activity 6: Your Own Records

By using a database yourself for your student records or curriculum planning ideas, students can get intrigued with the idea of trying it themselves. This is especially true if you just happen to use it when students are around.

HARDWARE AND SOFTWARE

Most database software, like most word processing software, is best used with a *monochrome (black and white) monitor*. Color monitors often make the text hard to read. A *printer* is essential in most cases. Searching the database can be done on the screen, but if the information is really of value to the students they'll want to print out a copy to save. Since it's unlikely your school will get database software before word processing software, the chances are that a printer is already available.

Many *database programs* can be used in conjunction with specific word processing programs. You use the word processor to write a general piece of text, leaving blanks (or whatever symbols you are told are necessary by the software instruction manual) for specific pieces of information stored in your database. The appropriate information from this database can then be entered automatically. Combining two pieces of software in this manner is called "integrating."

If integrating a database with a word processor is going to be useful to you, both pieces of software have to be compatible—sort of like a key and a lock. Usually database programs and word processing programs must be by the same manufacturer and sometimes from the same series of software programs. A single set of integrated software might be available for the particular brand and model of microcomputer you are using; ask the supplier.

As you might imagine from the short list of applications we mentioned, database programs vary widely. At least one, PFS FILE, has been packaged specifically for school use on Apple hardware, and offers a number of model files for use in social studies and science classes. There are many others for every brand and model of microcomputer. Below are some guidelines for selection.

- *Screen display.* The most important selection guideline is that students be able to see on the screen the format for recording their information. Some programs make you create a form by specifying field lengths in the form of a list and never let you see your field design on the screen. It's much harder this way to know if the field design will be adequate to your purpose.
- *Erasing records.* Be sure you can erase records. If a student accidentally adds a record to the wrong file or enters incorrect information, it shouldn't have to stay there forever. It's also important to be able to add new information to existing records and to update existing information.
- *Search capabilities.* Search capabilities should include: displaying records in the order you prefer—some programs do this alphabetically, others in order of entry, *and* multiple conditions for cross-referencing. In a file of animals, for example, you might want to retrieve all animals that are vertebrate *and* suckle their young *and* have tree-climbing ability. You might even want your students to try to find all the United States presidents born in Vermont *and* Massachusetts, just to make a point.

PREPARATION REQUIREMENTS FOR SOFTWARE USE

If you're planning to use a database program with students, you'll need anywhere from half an hour to ten hours or more to learn it yourself. The time depends, of course, on the complexity of the software. When you learn to use a database, just as with a word processor, it's better to set yourself a task that needs doing rather than following the tasks outlined in a manual. This way, in addition to learning the software, you've got something you want when you're finished.

DATABASE RESOURCES

For resources on online database subscriber systems, see Chapter 7.

Articles and Books

1. "Problem Solving with Data Bases" by Beverly Hunter, *The Computing Teacher*, May 1985, pp. 20–27. Perhaps the clearest short introduction to the subject. Gives a rationale, examples, and lesson plans incorporating a database in social studies classes.
2. "Enhance Your Students' Thinking, Problem Solving, and Research Skills" by Craig Burton, *AEDS Monitor*, May/June 1985. Emphasizes the information-handling skills students can develop from classroom use of database software.
3. *The Intelligent Schoolhouse: Readings on Computers and Learning*, edited by Dale Paterson, Reston, Va.: Reston Publishing, 1984. The section "Using an Information Retrieval System in a Junior High School" by Nerby and Hilgenfield (pp. 144–46) presents goals and objectives as well as class planning for using a telecommunications database.
4. "PFS News" is a newsletter from Software Publishing Corporation available to any person or organization that buys a PFS software product. Contains many ideas contributed by users for database applications and suggestions for integrating your database with other software. Write to: Software Publishing Corp., 1901 Landings Dr., Mountainview, CA 94043.

4 Number Crunchers

Menu

	GOTO PAGE
Subject Areas	53
Computer Activities 1–7	55
Hardware and Software	57
Preparation Requirements for Using Software	58
Number-Cruncher Resources	58

SUBJECT AREAS

SCIENCE	MATH	SPORTS
HOME ECONOMICS	HEALTH	SOCIAL STUDIES
SPECIAL EDUCATION		

Hundreds of software programs have been written to address the special financial needs of business, including accounting, payroll, sales, and forecasting. But there are others that are appropriate for number processing in schools, and in many more classes than just business education. A graph-drawing program and a spreadsheet program are two widely used number-crunching programs.

A *graph-drawing program* does just what you might expect—it draws bar graphs, line graphs, and circle graphs. It's useful in math, science, social studies, and any other subject where graphs are a learning tool, and is therefore an excellent addition to a school's software library. It's often easier to teach graph drawing and interpretation on the computer than with a book since this software, like word processing, removes the drudgery and lets students concentrate on the content and the meaning.

One important feature of a graph-drawing program is that students can easily switch from bar to line to circle graph representations of the same numbers. In comparing the graphs they can choose the one that best displays the data under consideration. For example, which of these graphs in Figure 1 do you prefer to represent data on how students spend their time during an average twenty-four-hour day, and why?

Most graph-drawing programs get their numbers from a database program or a spreadsheet and so have to be compatible with this software. Some integrated packages have database, spreadsheet, and graph-drawing capabilities all together.

A *spreadsheet* is even more versatile. It processes numbers—any kind of numbers, not just money numbers—the way a word processor processes words. It's a giant ledger page, usually at least sixty-three columns across and 254 lines down. Of course you can't see the whole thing all at once on a computer screen, but you can look at any part of it you like and often at several parts at once by splitting the screen into what are called "windows."

You can make a spreadsheet do almost any kind of calculation just by entering formulas in terms of the column and row to be referenced. It transfers information from one location to another au-

54   THE NEUTER COMPUTER

Figure 1 **A.** Line Graph. **B.** Circle Graph. **C.** Bar Graph

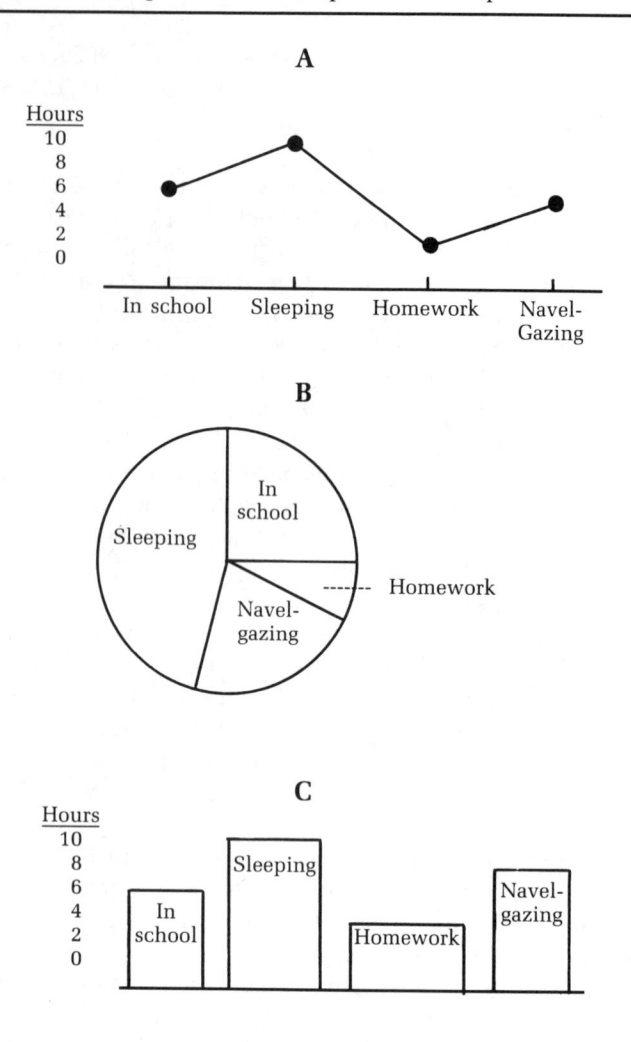

A

Hours
10
8
6
4
2
0

In school   Sleeping   Homework   Navel-Gazing

B

In school
Sleeping
Navel-gazing
Homework

C

Hours
10
8
6
4
2
0

In school   Sleeping   Homework   Navel-gazing

tomatically, has some graph-drawing capability, allows text entry, and does calculations in integers and decimals as well as dollars and cents. A spreadsheet is therefore a multipurpose tool. It's also an extremely powerful tool. Some people think that spreadsheets are too powerful to introduce in schools—"You wouldn't teach a kid to use a saw to cut butter, would you?"—but we think the analogy is wrong because a spreadsheet is just as useful for processing simple number relations as complex ones. The program is certainly not too difficult for girls and boys to learn, and it's a valuable tool for school and life experiences to come.

COMPUTER ACTIVITIES 1–7

Activity 1: Calculate Grades

Your students will have a more realistic perception of their grade-point averages if they calculate the average with a spreadsheet as the term progresses instead of waiting for your revelation at the end of the term. Ask them to enter their numerical grades and find test averages, weekly averages, and course averages. Letter grades can be entered as well if the letters are first translated into numbers: A = 90, B = 80, etc. When new grades are entered, the spreadsheet automatically adjusts the average—upward, we hope.

Activity 2: Analyze Polls

Analyze questionnaires, surveys, quizzes, or tests. How many answered A, B, C, or D? The spreadsheet can be programmed to calculate percentages and averages and adjust them as new data are added. If the survey is recorded on a database, a compatible spreadsheet can retrieve data directly. Use a graph-drawing program to chart the results.

Activity 3: Demographic Data

Have students make spreadsheets and graphs showing statistics on your school, community, state, or the country as a whole. Use the U.S. Census reports for information, or generate your own data by taking a community survey. Once the analysis is printed out, students can:

- Look for trends: home owners to renters, large to small households
- Discover reasons for geographic shifts of specific populations
- Explore relationships: education vs. job status, population density vs. number of children, sex of wage-earner vs. income level

56   THE NEUTER COMPUTER

What comparisons are significant? What appears irrelevant? Encourage students to think about the data needed for a particular purpose and how the information should be organized to make the best use of the spreadsheet's capabilities.

Activity 4: Budgets

Students can create budgets for their personal expenditures, class trips or activities, or a school project or event. The spreadsheet is wonderful for estimating break-even pricing. For example, students enter an event's expenses and the number of tickets they expect to sell, then they enter $2 as the ticket price. Bankruptcy! They next try $3, or $4, and even $5: could they sell that many expensive tickets? If not, how could they reduce expenses? The spreadsheet's "what if?" capability is perfect for identifying the conditions for turning loss into profit. Of course, formulas need to be set up to do this, but figuring out the formulas is part of the learning process.

Activity 5: Science Experiments

Students can enter the results of science experiments and let the spreadsheet do the calculations. Knowing what formulas to use on what data is an exercise in clear thinking all by itself. Presenting experimental results visually by means of a graph-drawing program reinforces and deepens their learning.

Activity 6: Mathematical Concepts

Mathematical concepts can be introduced earlier in the curriculum with a spreadsheet. It provides a way to experiment with functions, binomial series, slope, differential equations, simultaneous equations, and more. Students using a spreadsheet can examine the content of these mathematical ideas before they learn the fancy names of the concepts or how to make the calculations.

Activity 7: "What If . . . ?"

What if I had an allowance of a million dollars a month?
What if I shared my paper route with my sister?
What if I got 100 on the next test?
What if I'm ten years old and only three feet tall?

Charts that list age, height, weight, and frame figures can be programmed to let students play "What if . . ." by entering their own real or even fictitious statistics and reading the resulting growth predictions calculated by the spreadsheet. "What if . . ." is a favorite sport with spreadsheet programs, and the variations on the game are limited only by your students' imaginations.

HARDWARE AND SOFTWARE

Like word processing and database software, a spreadsheet looks better on a *monochrome (black and white) monitor*. If you have color monitors, be sure to check the legibility of the spreadsheet's video output (how it looks on the screen). On the other hand, it's quite nice to have a color monitor for graph-drawing purposes. If you're planning to use both a spreadsheet and a graph-drawing program, it might be worth spending the extra hundred dollars for a monitor that provides good resolution for color as well as monochrome.

You will also need a *printer*. Spreadsheet charts are often printed out sideways, so a fifteen inch or longer carriage is preferable to a twelve inch carriage. All graph-drawing programs require a dot matrix printer (with graphics interface if specified). An impact or letter-quality printer can only print letters, not graphics. If you have a color plotter, students' graphs will get a lot of oohs and ahs.

Spreadsheet software varies in complexity. For school use, you can avoid the highly complex (so-called "advanced") versions. Since no spreadsheet has yet been designed specifically for educational use, ask about those designed for family use. They tend to be simpler. Choose one that will allow you to:

58   THE NEUTER COMPUTER

- Replicate formulas
- Split the screen vertically or horizontally
- Enter text as well as numbers easily
- Change column width
- Format for integers, decimals, or dollars and cents
- Save or print a portion of the spreadsheet

In choosing *graph-drawing software*, be sure that:

- The program is compatible with the spreadsheet or database you have, and there are clear instructions on how to integrate them.
- The software lets you print a variety of graph forms from the same data.
- You can give a title to the entire graph as well as its axes or component parts.

PREPARATION REQUIREMENTS FOR USING SOFTWARE

Learning to use a spreadsheet well enough to introduce the tool to your students will take at least three hours, and more if you're a computer novice. Experiment with the principal commands to know which ones you'll need for your purposes. Learning it thoroughly can be a much longer affair. Some people believe that spreadsheet commands constitute a computer language of their own, and a rarefied one at that, but you needn't go that far. In-depth exploration of a spreadsheet's capabilities can be rewarding, however, since the more you learn about it the more classroom uses you'll find for it.

NUMBER-CRUNCHER RESOURCES

Articles and Books

1. "A Spreadsheet Way of Knowledge" by Stephen Levy, *Harpers Magazine*, November 1984. Describes the history of spreadsheet software and its impact on the use of microcomputers in business and industry.
2. *Hands On!*, Vol. 7, No. 1, pp. 19–21, gives suggestions for incorporating spreadsheet use into math and science classes. Write for the newsletter to Technical Education Research Centers, 1696 Massachusetts Ave., Cambridge, MA 02138.

3. "Social Studies, Spreadsheets and the Quality of Life," *The Computing Teacher* (December/January 1985–86, pp. 13–17. Discusses how students in social studies class can use a spreadsheet to assess cities' quality of life and learn about the "subjective nature of statistics."

People Resources

VINCE O'CONNOR
Milwaukee Public Schools
P.O. Drawer 10K
Milwaukee, WI 53201

Dr. O'Connor distributes copies of his paper, "Spreadsheets: Applications and Implications for Algebra" along with a VISICALC data disk. Send him a blank disk and specify the make and model of your computer. You must have VISICALC software for this.

JAN McDONALD
SUNY-Albany
Department of Teacher Education
1400 Washington Ave.
Albany, NY 12222

Dr. McDonald distributes a paper called "My Favorite Sources and Problems for Computer Solution," and a number of them are quite appropriate for spreadsheet use. Enclose a stamped, self-addressed envelope.

5 Programming Languages

Menu

	GOTO PAGE
Subject Areas	61
Choosing a Programming Language	61
Computer Activities 1–7	62
Hardware and Software	66
Preparation Requirements	67
Programming Resources	67

Programming Languages   61

SUBJECT AREAS

COMPUTER SCIENCE
PROGRAMS CAN BE WRITTEN FOR ALL SUBJECTS

A programming language conveys the instructions to a computer needed to create original programs or software. The better known languages include BASIC, Logo, FORTRAN, COBOL, Pascal, C, and LISP, although there are many others. Until recently, nearly all schools taught programming in BASIC, which stands for Beginner's All-purpose Symbolic Instruction Code. BASIC was the language originally built into most microcomputers, and for a long time it was the only language available for microcomputers in schools.

Today, software is commercially available for many computer languages. This fact, plus the College Entrance Examination Board's decision to require Pascal for advanced placement computer credit, have resulted in having to make a choice about the language used to teach programming before college. In particular, the availability of Logo, a computer language designed for young children with no previous academic experience, has stimulated widespread introduction of programming as early as in the first or second grade. Because Logo is a powerful language and structurally closer to Pascal than BASIC is, a number of schools are continuing Logo instruction into high school.

CHOOSING A PROGRAMMING LANGUAGE

If the debate about what programming language to teach is still raging in your school, we suggest you support Logo. Because Logo moves the student quickly to a position of control and because Logo programming is based on logical word sequences (unlike BASIC, which is based on number sequences), we find that Logo tends to appeal greatly to girls—and to many boys as well.

Another appealing feature of Logo is that initial programming can be learned through graphics. Of course BASIC can be introduced with graphics, too, and so, if BASIC is your choice we recommend you introduce it with graphics.

To illustrate the difference between the graphics approaches in the two languages, compare the following programs in Logo and

62 THE NEUTER COMPUTER

BASIC for drawing a square on the screen. We're not asking you to understand the programs; we just want your gut reaction.

```
         LOGO                          BASIC
TO SQUARE                      10 REM SQUARE
    REPEAT 4 [FORWARD 50 RIGHT 90]   20 GR
END                            30 COLOR = 1
                               40 HLIN 10, 20 AT 10
                               50 VLIN 10, 25 AT 20
                               60 HLIN 10, 20 AT 25
                               70 VLIN 10, 25 AT 10
                               80 END
```

Perhaps programs speak louder than words.

The choice of a programming language is only the beginning, however. Whether you're giving students their first experience of programming, or whether your students already have considerable programming experience—and this situation is becoming common as more students learn programming in elementary school—you'll want programming projects that challenge their abilities in interesting and productive ways. Some suggestions are given below; others can be found in the Programming Resources section at the end of this chapter.

COMPUTER ACTIVITIES 1–7

Activity 1: Interactive Computer Conversations

One teacher told us she got girls interested in computers by teaching them how to program conversations with the computer. Even the simplest kinds of computer conversations can lead to class discussions of artificial intelligence (AI in computerese), an area of computer technology that's intriguing more and more research scientists every year.

Conversation programs are also useful for illustrating and defining exactly what the computer "knows" and what it must be "taught." The following program, written in TERRAPIN or KRELL Logo (for the Apple) or Commodore 64 Logo, is an example:

```
TO CONVERSE
    PRINT [TELL ME SOMETHING ABOUT YOURSELF.]
```

```
    MAKE "ANSWER REQUEST
    IF FIRST :ANSWER = "I THEN PRINT  (SE  [ARE YOU TELLING
    ME YOU] BUTFIRST :ANSWER "? )
    IF FIRST :ANSWER = "MY THEN PRINT  (SE  [ARE YOU TELL-
    ING ME YOUR] BUTFIRST :ANSWER "? )
    IF NOT ANYOF (FIRST :ANSWER = "I )  (FIRST :ANSWER =
    "MY )
         THEN PRINT [YOU DON'T SAY!]
    CONVERSE
  END
```

To make this program work, remember that spaces are important to Logo. You have to type the spaces as indicated above or you'll get error messages. If you're using Apple Logo, use RL instead of REQUEST in the second line of the procedure. To run the program, simply type CONVERSE and press RETURN.

This Logo program enables the computer to hold a limited conversation with the person at the keyboard. A student can make the program fancier by introducing other conditionals; for example, IF statements that search responses for such key words as LOVE, HATE, MOTHER, FATHER, and so on. The student then has to figure out and program the appropriate replies for the computer to make.

If you don't have Logo, you can try this BASIC program. It's similar but not as powerful:

```
10 PRINT "TELL ME SOMETHING ABOUT YOURSELF."
20 INPUT A$
30 PRINT "WHAT DO YOU MEAN WHEN YOU SAY ";A$;"?"
40 GOTO 20
```

To use the program, type RUN and press RETURN.

Activity 2: Drill and Practice Exercises

Every subject involves some information that has to be memorized: math facts, spelling, English and foreign language vocabulary, states and capitals, the typewriter keyboard, the parts of the body or a leaf or the atmosphere. Computer programs that drill this information are easily written. In fact, the first classroom uses of the computer were programs of this sort designed by teachers who had become computer enthusiasts. Like those pioneering teachers, your students

64 THE NEUTER COMPUTER

can construct computer exercises for themselves and their classmates.

One teacher we know handed out the following Logo program to her students and asked them to alter it in any way they saw fit:

```
TO QUESTION
    CLEARTEXT
    PRINT [ HOW DO YOU SPELL FISH? PLEASE THINK CARE-
        FULLY AND THEN TYPE IN YOUR ANSWER. ]
    MAKE "ANS REQUEST
    PRINT [ THAT'S INTERESTING. AS I UNDERSTAND ENGLISH
        SPELLING, FISH WOULD BE SPELLED GH O TI. ]
    PRINT [ YOU THINK I'M WRONG? LET ME EXPLAIN... ]
    PRINT [ F IS THE SOUND GH MAKES IN ROUGH ]
    PRINT [ I IS THE SOUND O MAKES IN WOMEN ]
    PRINT [ SH IS THE SOUND TI MAKES IN MOTION ]
    PRINT
    PRINT [ SO YOU SEE, FISH IS SPELLED GHOTI! ]
END
```

This program can be entered using Terrapin, Krell, or Commodore 64 Logo. Press CTRL C to define it, and type QUESTION and press RETURN to run it. The students were so intrigued by the question form that some of them went on to develop really useful question-and-answer computer games for the class.

Activity 3: Teach the Computer

Teaching the computer requires programming knowledge. How much depends on what's to be taught, but it's a good measure of students' programming understanding. Any procedure that can be reduced to a simple testing rule can be taught to the computer. For example:

- Alphabetizing words
- Distinguishing between odd and even numbers
- Determining divisibility or distinguishing prime numbers
- Forming regular plurals
- Determining the measure of the interior or exterior angle of any regular polygon
- Playing a winning game of TIC TAC TOE

Activity 4: Design Simulations

Programs that simulate real events are more difficult to construct but are within the capabilities of some students. Their programs can be saved for use by other students as well. Although commercial simulations are slicker by far, you may have students who would like to write programs to:

- Trace the genetic characteristics in succeeding generations of fruit flies, kittens, or rabbits.
- Investigate angles of reflection by simulating a light source and a mirror that's manipulated by the person using the program.
- Probe the meaning of chance and probability by simulating coin tosses or dice throws. It's tiresome for anybody to toss coins a hundred times and record the results. The computer can do the job more quickly and accurately, and it never complains of boredom.

Activity 5: Explore Geometrical Relationships

Even a beginning Logo student can use programming to learn about angle measure, parallel and perpendicular lines, polygons, symmetries, perimeter and area, and properties of parallelograms, circles, and even three-dimensional figures. Perhaps that student can turn her exploratory program into an exercise for her peers.

Activity 6: A Student Message Center

Setting up a school model of an electronic mail service or electronic bulletin board is an entertaining challenge for more advanced programming students and one that appeals to many girls' desire for social contacts. Using the message center teaches students how to use an electronic mail network and how to avoid errors such as inadvertent erasure or impolite snooping in someone else's mail.

Writing a message center program involves establishing a menu so a user can choose whether to leave mail for someone or look to see if there is mail waiting for her. It involves sign-on procedures since messages have to be recorded and read from a disk. If this sounds like gibberish but you like the idea, talk to the programming teacher, ask a student, or look through computer magazines for a sample program, but don't give up just because you don't know how to do it yourself.

Activity 7: Interschool Computer Clubs

Making friends through computing, sharing ideas, and exchanging programs is attractive to girls as well as boys. If there is no school nearby to join in this activity, try finding one through a school computing magazine or, if you're using Logo, through the National Logo Exchange. Contact can be made by regular mail or if both schools have a modem, a device that allows computers to communicate via telephone lines, by electronic mail. See Programming Resources below.

HARDWARE AND SOFTWARE

As noted above, BASIC is built into most microcomputers. Logo isn't, so it has to be purchased as a piece of *software*—as must FORTRAN, COBOL, Pascal, or any other computer language. To complicate matters, there are sometimes different software versions of the same computer language for one make and model of computer. Usually, the most recent version from any given publisher is the best (and maybe the most expensive), since it incorporates improvements on earlier versions.

For any programming language instruction, it's good to have equipment that provides a wide range of opportunity for student experimentation. If students are to program in color, *a color monitor* is obviously a necessity. If they're going to create games, they'll need *paddles* or a *joystick* to test out their programs. A *printer*, preferably with graphics capability, is vital for any kind of programming. Students need to print out lists of the programming commands they've written, so the editing and reworking of this "hard copy" can be done away from the computer.

PREPARATION REQUIREMENTS

If you intend to teach programming, plan on thorough preparation. It's not that you need to be able to answer every question from every student. In fact, programming is best as a *discovery* process: the student tries and either succeeds or fails, but sees that making mistakes is a natural route to learning. But you should have some experience of this discovery process yourself to be able to guide students rather than tell them, and know when to take them a step further and when to let them continue exploring on their own.

Many school districts, colleges, universities, and adult education centers offer courses for teachers in Logo, BASIC, and other programming languages. If there's a course fee, your district may pay it for you. Before you sign up, ask teachers who already took the course whether they liked it. And if it doesn't include hours of hands-on computer experience, find another course.

If your students already know how to program and you want them to write programs in your subject area, there's no need to have extensive training in programming yourself. However, some knowledge of what programming is and what students can do with it at various skill levels will be useful. The programming teacher can give you this information, or you can ask the students themselves. "Do you think you might be able to write a computer program that would . . . ?" It's all right to admit that you can't do it but students can; it's not your fault you were born too early.

PROGRAMMING RESOURCES

The Logo Language

1. *Turtle Geometry: The Computer as a Medium for Exploring Mathematics* by Harold Abelson and Andrea DiSessa, Cambridge: MIT Press, 1981. A must for using Logo to teach calculus, it contains helpful information for middle school Logo teachers as well.
2. *Logo for the Texas Instruments 99-4A, Tandy Color Computer, and Apple II Computer* by Peter Ross, Reading, Mass.: Addison Wesley, 1983.

What can be done with turtle graphics for teachers of math and other subjects.
3. *Set-Ups for Logo Discovery* by Antonia Stone, Playing to Win, 106 E. 85 St., New York, NY 10028. Series of Logo explorations emphasize learning by discovery, providing enjoyable "set-ups" for adults to try before using them with students.
4. *Learning with Logo* by Dan Watt, New York: McGraw-Hill, 1983. Stepping through the basics and more advanced Logo material.
5. "Exploring Logo," designed by Karl Zinn and Gordon M. Leacock, Pleasantville, N.Y.: Sunburst Communications. Activity cards for use as a self-directed activity or as a teacher supplement.
6. *Nudges* by Tipps, Riordon and Bull, New York: Holt, Rinehart and Winston, 1984. Hundreds of ideas for teaching and using Logo. Written for IBM Logo but easily adaptable to other versions.
7. *Beyond Mindstorms: Teaching with IBM Logo* by Tobias, Short, Burrowes, Lough, and Riordon, New York: Holt, Rinehart and Winston, 1985. More "nudges."
8. *Microquests* has wonderful classroom uses for Logo and is published quarterly. Write Martin-Bearden, Inc., Box 337, Grapevine, TX 76051.
9. *The Computing Teacher* publishes a Logo column every month with interesting activities for different grades, written alternately by Kathleen Martin, Tim Riordon, and Tim Barclay.
10. The National Logo Exchange has an excellent newsletter for $25 per year in North America: Box 5341, Charlottesville, VA 22905.

The BASIC Language

There are many standard BASIC textbooks. Two that provide a nonstandard approach to BASIC programming through graphics are listed here. Both are written for Apple users, but may soon be available for other hardware.

1. *Using Graphics to Learn BASIC Programming* by William Barclay, New York: Harper and Row, 1986.
2. *Art and Graphics on the Apple II/IIe* by William H. DeWitt, New York: John Wiley, 1984.

Writing Simulations

1. "Build Your Own Computer Simulations" by Roy T. Tamashiro in *The Computing Teacher*, November 1985. Describes the process and provides a work outline and even a program template.

6 Computer-Based Instructional Software

Menu

	GOTO PAGE
Subject Areas	70
Computer Activities 1–8	71
Evaluating Software	75
Hardware and Software	78
Preparation Requirements	78
Instructional Software Resources	78

SUBJECT AREAS

ALL SUBJECTS

Eight to ten years ago, in the early days of classroom computing, educational software was called CAI (computer-assisted instruction). Most of it was modeled on workbook pages or flash cards and used primarily for drill and practice. CAI thus became associated with drill-and-practice software. Because the base of educational software has now broadened to include a variety of other instructional computer applications, we use the more generic term, computer-based instructional software.

Today's software manufacturers are using teams of teachers, educational psychologists, programmers, and graphic artists to produce effective and versatile programs that take advantage of the computer's capabilities for interaction, graphic display, rapid calculation, and simulation of real-life situations. With this software, teachers can conduct classroom explorations that previously were impossible: using the computer to model volcanic eruptions, river pollution, chemical explosions, and corporation management, to name only a few. Simulated consequences are a lot less risky than real ones.

In the past, you may have been forced to limit how you covered some topics in the classroom when the most instructive way was too complex, time-consuming, or boring for children to carry out. With a computer, however, your students can raise twenty generations of cats in twenty minutes to explore the mysteries of genetics, or toss dice one hundred or even one thousand times to learn about probability. They can collect and analyze scientific data fed directly into the computer, play "What if . . . ?" with history, write and learn about music, and much more.

Computers can transform learning from passive reception of information to active participation. And software manufacturers are producing more and more of these valuable classroom tools. Since some department heads in your school may not know that there's good software for their subjects, much less that it's within departmental budgets, you might want to call their attention to this chapter.

COMPUTER ACTIVITIES 1–8

Activity 1: Drill-and-Practice Games

Perhaps you think we harbor a certain prejudice against drill-and-practice software. While it's true that this type of computer-based instructional software is inherently less interesting than others, no one can deny there are skills that really benefit from rote drill, skills such as keyboarding, spelling, or arithmetic facts.

Drill-and-practice software still has its place in the classroom. Doing rote exercises on the computer is certainly more fun and the feedback is a lot faster than doing the same thing on paper. Pick these programs carefully (see Evaluating Software on page 75), but don't expect the fascination to last too long.

Most drill-and-practice programs are designed to be used by one student at a time. Since girls especially enjoy working with their friends, try to choose software that can be used cooperatively by two or more. Many students learn better when problem-solving or even drill is a joint effort. Also look for programs that are versatile: a spelling program that doubles as typing practice gets you double your money's worth.

If you have only one computer in the room, schedule an activity for noncomputing students that won't suffer unduly from conversation coming from the computer corner. Make sure the students know they'll all have a turn. It's very important to establish a schedule. We have learned that if you use a "first come, first served" approach, the computer enthusiasts will get there first. They are usually boys. See Teacher Strategy 2, Chapter 8, on how to schedule computer use equitably.

Activity 2: Editing Drill-and-Practice Programs

Many drill-and-practice programs can be edited to serve your specific curriculum requirements. Ask students to do the software editing for you as an individual or group project. Girls, and boys too, often enjoy helping the teacher in this way. The preparation of the data can be an ordinary assignment, while adapting the computer program can be a sort of bonus if you play it right.

Activity 3: Software Evaluation

Software evaluation can be conducted by a class or the entire student body. It has two major benefits. First, learning to evaluate anything by discussing and establishing relevant criteria is a worthwhile exercise on its own. Second, if you find that a lot of students or most of the girls absolutely loathe a piece of software, you certainly won't want to buy or use it. You'll need a software evaluation form, so we've included several samples among the Copyables in Appendix A.

Activity 4: Simulations

Simulations are computer programs that offer replicas of real-life situations. Students make decisions about aspects of these situations and enjoy or suffer the consequences of their decisions. In a simulation of a nuclear power plant, for example, a student who allows pressure to build beyond a certain tolerance will see the plant explode. The student's actions produce the result they would encounter in real life, but safely on the computer screen.

In programs of this sort, all decisions are acceptable: no opinions are programmed into the computer, nor is it programmed to advise or correct. Students learn from reflecting on and modifying their decisions in light of the observed consequences.

Good simulations, even though they are necessarily more limited than the almost infinite number of possibilities offered by real life, can add a richly experiential dimension to your classroom. Students can learn what's involved in campaigning for the presidency of the United States by running for office themselves, watch the effects of hazardous waste on the ecology of rivers and streams, operate businesses, perform chemical experiments, pilot airplanes, observe the effect of diet on families, conduct international negotiations leading to peace or war, and much, much more.

Many simulations can be used very well in classrooms with only one computer. In this case, decisions are made by groups rather than individuals. You can be the typist or the job of entering information into the computer can be rotated among students. Establishing a rule that the typist is not allowed to make alterations in the data being entered will reduce squabbles about what's being entered, and will make the person at the computer less envied.

Activity 5: Making Music

Most computers can produce a range of sounds and software is available to take advantage of this capability. At the simplest level, a program asks the student to trace a path across the screen and responds with a melodic line that matches the ups and downs, breaks, and horizontals of the path. More elaborate programs allow students to compose melodies and harmonies that can be played back in whole or in part. They appear on the screen as notes on a musical stave, and can be printed out as sheet music with a dot matrix printer. At the most sophisticated level, students can create the full range of musical sounds with special sound synthesizers or keyboards that are plugged into the computer.

Using a computer is a natural for teaching music, but music software can also be used in other subjects. One math teacher in New York City uses music software to reinforce fraction concepts. Another uses it to teach permutations and combinations. However you use it, you'll broaden your students' awareness of what a computer can do for them.

Activity 6: Computer-Based Labs

Scientific use of computers to take and record measurements and manipulate data has recently become the focus of a new kind of educational software. Intended especially for math and science classes but also useful in physical education, health, and social studies classes, computer-based lab software enables the computer to receive input directly from student-operated sensors that come with the program to measure heat, light, distance, pulse, and so forth.

The computer plots relationships between these data and other variables such as time. The hardware/software combination lets students focus on the process of the experiment and the content of the subject area, rather than on the technique of taking measurements—an activity we all know is fraught with error potential—or on the calculations needed to produce results. The students' task thus becomes one of interpretation, analysis, and extrapolation, skills that are increasingly necessary in our technological world.

Activity 7: Classwide Learning Projects

Classwide learning projects have been developed that cover large sections of curriculum and involve research, reading, writing, lab work, and film strips in addition to computer use. In projects of this sort, the computer's role may be to generate data based on measurements from lab instruments as described above, serve as a word processor or a database manager for report writing or journal entries, and/or simulate aspects of the problem situation.

For example, in an earth science learning project called GEOLOGY SEARCH, the class works in teams whose object is to discover, develop, and market oil. The computer is used as a tool by each team in turn as a source of information and a means of simulating the drilling activity. But coordinated classwork also includes library research into the makeup of the earth's surface, determining what conditions favor the development of fossil fuels, map making, and even investigation of current events in the world oil market.

An even more comprehensive program, THE VOYAGE OF THE MIMI, integrates the use of twelve taped television segments with computer work, laboratory research, and written materials to form the basis for a semester science class, or even for a complete year's curriculum. A last example, WRITE TO READ, was designed for the early elementary grades but is also valuable in special education classes for older students. It integrates computer use with keyboarding, drawing, clay modeling, and other manipulative materials, and has been quite successful in teaching reading and writing.

Naturally, such comprehensive programs are expensive and require considerable teacher preparation. Once in place, however, annual repetitions are virtually cost-free. The initial expense may be more than balanced by your continuing ability to bring the world into your classroom, offer opportunities for students to use computers and other problem-solving tools, and model an adult situation of work and learning.

Activity 8: Avoiding the Arcade Syndrome

To a harried computer teacher with upwards of twenty students at the computers, video games have the advantage of being self-directed, allowing the teacher to concentrate her or his time on a few students who need help. We have seen computer labs with extensive collections of video games brought in by the (usually male) computer teacher just because he likes them.

Nevertheless, we think video arcade games don't belong in a school. First, many girls don't like them: "boring" and "too predictable," girls told us when we asked for their opinion of the games. Stocking the software library with programs half the students won't use is unfair and exacerbates the computer gender gap. Second, the much touted hand-eye coordination skills supposedly derived from playing video arcade games is a pretty feeble excuse. A good gym class accomplishes the same end with much more constructive results. Third, these games often take antagonism, warfare, weaponry, violence, destruction, and death as their common themes. Even if they are vicarious, are these really the experiences we want our students to have?

If you remove the video arcade games from the school's software collection, you may nevertheless find students bringing their own in. A good policy is simply not to allow use of outside software. Such a rule brings the additional benefit of preventing, at least on school property, the illegal copying and distributing of copyrighted programs.

Outlawing imported software may still not solve the problem. Many computer magazines publish the programming code for video games. If students have the patience to type in the hundreds of commands, you'll find the games being played. The process of typing in this code and especially locating and correcting the errors (called "debugging") isn't a bad learning experience, but the resulting arcade game is a high price to pay.

While you want girls and boys to read computer magazines, some judicious controls on what is transposed from magazine to computer may be necessary to avoid the Arcade Syndrome.

EVALUATING SOFTWARE

We have been urging a viewpoint somewhat biased towards girls in these pages. In support of this bias, consider the following

76   THE NEUTER COMPUTER

excerpt from David Moursand's editorial in *The Computing Teacher*'s issue on computer equity, April 1984:

> For many years, I have not treated women equally. Rather, I have tried to treat them a little better than I treat men. . . . I feel that the nature of our society puts extra barriers in the path of a woman who seeks a professional career in science and math-related areas. . . . I cannot solve this problem, but I can certainly help, and I can help at a level that may make a significant difference for an individual woman.

If you're asked to evaluate software for purchase by your school, look at it with a special eye to the appeal it will have for girls. We hope you'll be aware of an attitude that says, "Oh, this is terrific. The boys will love it," without thinking about whether girls will react in the same way. This certainly doesn't mean you should look for "fluff"—programs about recipes and the care of houseplants—to appeal to girls. But good software that is educationally sound and highly motivating should have intrinsic appeal to girls as well as boys.

At the risk of sounding negative, here are some software characteristics that may well turn off many girls:

- It uses unnecessarily male-oriented rewards for correct answers, such as a football sailing over a goalpost.
- It has a central character who is identifiably male. This is okay if you're using other programs with identifiably female central characters as well, but watch out for the next characteristic.
- It has sex-stereotyped characters: the policeman is always male, the babysitter is always female.
- It involves irrelevant and unnecessary violence, such as a correct answer rewarded by a missile blowing up a target. This is not the same as necessary violence, such as the explosion of the nuclear power plant in the simulation mentioned earlier.

The best article we've seen on the hotly debated topic of software's appeal or lack of it to girls is "Girls Don't Like Fluffware Either," by Holly Brady and Twila Slesnick in *Classroom Computer Learning*, April/May 1985. We think nobody could say it better.

In addition to our obvious recommendation that software be free of stereotypes and racial or ethnic slurs, we offer these general software selection criteria:

- Is it worth the money? Many slickly designed programs address quite limited sections of the curriculum but are extremely expensive. As an alternative to purchase, consider asking students to write small programs as suggested in Chapter 6. Their products won't have the same polish, but they can serve the purpose adequately and save a considerable amount of money.
- Does it take advantage of capabilities unique to the computer such as simulations of experiments that are too dangerous for the classroom—like nuclear fission, or time-saving on calculations, or could the purpose be served equally well in a less expensive medium?
- Is the program truly interactive? Does the student have an active decision-making role or function only as an electronic page turner?
- Does it encourage social interaction, cooperative learning, questioning, and discussion? This is especially important for girls.
- If the purpose is drill, can you change the range or content of the data? In other words, can you easily edit the program to your specific needs?
- Very important: is it fun? Would you and your students enjoy using this program?

Help with Reviewing Software

Because the number of computer-based instructional programs is vast and increasing daily, several national evaluation services have been set up to review programs for educators. Three of them are listed in the Resource section. Your district's computer coordinator will know if you have access to one, and if so how you can see the published evaluations. Educational computing magazines (see Appendix B, Resources) also review new software. These articles are usually teacher-written, detailed, and helpful. Check the current and back issues.

These sources should be used to narrow down your options to a very few programs you think might be suitable for your purposes. At that point, and although it's time-consuming, it is important to do your own personal hands-on preview: there's no substitute for your knowledge of your own students. It's not necessary to work through every part of the program beforehand. To give some structure to your previews, look at some of the software evaluation forms designed specifically for teachers in Appendix A, Copyables.

HARDWARE AND SOFTWARE

Most drill-and-practice software comes with information on the package about the computer and peripheral equipment needed to run the program. If not, this is software you don't need. Generally, the equipment will be no more than a *color monitor* and perhaps a *joystick, mouse,* or *game paddles*. Often a *printer* will be recommended and is sometimes essential.

Lab software, simulations, and other curriculum-integrated software sometimes require additional computer equipment such as *measurement sensors* not provided with the program or a *VCR*. In terms of value for money, you may want to purchase these as well.

PREPARATION REQUIREMENTS

If you're planning to use mostly drill-and-practice software, just about all you need to know in advance is how to turn on the machine. Your preparation time will be limited to planning how to integrate it into your curriculum, which shouldn't take long if you've evaluated the software well.

Some software lets you insert spelling lists, capital cities, and other types of information you want your students to learn. You'll need additional time to learn the editing procedure and prepare the information you want to insert. An alternative is to ask a student to insert the data for you.

Simulations, lab tool programs, or more comprehensive software packages generally don't require greater computer knowledge, but they do take extra preparation time for building your lesson plans on them. You can gauge how much time by examining the software in question and the print material that comes with it.

INSTRUCTIONAL SOFTWARE RESOURCES

Annotated Software Catalogs

1. *Whole Earth Software Catalog,* New York: Quantum Press, 1985.
2. *Sterling Swift Catalog of Educational Software,* Sterling A. Swift Publishing Co., Austin, TX 78744.
3. Addison Wesley's guides to Apple, Commodore, and IBM software. Updated versions are issued annually.

4. TESS (The Educational Software Selector), published by EPIE. See the software evaluation organizations listed below.

In addition, the National Council of Teachers of Mathematics and the National Council for Social Studies both publish software evaluation guidelines. Software reviews are regular features of their journals. Also see the "Computer Magazines" section of Appendix B, Resources, for other sources of software reviews.

Software Evaluation Organizations

1. EPIE (Educational Product Information Exchange), Box 839, Water Mill, NY 11976. Subscriptions to EPIE's educational software evaluation service is available to state education departments. Your district's computer coordinator will know whether your state subscribes. If not, the TESS catalog listed above is updated annually and costs approximately $60.
2. MICROSIFT, Northwest Regional Educational Laboratory, 300 S.W. Sixth Ave. Portland, OR 97204. They also publish a catalog.
3. EDUCATIONAL SOFTWARE EVALUATION CONSORTIUM, ICCE, University of Oregon, 1787 Agate St., Eugene, OR 97403, CompuServe number 70014,2117. This group, a consortium of twenty-seven North American educational computer organizations, also publishes the *Educational Software Preview Guide* for $10.

Software Producers

Although this is obviously an incomplete listing—there are hundreds of educational software producers—the following organizations have issued some excellent software. They allow a thirty-day examination period on software purchases. Write for catalogs.

1. Conduit, University of Iowa, Oakdale Campus, Iowa City, IA 52242
2. HRM Software, 175 Tompkins Ave., Pleasantville, NY 10570
3. The Learning Company, 545 Middlefield Rd., Suite 170, Menlo Park, CA 94025
4. McGraw Hill Book Company, 1221 Ave. of the Americas, New York, NY 10020
5. MECC (Minnesota Educational Computing Consortium), 3490 Lexington Ave. N., St. Paul, MN 55112
6. Scholastic Inc., Box 7502, Jefferson City, MO 65102
7. Spinnaker Software, 1 Kendall Sq., Cambridge, MA 02139
8. Sunburst Communications, 39 Washington Ave., Pleasantville, NY 10570

7 Telecommunications

By Joy Wallace and Raymond M. Rose

Menu

	GOTO PAGE
Subject Areas	81
Computer Activities 1–10	82
Activity 1	
Hardware and Software	85
Preparation Requirements	87
Telecommunications Resources	89

SUBJECT AREAS

ALL SUBJECT AREAS AT ALL GRADE LEVELS
SPECIAL EDUCATION

Telecommunications is the system used to permit two computers to communicate with each other. A device called a modem connects to each computer and telephone lines transmit the data from one to the other. Modem stands for "modulator-demodulator," referring to its function of changing the sending computer's digital signals into the audible signals carried by the telephone line, and back again to digital signals at the receiving computer's end.

Assuming yours is one of the computers, the other can be in another classroom or in someone's home. Or it can be a commercial mainframe computer, such as the Source and CompuServe—services that offer electronic mail, news and business information, personal computing information, educational information (like an encyclopedia online), airline schedules, shopping information, teleconferencing, recreational activities, and much more.

The other computer can also be an electronic bulletin board that offers personal electronic mail or a message service as well as a public communication forum, much like a citizen's band radio. Some bulletin boards that are operated by computer user groups or computer clubs interconnect with other bulletin boards, offering communications to users across the country.

All these telecommunications uses have a valuable role to play in a school since they allow students to obtain up-to-the-minute information on a vast range of subjects and to send and receive messages. But they cost. In addition to paying for the modem, software, and cables or circuit boards, there are subscription fees and connect-time charges for commercial electronic database systems. The telephone company also charges. You may even need a separate phone line. (Costs are discussed further on in this chapter.)

Since telecommunications involves some trouble and expense, is it worth it? Some schools think not. But those that have the capability—and there are more of them all the time—are excited about the entry it permits their students into a world that, thanks to this technology, is a Global Village.

COMPUTER ACTIVITIES 1–9

Activity 1: Research Telecommunications Uses

Large firms use telecommunications for inhouse electronic mail between employees, avoiding long lines at the copying machine and long waits at the elevators, and for sending mail to branch offices, which sure beats the time needed to send something via regular mail. Farmers use it to keep abreast of prices in the commodities market. Stock brokers watch Wall Street activities as they occur, since even a fifteen-minute delay may mean thousands of dollars lost. Travel agents use it to find out the latest, most accurate, flight schedules and fares. Hospitals use it to send and receive urgently needed medical information. Having students research these and other uses of telecommunications helps them understand how linked communities and countries really are, and gives meaning to the phrase Global Village.

Activity 2: Interschool Electronic Mail

You can identify another school with telecommunications ability by placing an inquiry in one of the educational computing magazines (see Appendix B, Resources). With a phone call or letter to establish contact numbers and a schedule, your students are set to send and receive mail with a community that can be very far away.

Via telecommunications, students in Alaska and California are learning about their social, cultural, geographic, and educational similarities and differences. As these lessons are in effect taught by electronic pen pals of their own age rather than through impersonal books, students often learn more. And electronic mail is terrific for disabled and shy students: through a computer, everyone is the same.

Because you don't want students running up bills while they sit in front of the computer, thinking of what to type in, preconnect preparation is advisable. This can range from a short list of topics students want to communicate about or receive information on to a formal script.

Activity 3: Searching Online Databases

Whether students' reports are on current events, science, sports, business, social trends, or education, they can tap into the latest data via an online network such as the Source or CompuServe. Each service has a menu of individual databases on a vast number of subjects that go beyond the resources of any school or community library that depends on published information.

Activity 4: An Electronic News Project

If you subscribe to a commercial database, you can use a printed copy of UPI headlines and news briefs on a daily basis to introduce students to news services, news interpretation, and sources of news. It's instructive to read and discuss the headlines of the major news events of the day at school (especially attractive to students because almost no one else knows about them yet), and then analyze how the same stories are covered in the local newspaper, or better yet, two competing newspapers.

Activity 5: Take Advantage of Class Interests

When a topic of interest surfaces in class discussions, have the students search a database for more information. You'd need a subscription, of course. For instance, let's say your students become interested in recent incidents of racial harassment in their city. They will want to know how common the problem is in their state and in the country, what laws protect citizens' civil rights, and what communities are doing to promote racial harmony. They can search a large database (for example, UPI DATA NEWS) for state or national news by identifying one or several key words or dates the computer will use in a search of stories contained in the database.

After examining and possibly printing out the information, students can expand the search by selecting new key words, dates, or names they've learned are important, or narrow it if they find the subject of racial harassment is too vast to be researched properly.

Activity 6: Study Business Trends

Stock market information in electronic networks like CompuServe is continuously updated. Students who learn how to interpret the abbreviations and numbers can see the fluctuations and feel the pulse of market activity, a very different experience from the static closing price published in the newspapers. They can "buy" stock from one or more companies and follow their earnings and losses, and can analyze and try to predict market developments. Then they can read financial analyses in the newspapers to see how the pros do it.

Activity 7: A Community Bulletin Board

With the right software, a class can set up an electronic bulletin board accessible to anyone who calls the bulletin board's telephone number via the modem. In addition to offering communications opportunities, the bulletin board can provide announcements or information about school or community developments, solicit answers to specific questions, and suggest topics for discussion by community members.

If you'd like to introduce the class to someone else's community bulletin board, computer stores will know how to reach them. Try the telephone number yourself first, though: bulletin boards are sometimes set up by unscrupulous people to disseminate violent or pornographic software, or to provide illegally obtained software to users at less than the going market price.

Activity 8: Flight Information in Math Class

Airline information from electronic networks can be used to develop good word problems in math class. Questions can deal with amount of travel time, cost of airfare, arrival and departure times (taking time zones into account), routing among various cities, and comparisons among airlines on these and other factors.

Activity 9: Interschool Simulations

At the time of the American-Soviet summit meeting in 1985, a class of American students and a class of Swiss students had their own summit meeting. Using telecommunications and a simulation named THE OTHER SIDE, each class represented a country that had to make decisions about keeping its economy productive while trying to avoid war between them. The simulated experience of how difficult it was to keep the peace even with the best of intentions gave them a far deeper understanding of international relations than they could otherwise have had.

Activity 10: Telecourses

Small schools in rural areas can't provide the breadth of opportunities to their students that larger schools can. The small number of students they serve means that only a few are eligible for advanced placement or special education courses. Few school districts can afford to offer a course for three students. Similarly, students with illnesses or disabilities that make regular school attendance impossible have to make do with the sketchiest of educations.

With telecommunications, however, there's no limit to the number of educational opportunities you can offer even to a class of one student. State departments of education are increasingly serving as clearinghouses for courses taught via a modem, augmented by the telephone, U.S. mail, and occasionally closed-circuit television.

At pre-arranged times each week students attend class. They can listen to the teacher on the telephone. If the class has more than one student, an inexpensive speaker-phone enables them all to hear and speak. Text, numbers, graphs, and other information appear on the monitor through the telecommunications hookup, and students type in answers that are transmitted to the teacher's monitor, or answer questions over the phone. Individual teacher/student conferences can take place on the telephone, and exams can be conducted via electronic mail or the postal service. Thanks to telecommunications, no student need be deprived of a challenging, enriching education just because she or he happens to be in a minority.

HARDWARE AND SOFTWARE

A *modem* is, of course, essential. It can have a bewildering number of features, the most important of which are described below. Choose—and pay for—only those features you think will be important in a school setting, but if possible don't go for the bare minimum. A few months' worth of telecommunications experience may well lead to more sophisticated use, and it's cheaper to pay for a couple of extra features now than a whole new fancy modem later.

- *Direct vs. acoustical connect.* In a direct connect, the telephone line plugs directly into the modem by means of an ordinary modular telephone jack. In an acoustical connect, the modem rests on a rubber cradle which is hooked up to the phone line. Direct connect gives more reliable transmission.
- *Full- and half-Duplex.* Half-duplex is sufficient for receiving information from an electronic database, but if you want to communicate with another person a full-duplex is better because it lets you see on the screen what you're typing when you send a message.
- *Baud rate.* A baud is the measure of speed at which a modem transmits data. A baud rate of 300 is common but relatively slow. Modems with a baud rate of 1200 are four times faster, and there are now modems with a baud rate of 2400. The higher the baud rate, the faster the transmission and the less connect time you need. Commercial electronic database companies usually charge more for faster transmission: about 50 percent more for 1200 baud than for 300 baud. Since 1200 baud is four times faster than 300 baud, you still save money.
- *Originate and answer.* Your basic modem only originates, or sends, in plain English. It's nice to be able to answer as well, which isn't an unusual feature.
- *Auto-dial and auto-answer.* These features permit the modem to be used when you're not there personally operating the system, like the VCR you can set to record the 2:00 a.m. television movie when you're fast asleep. You can set the modem to dial a certain number at a certain time and set it to receive a communication all by itself.
- *Bell standards.* The telephone system establishes a Bell 103 standard for 300-baud modems and 212A for 1200-baud modems. Some inexpensive modems don't conform to these standards, and those that don't may not work with all telephone systems.
- *FCC approved.* It will say if it is, and it should be.
- *Software included.* A modem needs software to operate, so it's a good idea to get a matched set to make sure they get along well together.

Cables and circuit boards that connect the modem to the computer may be necessary, depending on the type of modem and computer you're using. Internal modems are on circuit boards and connect to a slot inside the computer. External modems are connected to the computer with special cables, and they sometimes require specific electrical connections which in turn necessitate a special circuit board.

Access to a *telephone line* that connects up with the modem is the essential link to the outside world. The telephone line itself may be the most difficult part of the telecommunications process for a school since switchboards and extensions are not nearly as reliable as direct phone lines.

A *monochrome monitor* is desirable for the same reason as it is for word processing: text is easier to read on it than on many color monitors. If you are going to use telecommunications as more than a glorified telephone, you need a *printer* to provide a hard copy (paper) of what is telecommunicated.

Communications software is needed to provide the instructions to the computer and the modem. The programs have different capabilities and are available for a variety of prices. Like all software, communications software must be matched to the hardware, including the modem you will be using. There are some public domain communications programs, essentially free and without copyright, available for most of the popular computers.

PREPARATION REQUIREMENTS

First, prepare to pay money. Commercial online database networks have a subscription fee, some annual and some one-time, which ranges from about forty to two hundred dollars or more. In addition, the networks charge you for the time you are connected to their systems. Connect charges range from a few dollars an hour to a high of three hundred dollars an hour, depending on the network and the time of day it is in use. Access to certain nonstandard databases in these systems involve additional charges.

To help you gauge the costs, a user who is familiar with the system needs about ten to thirty minutes of connect time for a typical search and printout. CompuServe and the Source, two popular online services, have a one-time membership fee of about forty and fifty dollars respectively. Their connect-time charges are approximately twenty-five dollars per hour during business hours and can go down to about ten dollars an hour late at night.

Then there are the telephone costs. The major commercial electronic database services have local access numbers in most metropolitan areas, so you'll be billed only for local message units. If you live in a rural area, you'll probably have to call a metropolitan area to get access to the system, which means long-distance charges. You'll be happy to know that public access bulletin boards, often run by user groups, can be accessed at no charge other than the telephone time. And telecommunications with another private computer, in a classroom for example, incurs only telephone charges.

Warning: when many people have access to a subscription database network, the access telephone number and the school's billing code number and password can become public knowledge. Once the codes are known, both students and faculty can use any modem at any location—and the school will be billed for the connect time. The solution is tight restriction on who actually accesses the system, giving the codes only to one or two teachers. The password should also be changed regularly. Use of the system needs to be defined and monitored to avoid school district bankruptcy. Plan this out carefully *before* you bring telecommunications into school, not after.

As you might guess, it's not cost-effective to learn your way around a complex information system while you're running up connect charges for each minute. Nor is it time-effective. There are now at least two telecommunications simulation packages whose price tags of fifty to one hundred dollars look expensive, but this is deceptive. You don't need a modem for them, and it only takes about an hour to learn the communications software and your way around the database simultaneously. Without a simulation, you'd need one to five hours to learn the communications software first (depending on the software), then three to five hours of minute-by-minute connect-time charges to learn how to use the commercial database. The simulations are listed and described below.

Exactly what you do to telecommunicate depends on the hardware and software you use, as well as with whom (or what) you're telecommunicating. So spend some time talking with people who are familiar with telecommunications and ask for information about your particular hardware and about the services you can access. Computer user groups are good sources of help, as is a knowledgeable computer store salesperson.

All these cautions may make telecommunicating sound like it's more trouble than it's worth. It is true that most people who take up telecommunications already know how to use a computer for other purposes, such as those described in Chapters 1 through 6. It's also true that getting connected can take time, certainly costs money, and is occasionally frustrating. But if you can find the time and the money and can survive a little frustration, you'll be giving your students a marvelously vast storehouse of information and a new way to turn strangers into friends.

TELECOMMUNICATIONS RESOURCES

Print Materials

1. "Sensible Telecommunications" by Richard Dalton, in *Popular Computing*, March 1985. What telecommunications can and can't do: common sense tips for deciding whether or not to take the plunge. Written for small businesses but applicable to schools.
2. *The Complete Handbook of Personal Computer Communications* by Alfred Glossbrenner, New York: St. Martin's Press, 1983. Everything you need to know about telecommunications. It's still current.
3. "Modems: What the Hardware Has to Offer" by Odvard Egil Dyrli, in *Classroom Computer Learning*, September 1985. Clear introduction to major features and costs of telecommunications.
4. "On-Line Contemporary Issues Bring Today's World to Social Studies Classrooms" by R. Pollak and G. Breault, in *The Computing Teacher*, May 1985. Using the MECC On-Line Network to create lesson plans for politics, government, economics, sociology, psychology, geography, history, and more.
5. "Telecomputing Diary," by Jean Tennis, in *Electronic Learning*, September, October, and November/December 1985. A three-part series: teacher's diary of trials, tribulations, and triumphs of bringing telecommunications into school.

Electronic Database Networks

COMPUSERVE INFORMATION
  SERVICE
5000 Arlington Center Blvd.
Columbus, OH 43220
(800) 848-8990

THE SOURCE
Source Telecomputing
  Corporation
1616 Anderson Rd.
McLean, VA 22102
(800) 336-3366

Telecommunications Simulation Programs

THE INFORMATION
  CONNECTION
Grolier
Sherman Tpk.
Danbury, CT 06810
203-797-3500

Available for the Apple II series, Commodore 64 and 128, and IBM PC. Provides a tutorial on telecommunications and simulates the use of the CompuServe network. This program doubles as real, unsimulated communications software.

PART TWO: STRATEGIES FOR COMPUTER EQUITY

The Basics of Equity

Every year, the town holds a race. On the first Sunday in May, hundreds of runners line up at the starting line. At the signal, they begin the ten-mile route—through town, out into the surrounding countryside, and back into town to the finish line. Spectators line the route, offering water to the runners as they pass and cheering them on. There are two judges at each side of the finish-line ribbon. Every effort is made to conduct the race impartially. Nevertheless, for the last eight years the same person has won the race. Does this outcome make you suspect that something isn't quite fair?

In fact, it turns out that the runner who keeps finishing in first place is a Boston Marathon winner, while the other contestants are only neighborhood joggers. Even though it looks like a fair race—everyone starts from the same place at the same time and runs the same course, and everyone seems to be in good physical shape—the Marathon runner can be sure of winning before the first yard has been run.

Computer equity for girls is very much like this race. Because most girls come into school assuming that computers aren't for girls (see Introduction)—unlike boys, who have positive associations and expectations about computers—many girls decline to take the computer electives, especially in programming. They don't spend free time with computers, even though it's available to them. Just as it's not fair to let a Boston Marathon winner compete in the same race with neighborhood joggers, it's not fair to offer computer opportunities evenhandedly when we know that boys and girls aren't in an equal position to take advantage of them.

We have to compensate for this imbalance. We have to demonstrate to girls that computers are for them too, that there's nothing unfeminine about using computers, and that their girlfriends won't criticize them if they do. Once this attitudinal obstacle is removed, girls will use, enjoy, and profit from computers just as much as boys.

The four chapters in Part Two provide the tools needed to remove the attitudinal obstacle. The computer equity strategy chapters for teachers, administrators, parents, and students contain many ways for using the excellent computer activities in Part One to hook girls' interest in computers. Suggestions for planning and evaluating a computer equity program in schools are in Part Three. As you read through Chapters 8 through 11 and choose your strategies, keep these six basics in mind.

1. Focus Specifically on Girls

Subtlety just won't work. To encourage girls to use computers, you have to say G I R L S loud and clear or else they'll assume you mean boys as usual. Girls didn't respond before when you invited "students" or "boys and girls" to take computer electives, or when you told them the computer room is open to "everyone" after school. They won't believe you mean "girls" unless you say so.

2. Target Girls in Groups

The good opinion of their peers is extremely necessary to adolescent girls. When you invite them to the computer room in friendship groups rather than individually, you're making peer pressure work for you for a change. Girls don't need to be afraid of being different when their girlfriends are doing the same thing. You expand the circle when you invite girls to bring another friend to the computer room next time.

3. Make Computer Use Social

Whereas many boys get so caught up in what they're doing at the computer that they couldn't care less who else is in the room, many girls strongly prefer to use computers with, or at least near, a friend. In addition, some studies have suggested that children learn more at the computer when they work in small groups instead of alone: the process of group sharing, analyzing, and deciding is beneficial.

In view of these two factors, assign two to four students to a computer when possible. When it's not, allow them to talk together about what they're doing.

4. Stress Usefulness

One of the important differences we found in the way boys and girls approach the computer is that while many boys seem to enjoy the computer for its own sake—"playing around" with it just to see what it can do, many girls seem to value the computer for how it can help them do what they want or have to do. In other words, computers are often means for girls but ends for boys. This may explain why programming tends to attract fewer girls than boys but applications courses tend to attract both sexes equally; the usefulness of programming may not be made clear.

Consequently, stress usefulness. Computer-based instruction helps girls learn their subject better. Applications such as word processing and database managers make their schoolwork easier and have many personal uses. Programming helps them solve problems that are important and otherwise would not be solvable.

5. Eliminate Sexist Computer Practices

Living in the same society that girls do, teachers and parents also tend to assume that it's natural for computers to interest boys more than girls. This can easily become a self-fulfilling prophecy. Be on the lookout for practices that actively discourage girls from computer interest or use:

- Don't ask only boys to move or demonstrate the computers, or to be computer assistants.
- Don't encourage only boys to sign up for computer electives.
- Don't schedule computer electives during the same period you schedule electives that are popular with female students.

Passively sexist computer practices are nearly as harmful. Since the deck is stacked in favor of boys to begin with, accepting the status quo guarantees that the imbalance will continue:

- Don't schedule computer use on a first-come, first-served basis; boys usually get there first.
- Don't ask for volunteers for computer-related tasks or privileges, but rather select girls and boys yourself.

Language and pictures can be passively sexist as well:

- Don't say "he" for the generic computer user, but rather "they" or better still, sometimes "she" and sometimes "he." The Logo turtle is not a "he," but an "it."
- When you invent problems or situations to illustrate a computer-

related point, choose examples that are equally relevant to girls and boys, or alternate them.
- If you have computer-related pictures or articles in your classroom, make sure they aren't exclusively male.
- If your computer textbook or curriculum materials are sex-biased in favor of males, don't ignore it but instead point it out and say it's wrong.

6. Eliminate Violent and Sexist Software

Arcade-type computer games—those that feature death, destruction, and war—tend to appeal to girls less than boys. Permitting such software in a school thus widens the computer gender gap. In our opinion, such software, whether billed as recreational or educational, isn't beneficial to children's social and moral development, and therefore has no place in a school. Don't purchase software that includes annihilating the opposition, and get rid of any you already have. It isn't necessary to blow up enemy aliens in order to learn math, typing, grammar, or anything else.

In our experience, educational software is rarely actively sexist. Applications are inherently sex-neutral in their design, although they can be presented to students in a sex-biased way ("You boys will really like this spreadsheet program"). Most tutorial and simulation programs put the student in the center of the action, rather than a male or female third person.

However, educational software may be passively sexist. For example, there's nothing inherently wrong with reinforcing a correct answer by showing a boy kicking a football over a goalpost. But if program after program has male figures and most of the activities are male-oriented, the cumulative effect is sexist. The message may be subtle, but girls get it: "We expect the person using this program to be male." Pay attention to the subtle messages, and choose software at least partially on the basis of its freedom from passive sex bias.

With these six basics of equity in mind, we invite you to read on and discover how you can achieve computer equity in your school.

8 Computer Equity Strategies for Teachers and Staff

Menu

	GOTO PAGE
Introduction	100
Classroom Strategies	100
1. Computers in Your Curriculum	100
2. Schedule Computer Use in Your Classroom	101
3. Have Girls Demonstrate and Move the Computers	102
4. Where to Put the Computer in Your Classroom	102
5. Make a Computer Bulletin Board	102
6. Discuss Notable Women in the Computer Field	103
7. Analyze Sexism in the Computer Media and Software	103
8. Conduct a Home Computer Survey	105
9. What to Suggest When the Lesson Is Done	106
10. Encourage Homework Done by Computer	106
11. Have Class Notes Taken on a Computer	106
12. Throw a Computer Pajama Party	107
Strategies 5, 6, 7, and 8	
Schoolwide Strategies	108
13. Schedule Student Computer Use	108
14. Girls' Day, Boys' Day: Temporary Strategy	109

Menu, Continued

GOTO PAGE

15. Girls' Course, Boys' Course: Temporary Strategy	110
16. Girls' Computer Committee	110
17. Student Computer Teachers	111
18. Computer Bulletin Board	112
19. Furniture Arrangement in the Computer Room	113
20. Computer Art Show or Contest	114
21. School Programming Contest	115
22. Literary Magazine	116
23. School Newspaper	116
24. Computer Awareness Day or Week	117
25. Raise Money for Computers in School	118
26. Computer Equity Score Sheet	119
27. Summer Computer Course	119

Strategies 24 and 25

Community Strategies	120
28. Invite Speakers and Role Models to School	120
29. Computer-Related Field Trips	121
30. Computer Career Fair	121
31. Computer Equity Evening for Parents	123
32. Computer Course for Parents	125
33. Send Computer Equity Information Home	125
34. Parent Task Force on Computer Equity	126
35. Area Conference on Computer Equity	126
36. Raise Money for Computers in the Community	128

Menu, Continued

GOTO PAGE

37. Involve Women's Organizations in
    Computer Equity   129
38. Summer Computer Camps   129

Strategies 28, 29, 30, 33, 34,
35, 36, and 37

INTRODUCTION

We have included more computer equity strategies for teachers and staff than for administrators, parents, or students. Quite rightly, too. It's usually teachers or staff in a school who notice the need to do something better, and it's nearly always the same people who are best able to carry it out.

In case you're a man and thinking that women might be more effective at computer equity, studies have shown that your gender is far less important than your attitude. Female or male, a teacher who actively encourages girls' computer participation is the one who closes the computer gender gap.

Whether you're a classroom teacher (computer, subject, bilingual, or special education), a librarian, a media specialist, or a counselor, the strategies in this chapter will help you involve girls with the computer. There are strategies you can use in your own classroom or with small groups of girls. There are others that are best done schoolwide and that take some team planning to pull off. (Please read Chapter 12 on how to go about forming a team and planning your computer equity program.) Still others involve the community: bringing community people into the school or taking students out into the community.

The strategies in this chapter range from the effortlessly simple to a mind-boggling extravaganza or two, with lots in between. The ones that don't require hands-on use of a computer are identified with

CLASSROOM STRATEGIES

Strategy 1: Computers in Your Curriculum

There are really two requirements for closing the computer gender gap. One is to actively encourage girls to use the computer and to overcome the negative computer associations they carry into school with them. The second is to make the computer an ordinary part of the school environment, because familiarity increases the likelihood of use.

Although it may be too optimistic to expect that the computer will soon be no more remarkable than a textbook in a classroom, the more you can integrate it into your curriculum the faster you will close the computer gender gap. You'll also be giving your students a powerful educational experience.

Chapters 1 through 7 contain dozens of ways you can use the following kinds of software to reinforce and extend what you teach:

Graphics
Word processing
Databases
Number crunchers (spreadsheets and graphing programs)
Programming languages

Computer-based instructional software (tutorials, drill and practice, simulations, and others)
Telecommunications

As you go through these chapters, we hope you see many intriguing possibilities for your students.

Strategy 2: Schedule Computer Use in Your Classroom

If you have too many students for too few computers, or if you allow your students to use computers during class time on an optional basis, you may well find that the boys beat the girls to the opportunity. A first-come, first-served system winds up favoring students who are the first to sign up because they're already familiar and comfortable with computers. These are usually the boys.

This is simple to fix. Have a computer sign-up sheet with a column for boys and one for girls. Make a rule that only equal numbers of boys and girls can use the computers. For example, the sign-up sheet may say:

GIRLS	BOYS
Carlotta	Wendell
Nikki	Christopher
Janelle	Kevin
	Mark
	Huang-Long

The first three girls and the first three boys can go to the computer now, but Mark and Huang-Long will have to wait until two more girls sign up. In a spirit of enlightened self-interest, Mark and Huang-Long are likely to take an active interest in recruiting a couple of girls. Strategy 13 contains information on how to schedule school-wide computer use.

102   THE NEUTER COMPUTER

Strategy 3: Have Girls Demonstrate and Move the Computers

Another way to break the computer/male association is to put girls into public computer roles. If you need something demonstrated on the computer for the benefit of the entire class, choose girls at least half the time. You might want to keep a checklist in your desk drawer to make sure you're not calling on boys more often in response to their waving hands.

Similarly, choose girls at least half the time when hardware needs to be moved around. One girl by herself or two girls together can handle any computer, printer, disk drive, monitor, or computer cart you have in your school.

Strategy 4: Where to Put the Computer in Your Classroom

If you have a single computer in your classroom and it's in a quiet, isolated corner, think about this teacher's story. She first put the computer away from her desk and the other students' to minimize interference between the computer and what the rest of the class was doing. Girls seemed reluctant to use it. Puzzled, she took a colleague's suggestion and moved the computer near her desk, with the back of the computer facing the class. That did the trick. Girls seemed just as eager to use the computer as boys were, and nobody was distracted, either.

Strategy 5: Make a Computer Bulletin Board

Ask students for contributions such as:

- Articles about women in computing
- Printouts of students' word processing or graphics work
- Photos of your students at the computer
- Pictures from magazines or even corporate reports about new or unusual uses of computers
- Software reviews from magazines or written by your students
- Historical anecdotes: Who Is Grace Hopper?

Announce that contributions must at least include information about women, if not feature them. If you notice you are getting mostly items about men, discuss it with the students. Why is this? What does it mean to girls? To boys?

Strategy 6: Discuss Notable Women in the Computer Field

As a homework assignment, ask students to do some library research that permits them to write an "autobiography" of Grace Hopper, for example. Did you know that Grace Hopper designed the famous ENIAC computer (which was operated by 100 female programmers), and that she led the team that created COBOL, the computer language that is still used for business applications? At age seventy-nine at this writing, Grace Hopper still works on computers in the U.S. Navy as a rear admiral.

Or students could learn about Countess Ada Byron Lovelace, who had a fascinating life. She was the first computer programmer, and the computer language ADA is named after her. Or students could do some research into more modern women achievers in the computer field. Suggest to them Ruth Margaret Davis, Jean E. Sammet, and Pamela Toni Surko. Steer them away from old encyclopedias and toward *Who's Who* and personal letters of inquiry.

You might expand the field to include technology more generally, which would let you include Sally Ride. The point of the assignment, of course, is to counter the notion that only men "do" computers—an understandable notion in view of the scarcity of women presented in magazines and advertisements.

Strategy 7: Analyze Sexism in the Computer Media and Software

Two effective eye-openers are to have your class do a computer magazine analysis and a software analysis.

Computer Magazine Analysis. Ask each student to go to the

library and choose one computer magazine for adults. Try to have them choose different issues to avoid duplication (the library may have a dozen or more). Then have them make one or more of the following counts for the entire issue:

1. Count the number of men or boys in the pictures and drawings and then the number of women or girls.
2. Of the males and females pictured, how many of each are shown in active computer use and how many are just watching someone else use a computer?
3. Count the articles written about men and those written about women.
4. Count the articles written by men and those written by women, as best as students can tell from the authors' first names.

On the day the assignment is due, ask the students to report on their results. They will be quite lopsided in favor of males. To initiate discussion, ask such questions as:

- Why do you think you counted so many men and so few women? Is it because it's mostly men who are interested in computers or because the magazines give women the message that they're not supposed to be interested in computers?
- Let's say a girl picks up one of these magazines. Do you think the male slant is likely to affect her? If so, how?
- Is the male slant likely to affect a boy who picks up one of these magazines? If so, how?
- If you were the publisher of the magazine you analyzed, would you make any changes in the male/female aspect? Which ones and why?

Software Analysis. Ask each student to go to the library and choose one computer magazine about family or recreational/educational computing. Again, have them choose different issues to avoid duplication. Ask them to answer the following questions for ten randomly chosen software reviews or advertisements they find in the issue:

1. What is the theme (goal, point) of this program?
2. Does the program involve any of the following?
    a. Violence

    b. Combat or war
    c. Weapons
    d. Adventure
    e. Fantasy
    f. Outer space
    g. Sports
    h. School subjects (e.g., math, typing)
    i. Science
    j. Problem solving

3. If there is a central character in the program, is the character male or female?
4. If there is an illustration, does it show boys or girls? If both, who takes the active role and who does the watching?
5. Do you think this program would appeal more to boys, to girls, or equally to both?

On the day the assignment is due, ask the students to report on their results. Students will probably have found a clear preponderance of macho characteristics and boys as the expected consumers of the software. To initiate discussion, ask such questions as:

- Why do you think so much of the software involves violence or conflict of some sort?
- Do you think the people who wrote the reviews or ads thought the software would appeal more to one sex or another? Why?
- How do you personally feel about this kind of software? Is there another kind you wish were more available?
- Would girls reading these reviews or ads find them inviting? Would boys? What would their reactions and feelings be?
- If you were the publisher of the magazine you analyzed, would you make any changes in its software policy? Which ones, and why?

    If kids get mad after doing either of these activities, so much the better; righteous indignation—or contrariness—can be powerful enough to make girls insist on their right to a computer, too. Maybe they can write a letter on the computer to the publishers.

Strategy 8: Conduct a Home Computer Survey

    You can conduct a home computer survey with the students in your class, or you can ask them to conduct it with their friends.

(Appendix A, Copyables, contains a simple questionnaire about ownership and use of home computers.) The results of the survey will probably reveal that while male and female ownership is fairly even, use is lopsided.

An interesting discussion ought to ensue. How can we account for these results? Why don't girls and women use computers as much as boys and men? What will it mean for girls' futures if they are less knowledgeable about and comfortable with computers than boys are?

Strategy 9: What to Suggest When the Lesson Is Done

What do your students do when they complete the work you've planned for the period but the bell hasn't rung yet? Go over their notes? Start their homework? Go to the library?

Instead, suggest the computer—especially to girls. This is easy if you have one or more computers in your classroom. If the school computers are elsewhere, check with the person responsible to find out if your students can use them on an ad hoc basis every now and then.

Strategy 10: Encourage Homework Done by Computer

Papers, compositions, reports with a word processor, as well as homework would benefit from the use of database, graph-drawing, or graphics programs. Make a point to invite girls to do their homework on a computer.

Sources of computers for homework purposes: homes (for home computer owners and one or two of their friends), school after hours, parents' offices with computers, community organizations with computers (libraries, community computer centers), museums, and computer stores that have slow hours after school and very nice managers. Perhaps you can think of a few others where you live. (See page 26, "When You Don't Have Enough Computers.")

Strategy 11: Have Class Notes Taken on a Computer

If you have a computer in your classroom, can get one, or can persuade a student with a portable lap-top computer to bring it in every now and then, appoint a class computer note-taker for the day. Alternate girls and boys. The note-taker's job is obvious. The other students' job is to take their own notes by hand, and then to contribute points the note-taker might have missed. The note-taker then adds these points to the official record.

There is educational value to having students search their memories and notes to find out if the notes are complete—it gets them to review the notes and clarify any uncertainties on the spot and you are left with a reliable set of complete class notes, useful for absent students and for test preparation for everyone.

Strategy 12: Throw a Computer Pajama Party

Okay, we admit that this idea is unusual, but is that bad? (If you can't arrange for an overnight stay in school, a computer pizza party held in the evening is a functional equivalent.) Unless you teach very young children, you'll actually have to throw two parties, one for girls and one for boys. Kids bring sleeping bags or blankets, pillows, and a change of clothes. If your classroom has computers in it, hold the party there by moving the desks aside. You could also hold it in the computer lab, in your own home if you have a computer, or in the home of a computer-owner student if you can get the parents to agree.

Choose a good educational game that would appeal to your kids, such as PINBALL CONSTRUCTION SET (lets total novices construct a pinball machine), any of several story construction programs (lets them write and illustrate their own stories), DREAM HOUSE (lets them plan the furnishings and landscape design of a house), ADVENTURE CONSTRUCTION SET (lets them invent their own adventure games), a graphics program, or another of your choosing. The basic principles are that the outcome should be complex enough that there can be no clear winner or loser, and that the program should not be overly academic.

Divide the students into at least two groups. For good interaction, the groups shouldn't be smaller than four students. Each group participates in solving the problem posed by the program you have chosen. Time the turns each group gets at the computer and for each turn have them choose a different keyboarder. Let them have as many turns as they like. If you have only one computer available, take the group that isn't using it to a different part of the room and do something else with them; it's not fair for them to peek at other groups' progress.

When the groups are satisfied with the results of their team effort, have them demonstrate and explain what they have accomplished to the others. Since all students will be knowledgeable about the program, they'll appreciate the clever solutions. Then try to get some sleep.

SCHOOLWIDE STRATEGIES

Strategy 13: Schedule Student Computer Use

The way to handle schoolwide optional student computer use so that it doesn't result in overwhelming attendance by boys is to rig the rules. A first-come, first-served procedure stacks the deck in favor of boys because they are initially more enthusiastic about the computer and tend to capture most of the time slots before the less committed students—some boys as well as many girls—even start to think about it.

Any of the following systems will work well:

1. Divide the sign-up sheet (at the computer room door, at each available computer, at the library where students check out software, etc.) in half by sex, and allow only even numbers of boys and girls to use computers.
2. Schedule the sign-up process itself. Students in grade seven or with last names starting A to D can sign up from 8:30 a.m. to 10:00 a.m., etc. Vary the process, however, or the ninth grader Pat Zaremba will never get a chance.
3. Ask all students who might want to use a computer in the coming month (or week, depending on how many computers you have and how organized you can be) to sign a list, and have the list available for signing for a good week or so to catch the dilettante computerists among them. The computer room supervisor can extend personal invitations from the list, taking care to equalize the sexes in the process. Renew the process each month, encouraging new (and preferably female) students to sign up.
4. Have a monthly (or weekly) sign-up list that requires students who have used a computer last month to wait a month before signing up again.
5. Personally encourage girls to sign up in friendship groups of three or more. Give them a tantalizing description of the wonders awaiting them. Then praise them for what they accomplished when they went and strongly encourage them to go again. A few of these treatments should hook them.

Strategy 14: Girls' Day, Boys' Day (Temporary Strategy)

We hate to say it, but one of the surest ways to get girls, especially those of middle school age, involved with computers is to institute sex segregation. Such a strategy is legal if it meets three conditions: 1) equal opportunities are available to both sexes; 2) it is designed to remedy a previous sex imbalance; and 3) the students involved will be sex-integrated as soon as possible.

If your students are allowed to use computers at optional times during, before, or after the school day, set aside certain times during the week when computers are limited to girls only or boys only. For example, you can reserve Monday and Thursday afternoons for girls, Tuesday and Friday afternoons for boys, and Wednesday afternoon for anyone. Be sure that the days you choose for girls don't conflict with other activities that are popular with them.

It is not true, as many people think, that girls avoid the computer room because the boys are there. In surveys of hundreds of girls in the Computer Equity Training Project, we found instead that girls avoid the computer room because their friends, likely at middle school age to be other girls, are *not* there. So by inviting girls in friendship groups, not individually, to come to the computer room, you are creating an environment that meets girls' social needs. Their computer involvement is therefore more likely to endure.

The strategy works, of course, only if you provide girls with interesting and useful things to do with the computer once they get to the room. If they don't already know how to use basic tool programs such as word processing, graphics, and database managers, offer to teach them during this time. Look at the computer activities in Chapters 1 through 7 for ways they can use their new skills. Challenging and enjoyable educational games (see Chapter 6) are appropriate for optional computer time, too. But remember that it's free time, not class time, so whatever they'd like to do with the computer ought to be okay.

Girls' Day and Boys' Day is a temporary strategy for two reasons. One is that the need for separate days for boys and girls in the computer room will disappear once the girls become intrigued by the computer. This should take only a few months at most. As a girl in one of our field test schools told us, "When I have something to do on the computer, I don't care who else is in the room—except maybe for my girlfriend."

The second reason is that we are opposed to sex segregation on principle, and suggest resorting to it briefly only because it works so well. Girls' Day, Boys' Day should be offered each year because new students are likely to enter school with the same negative computer associations that made the strategy necessary in the first place. You'll want to drop it as soon as they've developed enough of an interest in the computer to sustain their participation without an artificial single-sex prop.

Strategy 15: Girls' Course, Boys' Course (Temporary Strategy)

This is a variation on Strategy 14 for schools that can or want to offer mini-courses or structured after-school enrichment courses for students. Like the preceding strategy, it works because it gets groups of girls into the computer room together. Do remember, though, that you'll probably need to repeat it next year.

Since even a short course is more work for a teacher than drop-in computer time, you wouldn't want to offer the same course separately for girls and boys at the same time. Instead, you can alternate a course for girls with an identical one for boys, or you can publicize a course as especially for girls but open to everyone.

One of our field test schools chose this as a strategy and it was quite successful. The key is choosing course topics that you think will appeal to girls, and the best way to do that is to observe them using computers in class or during their free time: What do they seem to enjoy? Graphics? Programs that let them construct something (stories, adventure games, electronic circuits, pinball machines)? Logo? Music composition? Creative writing? Simulations in economics or political science? You could build an entire short course around an excellent simulation.

Strategy 16: A Girls' Computer Committee

This was a strategy carried out at two of the schools in the Computer Equity Training Project. In the opinion of faculty members at both schools, it was far and away the most successful one they adopted. The strategy is not exactly a girls' computer club, which implies that members join voluntarily because of a pre-existing interest in the topic of the club. It's precisely because girls *don't* have such an interest that computer equity strategies are needed.

Instead, you and other faculty members get together and identify girls who are leaders among their peers. These are not necessarily academic high achievers, but the ones who set the styles and trends the others follow. You surely know who they are. Personally invite them to a meeting and tell them that you are concerned about the educational and occupational consequences of girls' computer avoidance—in different words, of course—and that girls are missing out on a lot of fun that the boys are having. Ask for their help as school leaders in doing something about it. Most of them, judging from past experience with this strategy, will accept the challenge.

You might want to ask the principal to write a letter to each girl's parents that explains the reason for the committee, expresses confidence in their daughter's leadership abilities, and emphasizes the importance of her participation. Perhaps you can arrange some kind of service credit or special recognition for committee members.

The Girls' Computer Committee will need a faculty adviser for coordinating meetings and activities as needed, but the girls can plan most of the activities themselves. The committee meetings should focus on enjoyable and useful computer-related activities. Many of the computer activities in Chapters 1 through 7 and most of the computer equity strategies in this chapter, the parent chapter (10), and the student chapter (11) are easily used by the committee as things to do. Suggest these possibilities to them or give them the book to read themselves.

Some committees will want to take a hard-sell approach by convincing other girls that they should give computers a try, while others will prefer to use a "honey attracts flies" approach by having so much fun that other girls can't resist getting involved. The second way usually works better, so try to guide them in that direction. At one of our schools, the committee got totally involved with graphics: they made dozens of banners, greeting cards, party invitations, posters, and such things with PRINT SHOP, and showed off their creations to admiring and impressed friends in the hall and at the bus stop. Committee membership quickly doubled.

The major operating principle for a Girls' Computer Committee is: BRING YOUR FRIENDS. It's why you chose the leaders in the first place. It works.

Strategy 17: Student Computer Teachers

Having students (girls) teach computers to other students is exceedingly clever. In one fell swoop you achieve the following:

- Assistance for the beleaguered adult computer teacher.
- Ability to provide more computer instruction to students than your staff budget allows.
- Expanded supervisory coverage of the computer room, and at no or little cost to the school.
- Development of responsibility and maturity for the student computer teacher through school service.
- The visibility of girls as computer authorities, as role models for other girls, and as attitude-changers for those boys who think that "girls can't do computers."
- Since teaching is a role many girls enjoy, it attracts more girls to computing.

This strategy doesn't come free, however. Student computer teachers need to be computer-competent as well as moderately good teachers, and this requires some preparation. One of the schools that participated in the Computer Equity Training Project had a formal student "licensing" procedure with defined instruction components and achievement testing; another went about the selection process much more informally. You and/or your team will decide the best approach for your school. Whatever that is, be sure to make a point of actively encouraging girls to apply for the job. If you don't, you'll find that nearly all the applicants are male.

Make a list of the times during the school day that the student computer teachers are available, and the times before and after school as well if such optional access is possible. Student computer teachers can:

- Supervise the computer room when it would otherwise have to be closed, enabling students to use the computers for homework or fun.
- Assist the adult computer teacher in class by giving more instructional time to individual students who need more help.
- Assist students who are having problems with software or hardware.
- Give actual lessons in introductory computing to students, teachers, parents, or community members. This is also a way to raise money for more hardware or software (see Strategy 36 below).

Strategy 18: Computer Bulletin Board

A computer bulletin board in a school hallway, the cafeteria, or any other heavily travelled location can have all the items we men-

Computer Equity Strategies for Teachers and Staff   113

tioned in Strategy 5 for a classroom computer bulletin board, as well as:

- Hardware and software exchange or sale notices
- Notices about computer clubs, courses, or users groups in the community
- Notices about computer jobs wanted or available
- Notices of help needed and offered for programming and other computer projects
- Schoolwide computer art exhibitions

If you have an active Girls' Computer Committee (Strategy 16) or your computer equity program is otherwise well publicized in the school, a very good addition to the computer bulletin board is a weekly computer use chart showing the totals for girls and for boys. If you're maintaining a sign-up system for students' computer use (Strategy 13), these figures are easy to get. Consider having a student use a graph-drawing program to display the results each week in bar graph or pie graph format, with an accompanying line graph to show changes in boys' and girls' computer use over time. This can easily become a "Go, team, go!" kind of thing, which can't hurt the cause.

Strategy 19: Computer Room Furniture Arrangement

Arranging the computer room in the traditional way—with the teacher's desk in front and the computer tables and chairs facing the desk in rows and columns—isn't the only way to do it, and may not be the best way. Many computer education experts and classroom teachers have observed that when it comes to computing, students learn best when they can share ideas and comment on each other's work. In short, when they work cooperatively.

This is especially important for girls: our surveys of hundreds of them in the Computer Equity Training Project taught us that most of them prefer to work in pairs or trios than alone. So take a look at the furniture arrangement in the computer room. Are the terminals and chairs set up so that students can move and talk among themselves freely? Or are the computers and monitors blocking students' access to each other? Figure 1 shows some floor plan suggestions. Before you start moving the furniture, check out the electrical circuitry. Adding new outlets may cost, but it will be worth it.

114　THE NEUTER COMPUTER

Figure 1 Furniture Arrangements

Transform the traditional rows into islands, with the teacher's desk in the middle.

BECOMES

Put students on the inside of a U or a semicircle, instead of on the outside.

BECOMES

Position the students back to back, instead of putting the machines back to back.

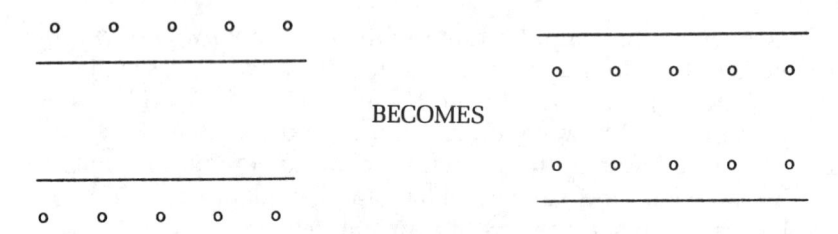

BECOMES

Strategy 20: Computer Art Show or Contest

We have been fascinated to observe how easily students develop a mania for computer graphics, especially girls. It may have something to do with the sensation of control over a powerful machine, or the ability to create something that looks much more professional than one could ordinarily create with paint or a pencil, or perhaps it's the simplicity and rapidity of creation made possible by PRINT

SHOP or KOALA PAD. (On the other hand, we know that kids happily spend many hours programming intricate drawings or designs in Logo or BASIC, so maybe it's not the simplicity or rapidity at all.)

Whatever the reason, you can take advantage of this appeal of computer graphics to boost girls' computer involvement. Hold a computer art show or contest. If you don't have enough printers, try to borrow a few temporarily from another school, a computer store (very nice free publicity if the event is covered in the local paper), or another source.

You can hold an art show simply by displaying all the computer graphics that students produce, perhaps with captions they write explaining how they did it. Or you can have student and faculty judges referee students' submissions and post the best ones—halfway between a show and a contest. Or you can take the Academy Award approach and have the entire student body be the judges—a show followed by a contest. You can take any of these approaches and use categories like: "First prize for the best abstract design done with Logo goes to . . ." "First prize for the best use of color done with MacPAINT goes to . . ."

Strategy 21: Student Nonprogramming Contest

Many schools regularly hold programming contests. If yours does and there are records of the winners, take a look. Dollars to doughnuts there won't be a girl among them. Well, maybe one. Clearly, however, programming contests are not an equity strategy even though they were a natural in the early days of educational computing when programming was just about all there was to do on the computer. They also provided schools with programs they needed because there was little commercial software available. Today, of course, that necessity no longer exists—there's plenty of good software for schools on the market.

The idea that kids can do innovative and creative things on the computer that can benefit the school is still valid, but now there are other tools besides programming. Databases, spreadsheets, or graphics programs, and Logo in addition to BASIC programming, give students opportunities to develop a wide range of serviceable products. And as we've emphasized before, these tools tend to make computing more attractive to girls.

So by all means have a contest, but make it a contest for the best computer product for a school activity or service. Students could, for example,

116   THE NEUTER COMPUTER

- Design a banner for the school newspaper.
- Design a cover for the literary magazine.
- Construct a database template for indexing library books.
- Make a spreadsheet template to record and analyze patterns of computer use.
- Integrate spreadsheet and database software to correlate student absences with events such as tests and boring assemblies.
- Design grammar game exercises as word processing utilities for language arts.

Students and faculty can brainstorm for other ideas as well. You'll get lots of female involvement, students will have a good time and learn something useful, and the school will benefit.

Strategy 22: A Literary Magazine

This strategy has obvious appeal to the writers in your school, and many of them are probably girls. Strongly suggest that submissions be via word processor and make sure that everyone with even mild interest in writing for the magazine receives instruction in word processing.

Strategy 23: A School Newspaper

Those of us who used to work on newspapers in school or later in college are envious of the kids who are doing that now. Do you remember the drudgery of correcting and retyping, correcting and retyping, ad infinitum? Do you remember cursing when the articles just refused to fit on the page, making us redo the layouts for the preceding five pages? Do you remember getting cartoons that were too big for the space, forcing us to choose between the cartoon and half an article? Do you remember the mastheads that looked like they were designed by a three-year-old with no artistic talent?

Those days are no more. With a computer, a dot matrix printer, and some newly available software, your students can design and produce a professional looking newspaper we couldn't even dream about. They can vary fonts and type sizes, compose mastheads and illustrations and adjust their dimensions, produce ragged-right or justified columns of any width, experiment with different layouts, select clip art, and more. And the software isn't even expensive. To find out what's available, look for reviews in educational computing magazines (Appendix B, Resources) or software catalogs (Chapter 6 Resources).

Strategy 24: Computer Awareness Day or Week

A Computer Awareness Day or Week is a good way to take stock of the sometimes surprising prevalence, opportunities, and uses of computers. It's a valuable educational activity for all students (and faculty), and when done properly it can also be an effective computer equity strategy for girls.

You can focus on any or all of the following aspects of computers:

- Modern uses, either visible (as in libraries) or invisible (as in washing machines).
- Computer-related careers, either direct (as in computer technician) or indirect (as in neurologist).
- Computer uses in schools, either for learning aids (as in science simulation software) or for practical tools (as in newspaper software).
- Computers-in-society issues, such as the ethics of unauthorized software copying, the computer's relation to citizens' privacy rights, computer crime, and computer equity.

Any or all of the following methods can be used as vehicles for imparting or thinking about the information:

Assemblies	Films
Hall or classroom displays	Classroom discussions
Student projects	Dramatizations
Guest speakers	Brainstorming games
Demonstrations (hands-on or not)	Pencil-and-paper games

How about a role play, where students take the roles of a software developer, a software publisher, a student who owns a copy of the software, and a student who wants one? How about a contest for the longest list of everyday objects that operate with computers? How about a "Guess My Line" game in which students must identify occupations from how computers are used in them? How about asking students to write short plays involving computer situations?

If you carry this strategy out in one day, you can suspend classes and devote the entire day to Computer Awareness, or shorten classes and devote the balance of the day to Computer Awareness, or feature Computer Awareness in each class as appropriate. If you choose to do it in a week, you can be much more thorough by devoting indi-

118   THE NEUTER COMPUTER

vidual days to specific areas (Monday for graphics and computers in the telecommunications industry, Tuesday for spreadsheets and computers in the business world, etc.) A Computer Awareness strategy can be done on as modest or grand a scale as you like.

Computer equity enters in when you plan the events with the girls especially, although not exclusively, in mind. Invite female speakers. Show a film about a woman in a computer career (see Appendix B, Resources). Display pictures of women using computers. Ask a girl to demonstrate some software. Pick a girl to play the role of a hacker in a dramatization. You don't need to be heavy-handed about this, and in fact it's better if you aren't—the emphasis on females is more matter-of-fact this way, less "Wow, look—a girl!" Girls will notice and appreciate.

Strategy 25: Raise Money for Computers in School

It's hard for girls and boys to use computers if there isn't enough hardware or software for them to use. Raising money to buy more is a legitimate computer equity strategy when the girls are actively involved in the effort: the pride they experience when they see the hardware or software bought with money they did so much to raise encourages them to take advantage of the benefits.

This strategy contains a few ways girls and boys can raise money for computers within a school; Strategy 36 gives other suggestions for raising computer money in the community.

- Raise the price of selected cafeteria items—preferably junk food like potato chips and candy—by a few pennies. They add up.
- Raise the price of tickets to school plays, dances, concerts, trips, and so forth by fifty cents or a dollar. Reserve some of the money you raised to pay for tickets for children who can't afford them.
- If you have a school bookstore, raise the price of nonessential items by a few pennies.
- Hold a raffle and make the tickets cheap. Choose things to raffle off that appeal to girls as well as boys, and either arrange to have the prize donated or set the ticket prices in line with how much you'll have to spend for it. Ask a few girls and boys to organize the raffle and select the prize, print and sell the tickets, and preside over the award. You can raffle off a camera and a roll of film, two tickets to the local movie theater, or a certificate for an audiocassette or a record at a nearby music store.

Or you can raffle off an experience, such as reserved time at a computer one hour after school every day for a week, choosing the cafeteria menu for one day, being the first person to use the new hardware or software, using the P.A. system for two minutes during homeroom period, or squirting a hose at a teacher or the principal.

Before you start your fundraising campaign, set a specific goal for what you want to purchase with the money. Post a picture of it in the hallway and next to it put up a fundraising progress chart in the form of a thermometer so kids can see how close they're coming to the goal. Make a grand announcement when you have all the money you need, and when the new acquisition arrives at school make a big fuss. It's all a lot of fun.

Strategy 26: Computer Equity Score Sheet

A good way to publicize the computer equity issue among students in the school and keep it going once strategies are underway is to announce at regular intervals boys' and girls' use of computers in school. You have to measure optional use though, otherwise you have a guaranteed fifty-fifty split and no drama. So use the records on students' free-time computer use before, during, and after school, as well as enrollment figures for computer electives.

Except for the elective enrollment figures, which are available only once a term or maybe once a year, update the chart of boys' and girls' computer use weekly. You can post the chart on the wall or you can announce the week's results at assemblies or over the P.A. system. The focus can be on girls' vs. boys' use, or on change from week to week for each sex individually. We prefer the latter focus, for the obvious nonadversarial reasons. If you want to heighten the suspense, you can call for predictions before the announcement from students on what they think the week's figures will be, somewhat like guessing the number of jelly beans in the jar.

You tend to get a healthy "We'll show them, all right!" response from the underdog—girls—in this sort of situation. Girls' educational and occupational futures are the winners.

Strategy 27: Summer Computer Course

If your school has summer courses and offers or can offer computer courses at that time, you have another strategy possibility.

Teach enrichment courses on computer topics you have noticed that many girls like or that consist of computer courseware that is fascinating but that you didn't have time for in your regular curriculum. Initiate a computer project that would take too much time during the school year, for instance, creating an animated cartoon with computer graphics. You could also do Girls' Course, Boys' Course (Strategy 15) over the summer.

However you choose to offer a summer computer course, be sure to target girls explicitly. Before school ends, give them printed information about the course(s) to take home. Talk to them personally and invite them to sign up. And for maximum success, remember to target girls' friendship groups.

COMMUNITY STRATEGIES

Strategy 28: Invite Speakers and Role Models to School

On the reasonable assumption that a school's faculty can't know everything about computing and its uses in the world, it makes sense to import some expertise. Students benefit from these contacts when their understanding of society is enriched and their potential career options broadened. When you invite speakers into classes or larger groups with girls' needs in mind, you have an excellent computer equity strategy.

While it's certainly important to invite many women—half or more of the speakers, if possible—being male is not at all a disqualification in computer equity terms. (For example, studies on women who enter nontraditional occupations reveal that the person with most influence on their career decisions was usually a male teacher.) In making your request for an expert in some aspect of computer use, specify that a major goal is to interest girls in computers. All speakers, male and female, need to point out that many women are involved in the field and extend clear encouragement to the girls to find out more.

Be a stickler on this point. Any speaker who cannot actively meet the computer equity requirement will do more harm than good. If he or she is only "evenhanded" about opportunities for boys and girls (or worse still, neglects to mention opportunities for girls at all), the computer gender gap will be strengthened. The negative notions girls bring into school with them can only be counteracted by positive and targeted encouragement.

The speakers you invite can range from a NASA astronaut—Sally Ride is a long shot but theoretically possible—to the business that uses computers down the street. Brainstorm for category ideas first with your colleagues: fire fighters, detectives, airplane pilots, cell biologists, precision tool and die makers, specialists in telecommunications law, whatever, and then work on possibilities for specific sources. Among yourselves, your acquaintances, the Yellow Pages, and back issues of the newspaper you are sure to find candidates.

Strategy 29: Computer-Related Field Trips

Instead of importing the expert to the students, export the students to the expert. Consider anyplace or anyone that uses computers; for instance, hospitals, graphic art studios, architects, accountants, stock brokers, department stores, police stations, and science museums. A computer exposition or fair held in your area can be a gold mine as a field trip. Call ahead to see if you can get one of the organizers to give a special talk or provide a guided tour.

A well-planned field trip is often worth the hassle of setting it up because students can see the environment and the work being done with their own eyes. A hands-on component, even if it only means "Hit this key, now hit that one," tends to be more impressive than simply listening to a description of what happens next. It's wise to visit the place before the field trip to explain your educational as well as your computer equity objectives, and to make reasonably sure they will all be met.

Strategy 30: Computer Career Fair

This requires great effort, but on the other hand it can be the highlight of the entire school year. A computer career fair is not only a marvelous career education activity, but it also enables you to present a smorgasbord of computer uses to students. With the range of applications thus widened, girls have many more reasons for becoming intrigued with computer exploration.

The computer career fair requires a team of faculty members, and preferably students as well, for the planning and preparation work. One of the schools in the Computer Equity Training Project recommends that you spend at least one term to put it together. If you have a Girls' Computer Committee as suggested in Strategy 16, this is an ambitious project for the committee to participate in.

Consider the following as components of your fair:

- *Speakers.* You can invite a speaker to talk about general computer industry career prospects as well as selected occupational representatives. See Strategy 28 for considerations in inviting speakers, who can include:

Accountant	Radio/TV representative
Architect	Newspaper/magazine representative
Artist or designer	
Dentist	Engineer
Farmer	Telecommunications expert
Medical professional	Automobile designer
Hospital administrator	Restaurant operator
Robotics specialist	Assembly-line worker
Chemist	Utilities worker (phone, gas, and electricity)
Banker	
Programmer	Transportation administrator

- *Demonstrations.* Using your own equipment will simplify life, but some demonstrators will be willing to bring their own if needed. (Be sure you have adequate electrical hookups.) A computer store may agree to lend demonstration equipment since it is a form of advertising. Demonstrations can include:
    - Speakers showing how they use computers in their business or profession. Describe to them ahead of time the age and knowledge levels of your students to ensure that demonstrations don't go over students' heads.
    - Students presenting creative uses of professionally developed or self-developed software. Especially encourage girls to do this.
    - Student tryouts of what has been demonstrated by the various speakers and students, or tryouts of newly purchased or borrowed software.

  You can hold demonstrations in booths set up in your gym or cafeteria, or you can disperse the demonstrations around the school, placing them in various classrooms. If the latter, you'll need a guide on what's where. It's best not to have demonstrations done from an auditorium stage if students are invited to participate: less confident students won't come forward, among them many girls.
- *Audiovisuals.* Appendix B, Resources, lists several sources of

films, filmstrips, videotapes, and other audiovisuals. These can include: career education audiovisuals on computer-related careers and audiovisuals showing computer-generated special effects. You can show these to large groups at a time (the whole student body, individual classes) or to small groups that gather around the audiovisual booth.
- *Printed materials.* Display books, pamphlets, posters, and other printed materials on computer careers, job prospects in high technology, computer software catalogs, hardware descriptions, and computer magazines. Trade associations and computer stores may have information available for distribution that students can take home. Insofar as possible, select printed materials that show women other than as secretaries or passive spectators.
- *Pictorial display.* Create an exhibit on the history of the computer industry; several women were major figures. You can also exhibit pictures of women who own or manage computer companies. Look through computer magazines for these.

Planning a Computer Career Fair. The following tasks need to be allocated among the planners to prepare a computer career fair:

- Scheduling: dates, times, space
- Contacts with presenters (after team decision on names or types of people to invite)
- Publicity: notices to students and parents, local media
- Logistics: tables, portable walls, electrical hookups, building maps, etc.
- Acquiring materials: printed material, films, borrowed hardware and software, etc.
- Refreshments

Regular meetings during the planning process are important since the functions overlap considerably—the publicity person must coordinate with the presenter-contact person, for example, who must coordinate with the scheduling person. We suggest a meeting every two or three weeks, changing to weekly for the last month before the fair. It's a lot of work. But it's worth it. (See Chapter 12 for more on planning.)

Strategy 31: Computer Equity Evening for Parents

The authors of this book have been in the business long enough to know that if you announce a program for parents specifically on the computer gender gap ("Parents: Is YOUR Daughter Being Left Out of the Computer Revolution?"), you're unlikely to get a standing-room crowd. This isn't because parents don't care about their daughters, or because they think it's right for their daughters to be left out of the computer revolution. Parents who are unaware they are treating their daughters and sons differently when it comes to computers have no reason to believe the topic applies to them. Without becoming aware, however, the problem is harder to solve—a Catch-22.

A computer equity strategy aimed at parents must therefore get past the "you're not talking about me" barrier. And once you get past it, you can't be accusatory. We all tune out blame. The solution is to sneak up on their blind side. They may not come to a computer equity evening, but they'll come to a session on the wonderful computer opportunities available to their children in school. Send home a notice describing an evening that will include a talk by the computer teacher about the computer education program the school offers, a tour of the computer facilities, and computer demonstrations by their very own children. This last event always goes over big.

But take advantage of the parents' status as captive audience and

- Using the Introduction to *The Neuter Computer* for source material, tell them about the national scope of the computer gender gap. Tell them you didn't believe it either until you saw it happening in your own school.
- Give them the student computer-use figures you've compiled.
- Have a few girls describe their feelings about computers.
- Ask them to fill out the parent questionnaire (see Appendix A, Copyables), and publicize the results.
- Having asked parents to bring their children, ask parents to observe how many boys vs. how many girls actually came, or how many boys vs. how many girls are clustered around the computers.
- Describe the educational and occupational consequences to their daughters if the gap isn't closed.
- Tell them about your computer equity effort and the strategies being carried out in school.
- Distribute copies of Chapter 10, Parent Strategies.
- Ask for their help in encouraging their daughters' computer participation. (See Strategies 32, 33, and 34 and the strategies in Chapter 10 for ways they can help.)

A few of our schools did a computer equity evening using these strategies and recommend it. Most of the parents who came had not been aware of the computer gender gap, but having heard about it felt it was an important issue that should be dealt with. This is valuable support for your computer equity program in school.

One school suggests not to call the session a "Computer Open House," as they did. Parents took them literally and drifted in and out between 7:00 p.m. and 10:00 p.m., with the result that some parents missed the computer equity part of the evening.

Strategy 32: Computer Course for Parents

If you want to go to more trouble—especially if you can be paid for your trouble—you can offer a mini-course of introductory computer instruction to parents in evening sessions, as several of the schools in our project did. The strategy has two goals. The first is to teach the parents how to use a computer; the second is to make them aware of the importance of encouraging their daughters to use it so that computer equity will be achieved.

In devoting evening sessions to word processing, database managers, spreadsheets, and the like, you have to be careful that the first goal doesn't swamp the second. By all means, teach them how to use a word processor, but then give them concrete suggestions for interesting and useful things they and their daughters can do with a word processor. The simplest way to do this is using the chapters in Part One of this book that focus on the computer applications you teach in your parent course. You can also devote the first session to an overview of the course, giving attention to computer equity as described above in Strategy 31.

A parent computer course can be combined with other strategies if it is taught by students, preferably girls (see Strategy 17), and if it is used to raise money for computers (see Strategy 36). Or faculty can teach it at no cost to the learners. Preregistration is essential for a free course to keep the number of learners from going over capacity and psychologically to make sure that those who enroll actually attend. Prepayment is naturally an even more effective guarantee, a good reason to charge a small fee for the course even if you're not doing it for fundraising.

Strategy 33: Send Computer Equity Information Home

This is simple and very effective. When you see a good article about computer equity, send copies home to all or selected parents. (See Appendix B, Resources, for a list of computer equity articles in addition to current articles you find.) Write up the developments in your own computer equity strategies, including updates in student computer-use figures and computer elective enrollments, for the newsletter that gets sent home. If one of your own female students becomes involved with the computer, let her parents know how pleased you are. If you think another girl would enjoy the computer and be good at it but refuses to consider the possibility, invite her parents to encourage her as well.

And keep it up. One of the important lessons we learn from Madison Avenue is that repetition yields results.

Strategy 34: Parent Task Force on Computer Equity

Parents who become concerned about the computer equity issue can be powerful allies for you, doubling your effectiveness in school by reinforcing it at home. A good way to channel their concern is by forming a parent task force. Invite parents who seem particularly ready to help to a meeting at school early in the morning or during the evening—not between nine and five—you eliminate too many working parents this way. Ask them to read as many parts of this book as you think they will need (at a minimum the Introduction and Chapter 10). Then, aside from providing information or serving as liaison between the parent task force and your colleagues in school, stand back and let the task force help.

The task force can operate through your parent/teacher association or independently. Either way, its mission is to promote computer equity for girls through activities carried out in or outside of school.

Strategy 35: Area Conference on Computer Equity

Now that you've gotten hooked by the computer equity issue, it's time for you to hook other people so that the girls they influence can benefit as well. If you think people won't be interested in attending a conference on computer equity for girls, you can call it "Crisis in Computer Education" or some such title. The rationale behind this is found in Strategy 31.

Consider any of the following groups as target audiences, since

Computer Equity Strategies for Teachers and Staff

each has an actual or potential impact on girls' computer involvement, and get the local media to cover the event:

- Educators from other schools or districts
- Parents
- High technology employers and computer businesses
- Women's groups
- Computer users' clubs
- Adult education and vocational education specialists
- Public library personnel
- Science museum personnel
- Professional associations in the computer industry
- College/university departments of computer science or women's studies
- Career placement specialists

You might consider a "name" speaker to draw the crowd—a popular local or state politician (an invitation to a U.S. representative or senator doesn't cost and an acceptance is possible), a well-known feminist, or a highly respected educator or businessperson. If your celebrity is intrigued and accepts, you may have to do a little educating first. Give her or him a copy of this book as a crash course in computer equity.

The program will of course need to fit the particular audience you have in mind, but consider these topics:

- Evidence for the computer gender gap—the audience, especially parents, is sure to add some evidence of their own, and the stories are very effective.
- Consequences of computer inequity, especially occupational.
- What you are doing in your school to reverse the problem, possibly discussed by a panel of teachers and girls.
- What the community can do to reverse the problem.

The goal of the conference should be action-oriented: now that the community is aware of the problem, what will it do to help resolve it? Media coverage is helpful in and of itself, but more long-lasting outcomes would be the adoption of the computer equity issue as a focus for action by existing community groups, or the establishment of an advisory committee for your school's or the district's computer equity program. One school we know had an advisory committee that met monthly over breakfast and provided help in many ways.

Strategy 36: Raise Money for Computers in the Community

In Strategy 25 we discussed how you can raise money for computers within your school, and talked about the computer equity dimensions of this strategy. The same dimensions apply to a community fundraising drive, which is often more tempting since the community has more money than the students do.

Consider the following, which can be carried out in the community by students, the parent/teacher association, and/or the faculty:

- Car washes and bake sales.
- A used book sale, with books solicited from community residents.
- A gigantic garage, tag, or rummage sale, with goods solicited from community residents.
- A raffle, with a prize (preferably donated) that would appeal to many community people, such as a computer, a television, a VCR, or a weekend vacation for two.
- Offer computer lessons for a fee (see Strategy 17), or any other lessons students or faculty members could teach and people would pay for.
- Hold a "Computathon." If students can hold walkathons, swimathons, jogathons, and other -athons for charity, why not a computathon to raise money for computers? They can obtain pledges for units achieved of the following:

Pages read	Yards jumped or hopped in burlap bags
Math problems done correctly	
Miles jogged, walked, or swum	Famous _____ named (mathematicians, composers, authors, astronauts, rock stars, etc.)
Lines of poetry memorized	
Presidents of the United States named (in order!)	Dates of historical events
Paintings identified by artist	Feet of rope climbed
Popular songs identified by singer or group	Drawings or paintings made

Choose a few varied activities and have students select what they want to do. After pledges have been obtained, hold the computathon events at school a few minutes a day for a week so that students who are absent a day or two aren't left out. An elementary school in Oregon chose reading, math facts, and jogging for their computathon, and raised over $12,000 for computers.

Strategy 37: Involve Women's Organizations in Computer Equity

Involving women's organizations is good if you want an outside group to co-sponsor a big-deal strategy with you, such as a computer career fair, an area computer equity conference, or a summer computer camp. Co-sponsor in this case means they share the work and raise most of the money needed. Another reason for pulling in an outside women's organization is when you want to apply gentle pressure on an educational establishment that doesn't consider the computer equity issue very important.

If you find yourself in either of these circumstances, contact local chapters of the following women's organizations and discuss collaboration. These groups may be able to offer you volunteer time, facilities, services, advice, and/or contacts. They are good allies to have.

- Service organizations, such as the League of Women Voters or the Junior League. Call the Community Affairs department at City Hall.
- Professional women's organizations, such as the American Association of University Women, the Federation of Business and Professional Women, or the National Federation of Women Business Owners. If you locate one, it will lead you to the others.
- Women's center or YWC/HA.
- Commission on the Status of Women (call City Hall) and your local chapter of the National Organization for Women.
- Citizens Advisory Committee on Sex Equity in Education. Call the school superintendent's office to find out if there is one.

Strategy 38: Summer Computer Camp

We know this is a little off the beaten track, but it's obviously a good computer equity strategy. A summer computer camp means that girls spend roughly half their time on the usual camp-type activities—arts and crafts, volleyball, river rafting, whatever—and the other half on computers.

If there is already a girls' summer camp in your area, or a Girls' Club or a Girl Scout group that meets during the summer, contact the people who run it and suggest expanding their program by offering a special camp session devoted to computers. If they like the idea but need computer facilities, ask your principal and superintendent if using the school's can be arranged. This might include offering the computer teacher a part-time summer job. If the school computers don't work out, try a local college or community college.

It's possible to accomplish the same goal when there is an existing co-ed camp or summer program that is willing to include a computer component. In this case, make the director aware that publicity and recruitment techniques that don't specifically target girls will probably result in a mostly male enrollment. Since you're familiar with the computer equity issue and with strategies that are successful in attracting girls, you can play an important advisory role to make sure girls sign up, possibly as a paid consultant. The same suggestion applies to an existing computer camp, which can probably use the same computer equity advice.

9 Computer Equity Strategies for Administrators

Menu

	GOTO PAGE
Introduction	133
Building-Level Strategies	133
1. In-Service Session on Computer Equity	133
2. Low-Key Education About Computer Equity	135
3. In-Service Session on Computers	136
4. Promoting Faculty Use of Computers with Students	138
5. Expanding Student Access to Computers	138
6. Obtaining More Hardware and Software	139
7. Ensuring Computer Equity Improvement	140
Strategies 1, 2, and 7	
District-Level Strategies	141
8. Make Your Peers Aware of the Computer Gender Gap	141
9. Build Computer Equity into District Policy	142
10. Publicize Computer Equity in the Community	143
Strategies 8, 9, and 10	
State and National Strategies	144
11. Educate Your Peers	144

Menu, Continued

	GOTO PAGE
12. Showcase Your Success	145
Strategies 11 and 12	

INTRODUCTION

Computer equity is nearly impossible to do without the active support of the school administrator. Your support is even more important to computer equity than many other programs because sex equity makes some faculty members uncomfortable. Computers do, too. If your faculty is to help girls avoid the serious educational and occupational consequences of saying "No, thank you" to the computer, you have to lead the way. Your leadership is the key to . . .

Awareness. Most of your faculty probably isn't aware of the computer gender gap or its consequences. Your leadership is needed to raise the issue, emphasize its importance, and provide staff development about it.

Accomplishment. The computer equity strategies in this book require varying amounts of time and effort from faculty members. They already have many responsibilities and obligations, and may not initially be keen about taking on more. Your leadership is needed to make resources available and create the expectation of sustained accomplishment.

This chapter contains suggestions on how you can exert your leadership on behalf of computer equity.

BUILDING-LEVEL STRATEGIES

Strategy 1: In-Service Session on Computer Equity

All the schools that participated in our Computer Equity Training Project held in-service sessions on computer equity of one sort or another—and all of the teachers felt they were essential. As one of them said,

> An in-service session is the only way to get the information about computer equity out to the whole faculty, not just the ones who are likely to be interested anyway. And if the principal or the assistant principal is there and participates in the session, people get the message that this is serious and they need to do something about it.

Some people think that if a school has had an in-service session on computer education, that's enough to deal with the equity issue. If this were true, there would be no computer equity problem in schools that have had an excellent computer in-service session. Unfortunately that's not what we see, partly because some computer education specialists are not aware themselves of the gender gap in computer use and therefore don't include it in their sessions. Your faculty needs a session on computer equity whether or not they've had one on computer education.

Content of the Session

- Evidence on the computer gender gap in your school.
- Information about the problem nationally: evidence, causes, and consequences to girls if nothing is done about it, as described in the Introduction. If your faculty isn't familiar enough with the general issue of sex equity in schools, material on this broad topic should be included (see Appendix B, Resources, for information suggestions).
- What teachers and staff can do to increase girls' computer use (Chapter 8), and what they can do to help parents (Chapter 10) and students (Chapter 11) get involved.

Selection of the Trainer. There are several possibilities for trainers, from a faculty member to a professional training consultant. It's especially important to get references for a computer equity trainer since computer equity can be a sensitive topic. A bad trainer can antagonize people and make the problem worse. This you don't need.

Here are some sources of computer equity trainers:

- *Sex Desegregation Assistance Centers* (Sex DACs). Ten regional federally funded centers offer expert in-service training on sex equity in schools at no cost to users of their services. They are listed in Appendix B.
- *State sex equity specialists.* There are three kinds: Title IV for sex equity (there are others for race and national origin equity), Title IX, and vocational education. They all do training or can recommend someone. Write or call them by job title at your state's Department of Education.
- *District Title IX coordinator.* In some districts the Title IX coordi-

nator is very knowledgeable about sex equity, while in others it's an empty title. Only the first kind is qualified to do training.
- *A local professor.* If there's a college or university with an education department in your area, find out if a professor specializes in sex equity in education.
- *A member of your school's staff.* Using this book and other resources listed in Appendix B, you or a colleague could deliver the training.
- *A professional trainer.* If you'd like an outside expert and have the money, hire a consultant. Write to one of the computer equity experts listed in Appendix B.

You may find that except for the consultants we list, none of the other sources is knowledgeable about the computer aspect of sex equity. Computer equity is a very new issue in education, and even some sex equity experts don't know much about it yet. A good solution is to invite a sex equity trainer and a computer education trainer to team up in preparing and delivering the in-service session—they'll educate each other and then educate your faculty.

If you can have only one trainer, choose the best sex equity trainer you can find, give her or him a copy of this book, and recommend that that they follow up some of the resources on computer equity in Appendix B. The trainer should have at least some familiarity with computers.

Strategy 2: Low-Key Education About Computer Equity

There are many ways short of formal in-service training to educate faculty members, other administrators, and parents about computer equity. Here are several.

Personal Inspection. Ask faculty members to drop by the computer room when it's open to students for free-time use. Drop by yourself, too. As one teacher in the field test told us,

> I thought I was convinced by the information you had in [the Introduction], but when I looked in the computer room and saw nine boys and two girls I was astonished. That's what did it for me, and now I REALLY believe it.

The Computer Neutrality Self-Test. Duplicate copies of the self-test from the copyables in Appendix A and distribute them to the faculty. At the next faculty meeting, ask them about their answers. An adapted form of the self-test can be distributed to parents, particularly before an evening session for parents on computer equity (see Strategy 31 in Chapter 9).

Post Student Computer-Use Charts. Your school may already keep track of student free-time computer use, either by signing them in at the computer room or signing out the software they use. It's a simple matter to have these lists summarized weekly, either just by sex or by sex and grade. The computer gender gap tends to widen with age—your figures will probably bear this out.

Have the computer-use chart posted every week where everyone can see it, for instance, in the Teachers' Lounge or near the mailboxes. Discuss it at faculty meetings or over coffee. (How about a lottery on next week's figures to heighten their interest?)

Have the Faculty Read the Introduction to the Neuter Computer. Several field test teachers told us they found the statistics very powerful.

Distribute Articles About Computer Equity. When you see a good article or study on computer equity, duplicate it and put copies in mailboxes. Ask for reactions at the next faculty meeting. (See the computer equity bibliography in Appendix B, Resources.)

Newsletters. Publicize the computer gender gap in newsletters to faculty or parents. Include your school's computer-use figures and stress the need for action about it.

Strategy 3: In-Service Session on Computers

What if your faculty is well aware of sex equity in general and computer equity in particular, but is still reluctant to carry out strategies to encourage girls' computer use? The obstacle might be faculty discomfort with or opposition to computers. People who don't know how to use computers naturally don't know what they're missing, and just as naturally don't see why they should encourage anyone else to do what they don't want to do.

Their opposition may spring from fear about computers, which are sometimes said to invade our privacy, breed computer criminals, prevent us from thinking for ourselves, turn nice kids into antisocial computer fanatics, put people out of jobs, and so forth. Many educators have additional concerns, such as whether a school should be spending a lot of money for computer hardware and software when there are other pressing needs, and whether computer instruction will drain class time away from other important subjects.

These issues are serious ones and deserve our best attention, but ignorance of the computer can't possibly lead to thoughtful, balanced conclusions. Computer training is a necessity.

Content of the Training. Whatever kind of computer training you choose, there are two essentials to keep in mind for the content:

- There is no substitute for hours of hands-on computer experience. Talking is less important than doing.
- Teachers must be taught computer skills that are useful to them. They can learn applications such as word processing for their own writing or spreadsheets for their own budgeting. They can learn classroom management programs to reduce some of the drudge work in teaching: making up and grading tests, calculating student course grades. They can learn how to use software in their individual subject areas with students. They can learn how to use applications with their students in class. But programming for its own sake or applications with no direction on what to use them for are pretty much a waste of time.

Selection of the Trainer. Here are some trainer possibilities.

- *In-house Trainer.* The computer teacher from your school or another school in the district may be willing to offer computer instruction on an informal basis before or after school. If you can pay her or him to provide scheduled sessions and if you can offer continuing education credit for them, so much the better.
- *District Computer Coordinator.* Teaching faculty members how to use computers is presumably part of the coordinator's job.
- *A Student Teacher.* It takes an unusual student and an unusual faculty, but some of the kids in school today are easily capable of teaching grown-ups how to use a computer.
- *Computer Teacher Center.* There are organizations that provide computer education services to schools in nearly all states. Ask your district computer coordinator about what the center offers.
- *College Courses.* A local college or university might offer a course on educational computing for teachers, and the district might pay for it. Before recommending it, ask previous students of the course whether it was good—the quality of computer courses nationwide is quite uneven.
- *State Computer Coordinator.* Write to this person—most states now have one—by job title at your state Department of Education.

She or he should be able to tell you about computer trainers in your area.

Strategy 4: Promoting Faculty Use of Computers with Students

Faculty members need to appreciate the usefulness and fun of computers, but an in-service session may not be enough to get them to the point where they actually use computers with students. The following suggestions may help.

Weekend and Vacation Computer Loans. Arrange for teachers to take the machines and software home over weekends and vacations. Yes, they'd have to sign out the equipment on Friday, transport it, and sign it back in on Monday morning. But computers are hardy things. No problems and many advantages have been reported by schools that do this.

Help with Choosing Software. Many teachers are overwhelmed by the sheer volume of educational software available. There are some good ways to make the task manageable: subscribe to a few of the educational computing magazines listed in Appendix B; they all review software. Since many software manufacturers permit review before purchase, establish a rotating review committee to share the work; refer to the resource section at the end of Chapter 6 which lists several software evaluation services and publications you can use.

Reviewing software takes less time than many teachers fear, but learning it for use in class is another story. Consider dipping into your substitute teacher budget occasionally to free teachers for learning instructional software.

Taking the Plunge. We've noticed that many computer-novice teachers are reluctant to leave the learning stage for the teaching/using stage. They remind us of graduate students who do endless research to put off the awful moment of actually writing the dissertation. Insist that total expertise is not essential—it doesn't even exist—and that the world won't come to an end if kids sometimes help teachers out. Make sure your computer training plans specify how and when teachers' new skills will actually reach students.

Strategy 5: Expanding Student Access to Computers

Many schools have perfectly good computer facilities that are severely underutilized due to lack of supervision. While it's true you can't risk theft and damage to hardware and software in unsupervised facilities, it doesn't do any good to encourage girls' computer use when the computer room is locked.

Here are some suggestions for opening it up by increasing your supervisor pool. All supervisors who are not already computer teachers or otherwise computer-knowledgeable will require some training first, which you can ask your computer teacher to provide. One school we worked with required supervisors to qualify by successfully completing a mini-course offered by the computer teacher.

Hire Computer Supervisors. If your budget can cover this, advertise for and pay adults with free time during the day and at least some computer knowledge to supervise the computer room.

Recruit Volunteers. One of our field test schools recruited parents to volunteer in two-hour shifts. Parents who work only part time or are full-time homemakers may be interested in helping out if they receive adequate training and support. Matching volunteers' particular interests to their responsibilities and giving them teaching rather than caretaking to do keeps them coming back.

Student Supervisors. You surely have some students in your school who have free time during the day or after school, and are expert enough at computers and reliable enough to serve as supervisors. If another junior high or high school is close by, perhaps students from there could be imported as computer supervisors. Some kind of credit or formal recognition, plus a record of service on their transcripts, could easily be arranged; or else you could pay them.

Computer Loans to Students. Faculty members needn't be the only ones allowed to take computers home on weekends or vacations. Students wanting the privilege should earn it by demonstrating responsibility and a level of computer competence acceptable to the computer teacher.

Opening School After Hours. Theoretically, you can more than double the time computers are accessible to students by opening the computer room up on evenings and weekends—it's so wasteful to have them unused most of the time. Any of the above supervision techniques or paying a faculty member for the extra time would enable you to extend computer access to evenings or weekends. This is also excellent for providing parents and other community members who don't have computers at home or work with an opportunity to use them.

Strategy 6: Obtaining More Hardware and Software

If your computers are in use all day long and your student/computer ratio is still impossible, here are some fundraising techniques to obtain more hardware and software than your normal budget allows.

Fees for Computer Lessons. A lot of people are paying a lot of money for introductory computer lessons that some of your teachers and students could teach, and at a lower fee. Lessons could be scheduled for early evenings or weekends, and proceeds would go to a Computer Fund. We suggest you require prepayment with enrollment rather than at each lesson: you increase learners' attendance and get all the money that way.

Hold a Computathon. If students can hold walkathons, swimathons, jogathons, and other -athons for charity, why can't they hold a computathon to raise money for hardware and software? They can obtain pledges for units of such activities as pages read, math problems done correctly, feet of rope climbed, lines of poetry memorized, important dates in history named correctly, astronauts named, and so forth. An elementary school in Oregon raised over $12,000 for computers this way.

PTA Fundraising for Computers. If your PTA raises money or could be encouraged to, they could go all out this year to raise money for the Computer Fund. You provide the goal and they'll figure out how.

Apply for Grants. Your district may have funds available that can be used for purchase of hardware and software. The district computer coordinator will know if your state has a funded program for this purpose.

Stretch Your Money. Hardware and software prices vary a great deal from place to place. You can stretch your computer budget considerably by taking advantage of bargains. At one junior high school in Brooklyn, New York, faculty members watch the ads for hardware and software sales. They don't mind making buying trips because they combine the errand with family day trips on weekends. They've made their computer budget go very far this way.

Strategy 7: Ensuring Computer Equity Improvement

The bottom line is results: increasing girls' computer use in your school as measured by their enrollment in computer electives or participation in extracurricular computer activities. The strategies above set the stage, while this one makes sure the play actually takes place.

Lead the Computer Equity Team. Or at least be a member of the group that plans and implements the computer equity strategies in your school. The planning process in Chapter 12 describes how a group of faculty members can select and carry out strategies that have a direct impact on girls' computer attitudes and behavior. The team will function better if you're a part of it.

Require Progress Updates. Demonstrate that you consider the computer equity situation important by asking for weekly reports on girls' computer use. Discuss the results at faculty meetings; publicize them in staff newsletters. If the reports are good, distribute congratulations. If they're bad, insist on improvement.

Reward Successful Faculty Members. Faculty members who are especially successful at getting girls interested in computers and keeping them interested deserve to be rewarded by any of the means you have at your disposal, for instance, public thanks, locating a computer in that person's classroom, incentive pay, paid attendance at a computer equity conference, and master teacher status.

Keep It Up Next Year. You may have raised girls' computer use 150 percent this year, but next year's girls will come into school with the same negative attitudes you just finished dealing with. Until we see equal numbers of females and males using computers in the workplace, the media, the home, and the school, computer equity will continue to be the school's responsibility.

DISTRICT-LEVEL STRATEGIES

A successful computer equity program in one school will surely make an important difference in the lives of girls at that school, but what about other girls in the district? Here are several strategies for widening your computer equity accomplishments.

Strategy 8: Make Your Peers Aware of the Computer Gender Gap

Your counterparts in other schools and the superintendent probably know as little about computer equity as you did at first, but now you can alert them to it.

District Meetings. Put computer equity on the agenda at a district meeting of school administrators. Tell them about the situation in your school and why you feel it's important to address it district-wide.

Meet with the Superintendent. Set up a meeting to discuss the computer equity issue. Urge district-wide action.

School Board Meetings. Arrange to have computer equity put on the agenda of a school board meeting, if necessary through indirect but politically advisable means. See to it that there are computer equity supporters in the audience that evening.

District Publications. Submit an article about computer equity to your school district's newsletter. If you're in a big district with a professional newsletter staff, invite a reporter to cover the story. It's naturally best to do this after you have impressive accomplishments to report. Our California field test school did this: readers in a thousand schools in the Los Angeles Unified School District learned they had a national computer equity model school in their midst.

Strategy 9: Build Computer Equity into District Policy

Like anything else in education, computer equity is easier to do if it's part of the official structure: policy and budget.

Make It Part of the Computer Curriculum Policy. Inequitable computer use is best addressed in a district's curriculum policy statement. It establishes legitimacy for the issue and informs faculty throughout the district that progress is expected. If you're not on the committee responsible for formulating district policy, tell those who are about the need for including computer equity.

The first policy step is to make computing required for all students. When it's optional, students with negative computer attitudes tend to avoid the course. More than half of them will be girls. The quality of the introductory computer course is critical however, since several studies have shown greater female discomfort with the computer after the course than before it. Generally, computer literacy courses that focus exclusively on programming run the greatest risk of further alienating girls. We recommend requiring a course in computer applications—word processing, graphics, database management—in the elementary grades. These tool programs have direct application, a characteristic many girls tend to value above all others.

The second policy step is to make computing an integral part of the rest of the district's curriculum. Regular classroom use of computer applications and instructional software diminishes girls' negative computer attitudes, which flourish when the computer is a strange and foreign machine surrounded by boys. Also essential are money for hardware and software, liberal student access to the computers, teachers trained in how to integrate subject-specific software into their lesson plans, and a time-efficient software review system. The educational benefits derived by girls—and boys—make this a wise investment, which needs to be anchored in district policy and budget.

Make It Part of the Sex Equity Policy. Your district, like all others, has a Title IX plan for sex equity. Chances are that computer equity, being so new an issue, is not included. Find out what must be done to change that.

Make Someone Responsible for Computer Equity. The district's computer coordinator, Title IX (sex equity) coordinator, both of them, or another knowledgeable person should be officially responsible for assessing the computer gender gap in district schools, assisting staff to close it, monitoring progress, and requiring accomplishment. See what you can do to get this responsibility assigned to someone who will carry it out well.

Get Funds Allocated for Computer Equity. Compared to most school district expenditures, this one is pretty cheap. Funds would be valuable for time and travel for staff development, in-service sessions, teacher stipends for after-school computer equity activities, and a few books and periodicals. A small discretionary fund to be used for computer equity strategies such as paying honoraria to computer career day speakers would also be useful.

Strategy 10: Publicize Computer Equity in the Community

An aware community will work with you rather than against you. Try these strategies.

Newspaper Stories. Ask the editor of your local paper to cover the story by sending out a photographer and a reporter. School stories are good copy for local papers, and with a computer angle they're even better. Wait until you have something to brag about before you do this.

TV and Radio. What works with newspapers will work with television and radio.

Community Computer Meetings. 1. Ask to be put on the program of computer user group meetings in order to discuss the issue. 2. If there's a computer dealer trade association in town, see if you can get computer equity covered in their newsletter or discussed at a meeting. The female computer market is virtually untapped and ought to be an attractive prospect to enlightened businesspeople. 3. If you're fortunate enough to live in a place that governs itself by town meetings, attend, bring up the issue of computer equity, and invite a community response.

STATE AND NATIONAL STRATEGIES

Computer equity is a national (indeed, a worldwide) issue, affecting the education and occupational future of girls and young women across the United States. There are things you can do, some of them quite easy, to make an impact.

Strategy 11: Educate Your Peers

Since you're reading this book, you already know more about computer equity than 90 percent of your peers. If you have a successful computer equity program in your school, you know more than 99 percent of them. Share what you know.

Professional Publications. Write a letter to the editor of your favorite educational journal. If you're really motivated, submit an article.

Raise the Issue at Professional Meetings. When you attend statewide or national professional meetings, go to a few sessions on computer education. If the speakers don't raise the equity issue, you raise it in the question period. Similarly, raise it at sessions on sex equity if the speakers don't. And if they do, reinforce its importance by describing your own experience with computer equity.

Be a Speaker at Professional Meetings. Present a workshop or invite colleagues to participate in a panel with you, and teach others what you have learned. Ask a faculty member to represent your school in this way.

Strategy 12: Showcase Your Success

Entirely too much reinventing of wheels goes on in American education. In addition to sparing your counterparts elsewhere the trouble of working out a successful computer equity program from scratch, there's also a fair amount of glory—a rather pleasant experience—in exhibiting your success for all to see.

Publicize Your Computer Equity Achievements. You can do this via professional publications of all sorts, conferences and professional meetings, and conversations with colleagues. Let it be known your school has accomplished something impressive.

Accept the Responsibilities of Modelhood. Modelhood takes time and a little bit of money: answering telephone and mail inquiries on your success, showing visitors around your model school, getting substitute teachers for your computer equity faculty leaders so they can accept speaking invitations. It's well worth it.

Produce Replication Materials. If you think you can improve on *The Neuter Computer*, write up the secrets of your success so others can copy it. Consider producing an audiovisual on computer equity to motivate girls to become involved with computers, or one to educate adults on the issue. Place ads for your materials in professional journals. Use the proceeds to expand your computer equity program or to buy hardware or software.

10 Computer Equity Strategies for Parents

Menu

	GOTO PAGE
Introduction	148
Home Strategies If You Have a Home Computer	149
1. Everyone Should Learn How to Use It	149
2. Family Computer Projects	149
3. Encourage Homework on the Computer	150
4. Host a Computer Party	150
Home Strategies If You Don't Have a Computer	151
5. Encourage School Computer Activities	151
6. Be on the Alert for Sexism	151
7. Subscribe to Computer Magazines	152
8. Discuss Computers at Home	152
9. Consider Buying a Computer	153
Strategies 5, 6, 7, and 8	
School Strategies—What You Can Do in a Group	153
10. Find Out About the Situation	154
11. Send a Delegation to School	154
12. Newsletter	154
13. Computer Equity Evening	154
14. Mother/Daughter or Father/Daughter Computer Session	154

146

Computer Equity Strategies for Parents 147

Menu, Continued

GOTO PAGE

15. Computer Workshops for Parents 155
16. Computer Career Fair 155
17. Fund-Raising Drive 155

Strategies 12, 13, 16 and 17

School Strategies—What You Can Do
As an Individual 156
18. Educate the Educators 156
19. Become a Volunteer Computer
    Supervisor 156

Community Strategies 157
20. Go to a Computer Store 157
21. Visit Businesses That Use
    Computers 157
22. Attend a Computer Show 157
23. Go to Movies That Display
    Computer Graphics 158
24. Visit a Science Museum 158
25. After-School Computer Programs 158
26. Summer Computer Camps 159
27. Help Your Daughter Get a Part-
    Time Computer Job 159
28. Join a User's Group 159

Strategies 21 and 23

INTRODUCTION

Your attitudes and values have enormous influence on your daughter. Some of the girls we met during the project said they became involved in computers because their mothers or fathers got them started. These girls were lucky. Our research tells us that:

- Some parents consider computer education more important for their sons than for their daughters. They discuss computer-related careers more with their sons, buy more home computers for their sons, and enroll their sons in summer computer camps more often than their daughters.
- In most homes with computers, mothers are the least likely family members to use the machines.
- In some families, boys are allowed to stay for after-school computer activities while girls are required to come home.

Some of those parents who have learned about the computer gender gap are going out of their way to make sure their daughters enjoy using a computer when they're young. This way, they figure, their daughters won't avoid the computer when they reach adolescence. It's a reasonable theory, but nobody can be sure it will work. Computers are too new in 1986 for many girls to have used them throughout their childhood, and we don't know yet what will happen when these girls enter middle or junior high school.

Using our crystal ball, we think this approach will work with some girls, but we suspect it won't work with all of them. A girl who still likes computers at age twelve or thirteen may decide to keep it to herself or even change her mind if she sees that her girlfriends think that computers are "yukky"—and that girls who like computers are "weird." Many adolescents aren't strong enough to resist peer pressure like that.

So you can't relax yet. Your role in making sure your daughter has the educational and eventual occupational benefits of computer knowledge is very important. This chapter offers you some suggestions on how to go about it.

Whether or not your family has a computer, there are many things you can do to encourage and support your daughter's interest in computers without even leaving home.

HOME STRATEGIES IF YOU HAVE A HOME COMPUTER

Strategy 1: Everyone Should Learn How to Use It

Especially mothers. In the schools we worked with, only 10 percent of the girls who had computers at home said their mothers used them. Only 13 percent said their sisters used them. This isn't a very good example to set.

Whether you're a mother or a father, if you don't already know how to use a computer now is the time to learn. It's easier than you may think, and it's both enjoyable and useful. Ask a computer-knowledgeable family member to teach you, take an adult education course, or teach yourself from a software manual. If this means your son won't be able to use the computer the six hours a day he's accustomed to, so be it: you live there, too.

Strategy 2: Family Computer Projects

Many home computer activities involve skills girls are learning in school. Or at least, we hope they are; if not, they need to learn at home. With your daughter, you can use a spreadsheet program for planning the expenses of a family trip, or a database program to make a cross-referenced file of the family's birthday and gift records, books, collections, recipes, VCR or audio cassettes.

You can use a word processing program to write a Season's Greetings letter from everyone in the family to all your relatives and friends. You can use it just for fun for an inhouse electronic mail system: set up files called MOM TO NIKKI, NIKKI TO MOM, NIKKI TO DAD, etc., and date your entries. Family members have to promise not to snoop in someone else's mail.

In ancient times before television, families used to spend evenings together reading aloud, doing jigsaw puzzles, and playing Monopoly. Many pleasant hours can be spent as a family with a good computer game, such as PINBALL CONSTRUCTION SET, ARCADE MACHINE (a program which lets you create original games that can be totally nonviolent), GERTRUDE'S PUZZLE, or ROCKY'S BOOTS. There really are good alternatives to the sadistic kill-the-enemy-aliens kind of recreational software. Magazines such as *Family Computing* have reviews of this kind of software; see Appendix B, Resources. Chapters 1 through 7 contain dozens of interesting and useful things that can be done with computers, many of which are appropriate for the home.

Strategy 3: Encourage Homework on the Computer

As authors of this book, we offer a personal testimonial to the value of word processing. Because corrections are so easy, we find we are far more self-critical of what we write and much more willing to take the trouble of improving it. Children who are lucky enough to have this marvelous machine at home have the best aid to good writing since the pencil eraser.

Graphics can be used to illustrate reports and database programs can be used to keep track of research notes. There is good software available for extra practice in math, spelling, and all other school subjects; call your daughter's teachers and ask.

Strategy 4: Host a Computer Party

A computer party can be the pajama-type, an evening pizza party, or the rainy-Saturday-afternoon kind. Recreational software you'd use as a family will go over big with your daughter's friends, and it won't hurt her social status any to have them see how expert she is with a computer. On a more informal basis, encourage your daughter to invite a friend or two over after school to use the computer.

If you're really civic-minded, and your daughter's school has limited computer resources, invite the class over. This may be the only chance some of her classmates have to see a computer in action. Very few schools have modems and subscriptions to commercial database systems such as the Source or CompuServe; if you do and are willing to foot the bill—it's a very deserving cause—invite her class over for a hands-on demonstration.

HOME STRATEGIES IF YOU DON'T HAVE A COMPUTER

Strategy 5: Encourage School Computer Activities

When we went to school, our parents insisted we take typing because it was an all-purpose useful thing to know. The equivalent for our daughters is computers. Insist that your daughter take at least the introductory course and learn the basic computer applications: word processing, spreadsheets, graphics, and database managers. If she exhibits any interest at all, suggest strongly that she take elective courses as well.

Encourage your daughter to use the school computers for homework or fun during her free time during the day or before or after school. If early or late transportation is a problem, it's worth the trouble of arranging a safe alternative. Some girls can't stay late at school to use the computers because they're needed at home for household responsibilities. This often can't be helped. Sometimes, however, parents assign the chores to daughters and not to sons. Boys are just as capable of babysitting, cooking supper, cleaning, and errands as girls are: think about whether you're unintentionally but unfairly restricting your daughter's computer opportunities after school.

Your daughter may resist taking computer courses or using the computer during her free time in school: "But Mom, I don't want to be the only girl there!" This isn't a trivial objection to a young person, so try to get a couple of her best friends to go with her.

Strategy 6: Be on the Alert for Sexism

Once you become aware of the computer gender gap, you'll notice the sexism that fuels it. For example, this is from a software ad for four- to ten-year-old children: "Now on your computer screen, your little girl can dress a Barbie Doll and change her clothes and her hair styles. Your boy can move a Hot Wheels car around a Hot Wheels garage, after actually designing the car on the computer screen. He can engage in a make-believe battlefield scenario with G.I. Joe pitted against Cobra." Notice not only the sex-stereotyped content but also the fact that while the boy is a "boy," the girl is a "little girl."

This is pretty obvious stuff, but often the sexism is by omission. In television ads for computers and in computers magazines, the people you see are overwhelmingly white able-bodied males. The next time you go past a store that sells magazines, pick one of them up and see for yourself. Buy it to bring home and show to your daughter. Whether the sexism is by omission or commission, the net effect is to tell your daughter that computers are not for her. If you don't counteract the message, she may believe it.

Talk about the sexism in the computer world with your daughter. Get mad about it together: "How DARE they say computers aren't for you?! We .\ show those bums that computers are for girls, too!" Make a collection of the most revolting computer ads—they're hilarious once you get over the initial shock. Make a collection of the good ones that include girls or women. Write letters of protest (on your word processor, of course) to the most offensive manufacturers of hardware and software and letters of congratulations to the best.

Strategy 7: Subscribe to Computer Magazines

Even if you don't have a computer, it's interesting to see what computers can do. Many magazines (see Appendix B, Resources) contain pieces on computer graphics and their uses that are fascinating even for noncomputer-owners.

Strategy 8: Discuss Computers at Home

In a questionnaire parents filled out at one of the schools we worked with, the results showed that while most parents thought computers were equally important for the futures of their daughters and sons, they actually talked more about computer activities and careers with their sons than their daughters. Parents with computers at home also used them more with their sons than their daughters. We're sure the gap between "what I say" and "what I do" is unintentional, but you need to make sure you're not just giving lip service to the goal of computer equity for your daughter.

Ask your daughter what she's doing with computers in school. If you use a computer at work, talk about it. Bring up computer-related careers in "what do you want to be when you grow up" discussions. If you see a newspaper or magazine article on the computer gender gap or on interesting new computer uses, show it to her. Ask relatives or friends who use computers in their jobs to talk about them when she's around to hear.

Strategy 9: Consider Buying a Computer

If you can afford it, buying a computer is a wonderful thing for a family with a child in school to do. While it's not cheap, prices are getting lower all the time. Enlist your daughter's help in talking to the computer teacher in school and her computer-owning friends for recommendations. Since everyone will tell you that their particular kind of computer is marvelous and everything else is junk, ask a few people if the two of you can come over to try out theirs before you buy.

The most important rule for buying a computer is to work backward from the software to the hardware, since all computer software cannot be used on all computers. (It's as if you could use only one kind of record on your particular record player.) You're interested in software for *home* use: applications such as word processing, spreadsheets, and graphics that are simple to learn and use, and lots of educational and recreational software. Most computer owners and any computer store can tell you which computers feature this kind of software, and which ones are more for business purposes.

SCHOOL STRATEGIES—WHAT YOU CAN DO IN A GROUP

If the faculty at your daughter's school is unaware of the computer gender gap and is doing nothing to close it, she and other girls are getting cheated out of the education they need for the world they'll grow up into. Someone has to bring computer equity to their attention, and it might as well be you.

On the other hand, your daughter's school may have recognized the problem and is trying to do something about it. They sure could use your help.

The PTA is a good vehicle for getting involved in computer equity. Make a date with the PTA president to discuss whether the organization is interested in carrying out one of the school strategies described below.

If you don't have a PTA or it's not active, perhaps there's a parent advisory committee or task force on computer education or sex equity that can get involved. If you have friends with children in that school and they're just as concerned about the computer gender gap as you are, maybe you could all start a new task force on computer equity. Either way, here are some strategies for educating the faculty and/or helping out with solutions.

Strategy 10: Find Out About the Situation

One or more of you can go to school and observe the computer room at nonclass times to count the boys and girls in the room, or you can ask your daughters to do that. You can ask the school secretary, the computer teacher, or the principal to tell you what percentage of the computer elective course enrollment consists of girls.

Strategy 11: Send a Delegation to School

If the computer sex ratio is more imbalanced than forty-sixty, make an appointment with the principal to express your concern and ask that the issue be addressed in school. If you get no satisfaction at this level, talk to the superintendent or a member of the school board and get computer equity put on the agenda of a school board meeting. Pack the audience that night with computer equity supporters.

Strategy 12: Newsletter

PTA's usually have newsletters that go home to all the parents. Write an article for it about the computer gender gap situation in your daughter's school, including the data you gathered by carrying out Strategy 10.

Strategy 13: Computer Equity Evening

Your group, preferably working with the faculty, can schedule an informational session for parents and faculty about the need for computer equity action. Set up a panel composed of girls, teachers, and parents.

Strategy 14: Mother/Daughter or Father/Daughter Computer Session

This can be done at school as a breakfast activity before school and work (just don't spill the coffee on the computer). Or it can be done in the evening. Your daughter will be thrilled to show off her skills to you.

Strategy 15: Computer Workshops for Parents

Your group can sponsor adult education workshops for parents who want to develop computer skills. This project is best done in cooperation with the faculty, too—especially the computer teachers. If you do this, be sure computer equity doesn't get forgotten in all the attention to computer education.

You can offer a one-evening session of hands-on demonstrations of common computer applications (word processing and graphics, for example). Then you can talk about how important it is that girls develop these skills. A one-session workshop is a valuable ice-breaker for parents who know nothing about computers.

Or you can offer a series of workshops, each of which focuses on a particular aspect of interest to parents: spreadsheets, word processing, graphics, databases, educational software. Work the problem of computer equity into each session by distributing chapters from this book and reprints of articles that have appeared in the media. Having the parents' daughters act as computer teaching assistants. The computer facilities need to permit lots of hands-on use, preferably no more than two people to a machine.

Strategy 16: Computer Career Fair

The group can arrange a computer career fair on a Saturday. This involves contacting speakers (preferably female) for the event, obtaining demonstration materials, and so forth. It's a big deal, but it's important and a lot easier to do if the faculty will help you. (See Strategy 30 in Chapter 8.)

Strategy 17: Fund-Raising Drive

Your group can make computer hardware and software purchases the object of its fundraising activities, either as an ongoing activity or as a special drive. In exchange for your assistance, you can insist on assurances that the faculty will make special efforts to interest girls in computers.

SCHOOL STRATEGIES—WHAT YOU CAN DO AS AN INDIVIDUAL

Of course, trying to organize something like a computer career fair for the entire student body all by yourself is next to impossible, but there are other things you can do on your own to promote computer equity in your daughter's school.

Strategy 18: Educate the Educators

Let's say you've learned that most of the children who make free-time use of the school computers and who sign up for computer electives are boys. Let's say you've learned that only the computer teacher and the math teacher (both male) actually use computers with kids in class. Or let's say the school has no computers at all or just a couple.

Make an appointment with the people who teach language arts, social studies, science, art, and other subjects, and suggest firmly but nicely that as a parent you consider it essential that your daughter have the advantages of the computer in these subjects. Then go to the principal and repeat your message. Discuss the situation with friends who have children in the school and urge them to do the same thing. No school can resist determined parents for long.

Strategy 19: Become a Volunteer Computer Supervisor

We have seen that many schools keep perfectly good computer facilities locked up because there's no one available to supervise the computer room. This is a real problem. If you have time during the day and have computer skills (or are willing to learn), covering the computer room for an hour or two at a time would expand children's access to the computers considerably. Insist on training as a precondition. Also insist that you be allowed to recruit girls to come in and use the facilities. You can do this by starting with your daughter and her friends, and then encouraging them to bring their friends.

If you work for a living during the day, offer to supervise the computer room once a week on an evening or a Saturday. They might well be able to open the school up for that.

COMMUNITY STRATEGIES

There are many community resources you can tap to encourage your daughter's interest in and involvement with computers. Here are a few.

Strategy 20: Go to a Computer Store

At a computer store you and your daughter can try out things you wouldn't buy in a million years, but you needn't announce it out loud. On the other hand, you might wind up buying something. In all fairness, go at a time when the store isn't too busy. The store will probably have color printers to go with their demonstration graphics software, which makes a nice souvenir. It's possible to try one piece of software in versions for different computers, which lets you compare them.

Strategy 21: Visit Businesses that Use Computers

Many public-sector organizations such as police and fire stations, libraries, and hospitals use computers extensively. Call and ask if you and your daughter could come in for an explanation and a demonstration. If you phrase the request right, you're sure to find someone who will say yes.

There are many private businesses that use computers in fascinating ways, such as graphic design companies, law firms, manufacturing plants, and newspaper publishers. You could visit the places where your friends and relations work. Or you could be more adventurous—open up the Yellow Pages, and start calling.

Strategy 22: Attend a Computer Show

Many large cities have computer trade shows that bring together a good number of hardware, software, and computer accessory vendors under one roof. Despite the disadvantage of having to pay to get in (some computer stores have discount coupons) and possibly the disadvantage of having to take a day trip if you don't live nearby, your daughter will love this. It's like a hundred-ring computer circus.

Ask people who staff the booths lots of questions and ask for demonstrations: it's their job to show you as much as you want to be shown. And even though everyone there looks like a computer genius, it's not true. (You might pay attention to the sex and racial composition of the crowd while you're there, too, for a sad but instructive lesson.)

Shopping malls are increasingly scheduling free computer exhibits. Hardware and software manufacturers set up booths you can explore to your heart's content. The exhibits are sure to be advertised in local newspapers, radio, and television, so keep an eye out.

Strategy 23: Go to Movies That Display Computer Graphics

If you have a strong stomach and can stand to take your daughter to a movie about invading enemy aliens, the graphics are often terrific. Check the newspapers for current films; older ones are listed in Appendix B, Resources.

Strategy 24: Visit a Science Museum

More and more science museums across the country are setting up hands-on computer demonstration areas. A few large cities such as Boston even have special museums devoted to computers and other technologies of interest to the general public. You and your daughter will be entranced for hours.

Those museums that don't have these attractions usually do have exhibits that involve computers in one way or another: computer-generated weather maps, computer-processed photographs or galaxies and planets, and computer-driven population counters.

Strategy 25: After-School Computer Access

There might be several community organizations nearby that offer computer drop-in access or enrichment programs for children after school or on Saturday. Check out the nearest science museum, organizations such as Girls Clubs or the YWC(H)A, or the library. Playing to Win is an organization in New York City that provides computer access to community residents on a membership basis; do you have such an organization where you live? A few towns and cities have mobile computer vans that serve neighborhoods on a rotating schedule. Art schools or your local art museum may offer a course in computer graphics for children.

Strategy 26: Summer Computer Camps

Day and overnight camps for children that include or specialize in computers are springing up all over. For local ones, check your newspaper. For overnight camps farther away, the Sunday magazine of many large-city newspapers, especially *The New York Times*, runs many pages of camp ads from late winter through spring. You can also identify summer computer camps by asking your reference librarian how to find the names of camp referral services.

Strategy 27: Help Your Daughter Get a Part-Time Computer Job

Depending on the laws where you live, children as young as fourteen or even younger can have jobs after school, during the weekend, and over summer vacation. Lots of businesses have occasional need for people to do data-entry and other kinds of computer work. If your daughter enjoys the computer—a high skill level is assuredly not necessary for the type of job teenagers can get—a part-time computer job will reinforce her interest, make her feel very grown up, and pay her real money to boot.

Unless you are unusually persuasive with strangers, the best way to arrange a job for your daughter is to sound out people you know who work at places where computers are used. One of the authors of this book arranged a summer data-entry job for her fifteen-year-old at her brother's company. It was a smashing success.

Strategy 28: Join a User's Group

If you have a computer at home or are considering getting one, a user's group is a marvelous way to find out new things to do with a computer, meet other people who are interested in computers, and often get discounts on software and supplies. Parent/child participants are not at all unusual. These groups are located around the country and are organized by type of computer, e.g., Apple Macintosh User's Group, IBM PC User's Group, etc. Computer stores know where and when they meet.

11 Computer Equity Strategies for Students

Menu

	GOTO PAGE
Introduction	162
School Strategies	162
1. A Girls' Computer Committee or Club	162
2. Start an Equity Publicity Campaign	163
3. Start a Computer Information Campaign for Girls	164
4. Use Computers Yourself for Homework or Fun	166
5. Take Computer Electives	168
6. Use the Computer for School Service	168
7. Organize a Valentine Heart-To-Heart Campaign	169
8. Set Up a School Message Center	169
Strategies 1 and 2	
Home Strategies	170
9. If Your Family Has a Home Computer	170
10. If Your Parents Use a Computer at Work	171
11. If Your Parents Don't Know Anything About Computers	172
12. Getting Your Family Involved in Computer Equity For Girls	172
Strategies 10 and 11	

… Computer Equity Strategies for Students 161

Menu, Continued

	GOTO PAGE
Community Strategies	173
13. Publicize Computer Equity	173
14. Volunteer Your Computer Services	175
15. Attend Computer Shows and Exhibits	175
16. Organize a "Computathon"	176
17. Get an After-School or Summer Computer Job	177
18. Join a Computer User's Group	177

Strategies 13, 15, and 16

162   THE NEUTER COMPUTER

INTRODUCTION

When you look into your school's computer room when there's no regular class being held, what do you see?

(a) No one using the computers.
(b) Mostly boys using the computers.
(c) Girls and boys using the computers.
(d) Mostly girls using the computers.

Your answer is probably (a) or (b), which means there's a problem in your school about girls and computers. This is not good. Girls are going to need computer skills for the jobs they have when they grow up. Even for girls who aren't planning to be computer specialists—although these jobs are interesting and pay very well—computer skills are important. They are often used in jobs such as doctor, librarian, engineer, nurse, architect, teacher, and scientist.

You can do something about this problem, which is called the computer gender gap. The solution to the problem is called computer equity for girls: getting girls involved with computers as much as boys.

It's possible that you couldn't answer the question at all because your school doesn't have a computer room. Maybe it doesn't have any computers at all. This means that girls, and boys too, have even less opportunity to use computers. You can do something about that, too.

As a student, you might think you don't have the power to make an important change in your school. Maybe you can't make a big change right away, but you can certainly start. If you can get your friends involved, change can come about sooner. This chapter suggests some things you can do to get girls (and boys) interested in computers—for fun and learning.

SCHOOL STRATEGIES

Strategy 1: A Girls' Computer Equity Committee or Club

Getting friends to do something together is more fun than doing the whole job yourself, and probably works better, too. So start by getting your friends interested in a girls' computer committee or club. If your school is large and you don't know other girls who might be interested in computer equity, put a notice up on the bulletin board or ask your guidance counselor how to get in touch with them. Remember, you don't have to be a computer expert to be interested in computers. As people begin to respond to your notice, explain the computer gender gap problem to them and ask them to help you solve it.

Set a regular meeting time; maybe lunchtime is good. Get a faculty adviser. Meet in the computer room (if there is one). And don't forget to advertise your meetings.

Once your club is established, here are some things you can do at your meetings:

- Invite a guest speaker. Poll the members: does somebody's mother, aunt, or sister work with computers? Would she come to a meeting to talk about it? Invite other students and teachers to come, too.
- Send representatives of your group to interview the principal. How can the school make the computers more available to kids during the week, or maybe even over the weekend? Think about what might be done to prevent theft or vandalism, because the principal will surely be thinking about it. Write an article for your school newspaper about the interview. Remember that good reporters always check the accuracy of their articles with the person they interview before publication.
- Make a presentation to the student government or council, outlining ways you'd like to see computing opportunities for students expanded.
- Find out if there's a computer club or committee in a nearby school, and set up a joint meeting to discuss your ideas.
- Consider some of the other projects in this chapter or in Chapter 8, Teacher/Staff Strategies.

Strategy 2: Start an Equity Publicity Campaign

You're one of the special ones. You knew there was a problem about girls' equal opportunity to use computers or you wouldn't be reading this. But you have to get other people to see that it exists, too.

The first thing to do is spotlight the computer gender gap in school. When your school has a fund drive, is there a chart that looks like a big thermometer near the entrance that shows how much money has been contributed so far? Well, you're starting a drive of your own. Drop by the computer room when classes aren't in session.

Count the number of girls and boys using the computers. Keep a record and turn it into a temperature chart. Put it where everyone will see it.

One school we know went from two girls who used computers in January to fifty-nine girls in May. They had quite a dramatic chart! The more girls used computers, the more other girls wanted to. Suddenly the problem in this school was how to let the boys have equal time.

You could post a copy of your chart in the teachers' lounge as well as the hallway since the teachers need to know what you're up to. Or you could ask your school newspaper to print it, along with a story you write about how you got interested in the problem and about how important computers are to girls. Look at the Introduction and Appendix B for information for your article.

Strategy 3: Start a Computer Information Campaign for Girls

Maybe some girls don't use computers because they don't know they can: they don't know where the computers are, what time they're available, what they're good for, what software they can use, or what software other girls like. You can start an information campaign all by yourself, but it would be a lot easier if you had a group working on it. There are several things you can do.

Let Girls Know When Computers are Available. When are the school computers available for girls who want to drop in during their free time? To find out, talk to the teacher in charge of the computer room if there is one, or to teachers who have computers in their classrooms.

Make posters showing the schedule of free hours and ask if you can put them up where other girls will see them. The girls' locker room and girls' bathrooms are good places. If your school has a poster-making software program (like PRINT SHOP), you can make wonderful posters on the computer. Girls in Nobel Junior High School in Los Angeles, California, used the slogan "GIRLS AND COMPUTERS GO TOGETHER" for theirs. It was a big success. Get the school newspaper to publish your schedule. Maybe you can get a regular column to report on computer activities.

Start a Computer Newsletter. You might start a computer newsletter for students. You could print lists of software the school owns,

Making a poster is fun. Here is one created by a student from Nobel Junior High School.

tips on what to do with it, programs students have written, and reviews of software you've seen outside of school that you wish the school would buy. You could print reports on what different teachers are doing with the computers. Does the art teacher use them? How about the science teacher, or the special ed teacher, or the gym teacher? And if not, why not? If your school has word processing software, you can do the whole newsletter on the computer.

There's More to Computers than Arcade Games. There are lots of things a computer can do besides arcade games for shooting down missiles launched by hostile aliens. Chapters 1 through 7 describe many ways to use a computer, and they're a lot more interesting and useful than arcade games. Your school probably has some of the software we mention in those chapters, but some students may not know it's available or how to use it.

Girls tend to get interested in computers when other girls tell them how much fun computers are. If you've gotten hooked on computers, invite your friends to come share the fun. When they get hooked, they can invite their friends, too.

You can make posters describing software girls especially like. You can also make tip-sheets to post wherever the computers are, to help people start using new software. If you get different student "experts" to write these tip-sheets and sign their names, other students will know who can give them help with a particular program. If you have a computer column in the school newspaper or are writing a computer newsletter, you could use the tip-sheets as part of your copy.

Opening Up the Computer Room. In some schools, computers are never available for drop-in use at lunchtime, during study periods, or before or after school. The computers are probably locked up when they're not used for classes because there's nobody to supervise them. This is reasonable: supervision means not only helping students but also making sure there's no vandalism or theft. Computer hardware and software are very expensive to repair or replace.

If that's your situation, you'll need help in freeing up the computers. Talk to your principal, your teachers, and your counselors. Take the problem to the student council. Write an article about it for the school paper. Ask your parents to discuss the problem at a parent/teacher association meeting.

There are several solutions to the supervision problem:

- If teachers can't do the supervising, maybe trustworthy and computer-knowledgeable students can.
- Perhaps your school has a School Service program that would give students credit for supervising the computer room.
- Perhaps some students would be willing to trade off hours supervising in exchange for hours using a computer themselves.
- Find out if some parents would be willing to volunteer some time every week to supervise the computer room.

You won't be able to set up this kind of supervision by yourself, but you can give the school administration ideas. You can also bug them to make sure they don't forget about it.

Strategy 4: Use Computers Yourself for Homework or Fun

Using computers yourself for lots of different kinds of things is one way to show other girls that computers are helpful, interesting, and fun. You'll enjoy it even more if you use the computer with a friend.

Computer Equity Strategies for Students 167

Students from Nobel Junior High School proudly display their computer-generated banner.

If your school has the right software, you can:

- Use word processors to write letters, stories, poems, essays, and reports. You might not realize what marvelous freedom this gives you until you try it, but then you'll probably never want to write any other way.
- Use a graphics program like PRINT SHOP not only to make banners and posters, but also for party invitations, greeting cards, flyers, and printed announcements.
- Teach the computer to do anything you want it to do if you know enough programming in Logo, BASIC, or another computer language.
- Use a database program to record information about your favorite hobby, or your favorite people or artists or even enemies.
- Design your own adventure game.
- If you want more ideas, look at Chapters 1 through 7.

If you have a report or an essay to do and you can choose the topic, consider a report on computers. You'll probably teach your teachers a thing or two.

- You could write about computers in the job market—one source says that by 1990, most jobs will depend on computers to some extent.
- Or about computers in the home. How many of your fellow students have computers at home? Who uses them, and for what?
- Or about some of the women who were involved in the development of computers, such as Ada Byron Lovelace or Grace Hopper.

Strategy 5: Take Computer Electives

Some schools have required computer courses. These can be great and really teach you a lot about computers, but sometimes they can be real turn-offs. If your course is boring, don't rule out computers until you've had a chance to try a better course.

Take the elective computer course that interests you most as soon as you can. There are a lot of adults taking computer courses these days: they couldn't take them when they were in school, and now they need them for their careers. So if you have the opportunity to learn how, grab it. Talk a few of your girlfriends into taking the course with you. It's more fun that way.

Strategy 6: Use the Computer for School Service

You're growing up in the computer age, but many of your teachers grew up in a world without computers. They might not realize how useful computers can be. You can help your teachers by talking to them about computers, designing your own computer programs to make their jobs easier, or even teaching them how to use a computer. You can:

- Show the librarian how a database could be useful in the school resource center. You might actually design the system and get a bunch of friends together to help enter the data.
- Keep team statistics with a spreadsheet program for the physical education department.
- Make posters and banners with a graphics program for school events.
- Show your teachers how you keep your own weekly grades and averages on a spreadsheet, and suggest ways for them to use it for their class records.

Strategy 7: Organize a Valentine Heart-to-Heart Campaign

This is a project for a person who knows how to use database software. If you do, then a Heart-to-Heart Campaign is a terrific way to get a lot of kids involved in computing. It's also a great way to raise money for a girls' computer club or committee, or for hardware or software.

Valentine's Day is February 14, that means everything has to be in place and operating by then, so you'll have to start in the fall. The idea is to create a database where, for a small fee, any student can enter his or her characteristics, likes, and dislikes into the computer. Then on Valentine's Day, anyone who pays another small fee can search the database to find the Heart who matches their Heart. Because most kids love this kind of thing, the small fees do add up.

You'll need to figure out carefully what kind of information you want kids to enter in. Of course, you'll need names and gender, and perhaps age or grade. Beyond that, you might ask for information about interests like sports, school subjects, their favorite flavor of ice cream, what kind of music they like, favorite places to hang out, what they'd do with a million dollars if they had it, and all that sort of stuff. You know what's important to your crowd.

You'll also need to make sure you can get the information back out again once it's been entered. You do this by using "dummy data"—that's really what it's called. Once you've designed your database record, enter a bunch of made-up (dummy) data. Then search your system to see if it gives you back your information.

On February 14, you'll have to teach some kids how to use the database system, but it's so easy they can teach others. Sit back, watch the fun, and see the money add up.

Strategy 8: Set Up a School Message Center

If you can pull this off, everyone in the school will want to use it—girls, boys, teachers, staff, even the principal. Your parents might even drop in to leave a message for you.

Setting up a successful message center requires considerable computer smarts. There are some shortcuts, especially having electronic bulletin board software. This can be bought or perhaps borrowed through a user's group or from another school's computer club. If you can't get ahold of prepared software, making your own is possible. First, find someone who has access to or operates an electronic bulletin board, which is what a message center is, and try it out yourself before you create your own. Next, get an expert involved, your school's computer teacher or someone outside the school, to help you with the programming. If you put a computer message center into operation, you will have a sure-fire way of getting everyone in the school involved with computing.

HOME STRATEGIES

Strategy 9: If Your Family Has a Home Computer

Who uses the computer? Who uses it most? If there are girls or women in your family and the answers to these questions are men or boys, then you have computer equity work to do at home. What can you do?

Teach your mother and sisters how to use the computer. Maybe they don't know how because they think it's too hard, they're scared they'll break it, they're afraid they'll do something wrong, or they don't know what to use it for. Tell them it's not too hard—you'll teach them. It won't break—a computer's a tough old bird. They *will* do something wrong, however. Everybody does. But the computer will never yell at them, and no one ever has to know.

If you've learned how to use a database at school, there are ways to use it at home that are fun for everyone in the family. You can teach them all how to use it for:

- Cataloging record, tape, or book collections
- Recording birthdays, anniversaries, cards, and gifts given
- Recipe collections (if you have a printer, this is an easy way to exchange recipes with friends)
- Information about books you've read or want to read
- Recording plantings in the garden, or wildflowers, or sightings of birds
- Family phone book, with categories for each person's friends, relatives, business contacts, etc.
- Plays or concerts attended, with performers and reviews—your own or from the newspapers—of the performances.

Ask your parents to subscribe to a computer magazine about home computing; several good ones are listed in Appendix B. They all offer ideas, sample programs, software reviews, and stories about how other people are using their computers. There's sure to be something in these magazines to intrigue somebody in your family into using the computer.

Use a word processing program to write a family newsletter to send to relatives at Christmastime or other times during the year. Each family member can write his or her own part. In fact, make sure everyone in the family gets time with the computer if they want it. Don't tolerate family "computer hogs." Set up a schedule, and don't let anyone beg, borrow or steal someone else's time.

And use the computer yourself, for homework, graphics, making notices of your neighbor's garage sale, or making party invitations. Or just for fun. Explore the stars: there's a special piece of software designed to take you along. Run for president with PRESIDENT ELECT. Design a robot with ROBOT ODYSSEY. There's lots of fascinating computer software you probably won't find at school because it doesn't fit into your classes exactly. Nevertheless, it's exciting and fun to use.

You think this is all very well, but you don't have much software at home? Okay, that's a problem, but there are some things you can do about getting some software.

- Buy it. This takes money, of course, but it also takes patience because you have to try out the software before you plunk that money down. You need to know if you really want it, so try it out first in the store.
- Exchange software with a friend who has the same kind of computer you do. It isn't legal to make copies of copy-protected software, but there's no law against swapping, even on a temporary basis.
- Borrow the software from your school, public library, or another local organization that has a software lending program.
- Some computer books and magazines print the statements for lots of different kinds of programs, even word processing programs. It's work to type them all in, and of course if you make a typing mistake the program won't run (in fact, it may not run anyway if the book or magazine has made a printing error). But if you can make it work, the program will only cost you a blank disk.

Strategy 10: If Your Parents Use a Computer at Work

Computers are used in all kinds of businesses: manufacturing plants, newspapers, hospitals, offices, postal services, restaurants—

practically every kind of business there is. So it's quite possible that one or both of your parents either uses a computer at work, or at least works where computers are used. Ask them to tell you about it. What do they do with the computer? How did they learn? Was it easy or hard? Was it fun?

If it's a visible computer, go with them to work on a day school is out and watch how the computer is used. Did you know there are visible and invisible computers? The computer we wrote this book on is visible. The computer in a washing machine is invisible. You and your family can play a game of who can think of the longest list of different kinds of visible and invisible computers . . . kind of a computer trivial pursuit.

Talk to your parents about the computers at school and about what you're learning. Check it out against what they know from their experience with computers at work. Perhaps they have special experience that would be interesting to your friends at school, and to your teachers. If so, ask them to come to school to talk about it.

Strategy 11: If Your Parents Don't Know Anything About Computers

Suddenly you're the computer expert in the family. But don't rest on those laurels and let your parents get away with thinking that only kids have to know about computers.

- Talk to them about what you're learning about computers.
- Show them what you've done on a word processor.
- Bring home samples of your computer graphics work.
- Tell them about computer equity and what you're doing to make sure girls and boys have equal chances for computer education.

To show them what computers can do, how about dragging them to the local computer store, to school, to anywhere where computers are? Once they get interested, they might even decide to buy a computer for the family. Getting down on your knees might help.

Strategy 12: Getting Your Family Involved in Computer Equity

Your parents, sisters, and brothers might not know that a lot of girls and women are being left out of the computer revolution. They might not have thought about why it matters. Make sure your family understands how important computers are for your future. Ask them

Computer Equity Strategies for Students 173

An intricate design and its proud creator—a student from Nobel Junior High School.

to read the Introduction to this book—it ought to convince them that computer equity for girls is serious business.

If girls (and boys) can't get at the school computers when they're not being used for classes, maybe someone in your family could volunteer a couple of hours a week to keep the computer room open by supervising it.

Ask your mom or dad to bring up the subject of computer equity at the next meeting of the parent/teacher association. Some things they could suggest are: parent/student computer sessions, fund-raising projects for computers or software, car-pooling to get you home when you stay for after-school computer sessions, opening up the school computers on weekends or during vacations, and establishing a lending program for school hardware and software.

COMMUNITY STRATEGIES

Strategy 13: Publicize Computer Equity

There are several things you can do to let people in your community know about computer equity.

174 THE NEUTER COMPUTER

A Newspaper Article. If you're working on equal computer opportunity for girls in your school or at home, you have a story to tell. Write it. Describe what you're doing. Your local paper might want to print that story, along with a picture of you working at a computer.

Computers in Your Community. Find out how computers are used in your community. What businesses use them and for what? Is there a computer-related business in town? Can you visit? Since most large corporations have Community Relations departments, write or call the director of that department. When you get there, pay attention to the numbers of men and women working in computer-related jobs. Are the numbers equal? Are there more men or more women in the top jobs? If you don't see many women, ask why not. If they tell you they can't find many qualified women for the computer jobs, tell them you and your girlfriends will be available in a few years.

Library Exhibit. Perhaps your public library will let you put up a computer equity exhibit of articles, pictures, "Did you know . . . ?" posters, graphs, and other things that show women with computers in school and at work, and that show the need for more of them. If

A Nobel Junior High School student is happily engrossed at her computer's keyboard.

the library already has a computer for public use or is thinking about getting one, a computer equity exhibit would be timely. Certainly the library staff will help you research the idea. Ask your family and friends to help with this one since it can be a lot of work.

Visit Your Local Computer Store. Talk to the manager about computer equity. Ask how many of the customers are women, and if the number is low, ask why that is. Notice the gender of the managers and salespeople, and if there aren't many women (or none at all), ask why not. Tell the manager that maybe they'd have more women customers if they had more women salespeople. Some computer stores hold classes for people to learn about computers. Does your store do this? Who comes? This is another place that might let you exhibit.

Strategy 14: Volunteer Your Computer Services

There are probably children in your community who don't have an opportunity to learn about computers. Perhaps you can persuade your school to hold a computer open house for them, with students like yourself acting as teachers.

Are there community programs that have computers—day care centers, community centers, Y's, or senior citizen centers? If so, they probably need volunteers to help supervise. They'd be glad to have your help. Suppose there's a community center near you that doesn't have a computer, but you have one at home. Perhaps your parents would let you take yours to the community center one afternoon a week and give your own class.

If you do volunteer, keep the idea of computer equity in the front of your head. Make sure that boys don't elbow girls away from the computer. Suggest computer activities that appeal to girls as well as to boys.

Strategy 15: Visit Computer Shows and Exhibits

Many cities and large towns have computer trade shows in convention halls, hotel exhibit rooms, and shopping malls. You have to pay to get into some of them, but it's worth it. (The shopping mall computer shows are free.) They all have different kinds of computers and software you can try out, and salespeople to answer your questions. If you go, ask lots of questions and get demonstrations of all the hardware and software. This is your opportunity to look at the marvels of the computer future—robots, computers that talk, even computers that listen.

If you don't live in a big city, perhaps your parents would take you there on a day when a computer show is scheduled. Find out if there's a computer museum or a museum of science and technology that has a computer section you can visit in the city, too. Sometimes large businesses, colleges, or universities have computer-related exhibits you can go to. They'll be announced in the newspaper.

Strategy 16: Organize a "Computathon"

If you can raise money for charity with marathons, swimathons, or jogathons, why not raise money for computers with a computathon? If your community center, library, synagogue or church youth group, or school could get a computer, think of all the girls (and boys) who would love to use it!

Get a group of kids together, the more the better. Brainstorm with them for ideas of things you could collect pledges for from your families and neighbors, such as:

Pages read	Yards jumped or hopped in burlap bags
Math problems done correctly	
Miles jogged or walked or run	Feet of rope climbed
Laps swum	Lines of poetry memorized

When you've got a long list, each person should pick the one she or he likes best. Decide on how much money you want to ask for each activity unit you complete: a dime? a quarter? a dollar? The amount should match the activity: you can read more pages than you can run miles, so the mile pledge should cost more than the page pledge. Don't charge too much, though, or nobody will buy.

You'll need pledge books made up ahead of time. This can be done on a word processor, of course, Put four or more pledge forms on a page, photocopy them, cut them up, and staple them. Then go forth and collect pledges.

You could hold the computathon all on one day, or you could run it over several days, even a week, so that more people get to participate. Because you'll need judges to verify the results of each computathon activity, you may want to limit the number of activites you do.

Plan carefully, get lots of people involved, and you can raise a lot of money. An elementary school in Oregon held a week-long computatathon using reading, math facts, and jogging. Four hundred students participated and they raised over $12,600 for computers.

Strategy 17: Get an After-School or Summer Computer Job

If you get real friendly with your computer store owner, maybe you can get a job helping out after school or on weekends. It's good for people to walk into a computer store and get help from a knowledgeable girl. Ask your parents and their friends for the names of people they know in businesses that use computers. Contact them and ask about part-time or summer computer jobs. A lot of businesses take advantage of summer student help for tasks their regular employees haven't had time to do the rest of the year, including computer-related ones such as data entry or word processing.

Don't expect glamor, though. Lots of jobs, even if they involve computers, are just plain hard work. But they provide a nice income and experience with using computers in the real world, *and* a valuable reference letter for your next job.

Strategy 18: Join a User's Group

Computer users often form clubs with others of all ages and both sexes who use the same brand of hardware. Computer stores know about the users' groups in town. Their meetings are great for swapping software, as well as getting tips on new and better ways to use your computer.

PART THREE: THE COMPUTER EQUITY PROGRAM

Putting It All Together

In Part One we presented fifty-six activities kids can do with computers. In Part Two we presented ninety-six strategies for getting girls involved with computers. With so many computer activities and strategies to choose from, method is needed to prevent madness. The Part Three chapters on planning and evaluating a computer equity program in a school ensure that your efforts lead to a sustained increase in girls' computer participation without driving you crazy.

The two authors of this book have had many years of classroom teaching experience. We know that school teachers, staff, and administrators don't exactly find time lying heavy on their hands. We also know that computer equity is far from the only deserving cause to clamor for your attention. We therefore suggest a way to put your computer equity program together that keeps your time and effort commitment as low as possible while making the likelihood of success as high as possible.

The basis of our approach is *shared ownership,* and it has several irresistible advantages. First, it's appropriate. The computer can and should be used in all subjects and departments, not just the computer class and the math class. Having special education teachers, French teachers, resource center specialists, assistant principals, and health education teachers on the computer equity team ensures that it will be.

Second, it's effective. When a variety of faculty members, parents, and students participate in the computer equity program, the kinds of computer equity strategies that can be carried out multiply. A girl may ignore a faculty member or a parent or a friend who offers a computer opportunity to her, but she's unlikely to resist the blandishments of all three together.

Third, it's pleasant. Work done alone can be drudgery, while work done with your colleagues and friends can be a social occasion ennobled by being on the side of the angels.

Fourth, it's healthy. Many hands make light work. We really don't think you have to worry about too many cooks. . . . So see to it that teachers and staff, administrators, parents, and students share in the ownership of your computer equity program. Life is too short, and energy too scarce, for heroic solo efforts.

12 Planning a Computer Equity Program

Menu

	GOTO PAGE
Introduction	184
Team Membership	185
Preparation for the Planning Session	187
Conducting the Planning Session	187
Follow-up Meetings	190

INTRODUCTION

Computer equity—increasing girls' computer use until it roughly equals that of boys—doesn't happen by itself. In this chapter, we recommend an efficient planning process for you to use that will increase girls' use of the computer dramatically.

There is no hard-and-fast rule about what constitutes a computer gender gap. But if the boy/girl ratio in your school is close to fifty-fifty and students' computer use is more uneven than forty-sixty, a computer equity program is needed. Find out by taking the Computer Neutrality Self-Test in the Introduction.

Computer equity is actually pretty easy to accomplish, in our opinion. Just about anything interesting you offer girls to do with or about computers will succeed in getting them involved. However, we want to warn you about a couple of fundamental errors we observed when we tested this book, errors that can seriously sabotage your efforts:

Error #1: Girls are Half of All Students, Aren't They?

Of course they are, but what happens if you target your strategies evenhandedly to both sexes rather than specifically to girls? Since boys are already more interested in computers, they're likely to be the majority of the kids who respond to your invitations. You can't close the gender gap that way.

Error #2: We Have to Teach the Teachers First

It's true that using computers with students means that faculty members have to be computer-knowledgeable, but that's not the final word. For one, many of the computer activities and computer equity strategies in this book don't require computers. They're identified by this symbol   These activities and strategies can certainly be done by faculty members who have no computer skills at all. Second, while ideally all faculty members should be computer-knowledgeable, they don't all have to be.

Third and most compelling to us is a situation it took us some time to understand. A few of our schools chose to approach the computer equity problem by concentrating on providing computer training to the faculty. They assumed it to be a necessary first step which would be followed by widespread computer use with girls and boys. That assumption was often proved wrong. Many faculty members apparently felt they needed to delay The Big Moment until they were 100 percent comfortable with computers themselves. This can take an awfully long time, to put it mildly. In the meantime, all you've got is an adult education program. No girls get near a computer—and no boys, either. This is no way to close the computer gender gap.

We're not saying that to do computer equity you can't teach boys or teachers how to use computers. What we are saying is that to achieve computer equity there is no substitute for strategies that target girls to become involved with computers. It's the difference between:

> I'd like to invite any members of this class who are interested to come to a demonstration of ROCKY'S BOOTS this afternoon.
> ... and ...
> I'm going to demonstrate ROCKY'S BOOTS this afternoon. Nikki, Sylvia, Antonia, Dondeena, and you too, Mark and Dave—I know you'd like it. Why don't you come?

And between:

> The computer teacher will give word processing lessons to any teachers who want to learn on Tuesday and Wednesday after school for the next three weeks.
> ... and ...
> The computer teacher will give spreadsheet lessons to teachers on a sign-up basis on Tuesday and Wednesday after school for the next three weeks. In two months, these teachers will report to the rest of us how they have used spreadsheets with their students and what is especially effective in involving the girls.

So, for a successful computer equity program, keep your eye on the girls—and on the computers.

TEAM MEMBERSHIP

Depending on the scope and number of strategies you implement, planning a computer equity program can become a major undertaking. You'll need a group to do it with you—the more varied, the better.

Before you put together a computer equity team, find out whether academic or in-service credit can be granted to participating faculty members. The planning team at one of the schools we worked with recevied academic credit from the local university and a professor of education from that university was a member of their group. The ability to earn promotion credits helps to compensate team members for the time they devote to the program.

Here's a list of people who would be very helpful to a computer equity program:

- *Administrators:* school district personnel, principals, assistant/vice principals, and department heads can adjust procedures and schedules if necessary, provide in-service time, obtain funds if necessary, and talk up the program with other administrators.
- *Teachers:* from any and all subject areas, since computers can be used with students in all kinds of classes.
- *Staff:* librarians, media or resource center specialists, guidance counselors, aides, the school secretary, the nurse, and others. Since they all have contact with kids, they can all help.
- *Girls:* By all means! A few girls who already like computers may know things to interest their peers you'd never be able to come up with.
- *Parents:* They can be essential for carrying out strategies conducted by or aimed at parents.
- *Outside sex equity experts:* Consider district, regional, or state Title IX coordinators, or local sex equity activists or consultants. They might deliver an in-service session on computer equity to your faculty, too.
- *Outside computer experts:* district, regional, or state computer education specialists, a professor of computer education, a staff member at a nearby teacher computer center. They can assist with training faculty in computers, help you evaluate or even obtain software, and help resolve computer management problems (such as too many kids for too few computers).

How Many Team Members Are Enough?

It depends of course on who they are and how much they can contribute, but a school with a couple of hundred students should be able to carry out a good computer equity program with five or six team members. A larger school would need more. Some faculty participants in the Computer Equity Training Project felt that a relatively small group was more efficient, while most of the others felt that a widely "owned" program had more resources to call on. We guess it's a matter of a school's preference. Be sure you get a good mix of team members, not just computer and math teachers, to take advantage of the multi-subject variety of computer activities and computer equity strategies listed in this book.

PREPARATION FOR THE PLANNING SESSION

We're assuming that all team members are volunteers and therefore know why they're participating. If not, that's first. You'll find a number of suggestions for raising team members' computer equity awareness in Strategy 2 in Chapter 9.

We've tried to include a broad range of computer-related activities that appeal to girls (and boys), as well as a variety of computer equity strategies for teachers and staff, administrators, parents, and students. While the four strategy chapters (8 through 11) are written for primary use by the people in their titles, many of the ninety-six strategies they contain can easily be adapted for use by others. We therefore suggest providing each team member with a copy of this book.

You'll save a lot of time at your first team meeting if each member does some homework beforehand:

1. Reads or at least skims this book.
2. Chooses two computer equity strategies she or he thinks are especially promising.
3. For each strategy, sketches out how it could be implemented: what would be involved, who might do it, and when it would be done.

This gets the initial familiarization stage, as well as the beginning of the strategy selection process, over with before the meeting, enabling you to get down to business right away.

CONDUCTING THE PLANNING SESSION

The computer equity team needs a leader. For the sake of stylistic simplicity, we're assuming you're it. Depending on the size of the group, how well they've done their homework, and how ambitious their intentions are, one to two hours should be enough to develop a workable plan. (Periodic follow-up sessions will also be needed—see below—but these should take no more than half an hour or so.)

How many strategies are enough? Our schools chose four to six strategies, some simple to carry out and some complex, and drawn from all four strategy chapters. They all felt comfortable with that level of involvement.

Suggested Agenda

- Introductions. Only if necessary—five minutes.
- Brief discussion of the computer gender gap. Ask for members' observations of the computer gender gap. Ten to twenty minutes.
- Strategy recommendations. Ask team members to present the strategies they chose before the meeting and to explain why they chose them. Write the nominations on the chalkboard with corresponding page numbers so people can refer to them during discussion. Fifteen to thirty minutes.
- Choice of strategies. Suggest that strategies should be varied, addressing a number of computer activities requiring different effort levels and involving all relevant groups (students, teachers, parents, and administrators), if possible. The team can choose by consensus or by vote. Fifteen to thirty minutes.
- Making strategy plans. Using the planning form described below, work out the details of each strategy you select. Thirty to sixty minutes.
- Date of next meeting. Schedule the first follow-up meeting. Five minutes.

Making Strategy Plans

This is the most important part of the meeting. Vagueness here about who does what, when, and how is usually a tip-off that the strategy will turn out to be more talk than action. The details need to be pinned down in the planning session. Use a Strategy Planning Form to structure the discussion and ensure that necessary planning gets done. A sample form is shown here, the blank form is in Appendix A, Copyables. Duplicate a pile of them for team members to work with.

In the upper right-hand corner of the planning form is a space for the strategy coordinator's name. This person will be responsible

COMPUTER EQUITY STRATEGY PLANNING FORM

STRATEGY: Parent Workshops   **GOAL:** 40 GIRLS REACHED   **COORDINATOR** Reid
                                         via 40 + Parents

ACTIVITIES	DATE	RESOURCES NEEDED WHAT ?	WHEN ?	HOW ?	PERSON RESPONSIBLE
Prep. letter, registration	2/1 - 4/3	none - send letter by 3/1			Mary
Plan Workshops	2/1 - 2/28	none			Reid, Jeani, Ann
Workshop 1: Comp. Eq., Wordprocessing	4/3	speaker, refreshments	3/5, 4/3	Call Ms. Rodriguez, PTA	Jeani
Workshop 2: Comp. Eq., Graphics	4/10	color printer, refreshments	4/9, 4/9	Borrow from Ann, PTA	Reid
Workshop 3: Comp. Eq., Communications	4/17	speaker, modem, refreshments	4/1, 4/15, 4/17	Call Library, Borrow from College, PTA	Phil

EVALUATION: HOW, WHEN, WHO?

1. Parent questionnaire for workshops. Prepare 2/1 - 3/31 by Phil with comments from Reid and Jeani. Fill out at workshops. Analyze 4/17-23. Report to team 4/24.

2. Reid to give Ann list of girls whose parents attended workshops by 4/24. Ann observes how many come to use computers and reports to team on 5/1 and 5/31.

for making sure that the strategy is carried out and keeping everyone posted on its progress. The coordinator is best chosen by consensus after all the other details on the form have been worked out; the discussion will indicate pretty clearly who the strategy leader has been.

Ask each coordinator to give a clean copy of the plan to everyone involved in it to prevent misunderstandings. You as leader should also have a copy. Circle the important dates to remind you when to ask coordinators about how their strategies are progressing: you'll need to know this for the follow-up meetings.

FOLLOW-UP MEETINGS

Follow-up meetings of half an hour to an hour are needed once a month or so for exchanging news on how each strategy is working out. Ask coordinators for summaries. If anyone is running into a problem, the rest of the team can help. This is also the time to discuss whether any action plans need to be altered in light of evaluation results or other indications the strategy hasn't worked out as planned. (See Chapter 13 on evaluation.) For example, if only fifteen of the expected seventy-five parents show up for the parent workshops, you'll want to find out what went wrong and correct it for next time. Team members' time is too valuable to spend it unproductively.

Follow-up meetings are also good occasions to bring new people into the team. This can provide an opportunity to work out an expanded or additional computer equity strategy. Finally, follow-up meetings are perhaps most needed to maintain the participation of team members. Everyone on the team has many other things to do and think about besides computer equity. These sessions are essential for keeping up morale.

13 Evaluating a Computer Equity Program

Menu

	GOTO PAGE
Introduction	192
Program Evaluation	192
Accountability Evaluation	195
And for Next Year...	197

INTRODUCTION

There are actually two kinds of evaluation. Although they have different purposes, both are valid and useful. *Program evaluation*, otherwise known in the trade as "formative evaluation," is expressed primarily in English and is only for computer equity team members. It tells you what's happening, what's working, and what needs fixing. *Accountability evaluation* (trade name: "summative evaluation") is more for public consumption. It consists primarily of numbers, along with a few choice words, that indicate what a smashing success your program is. This chapter gives you easy ways to do both.

PROGRAM EVALUATION

You've planned a special after-school session on computer graphics because you thought girls would be very interested. Four boys and one girl showed up. Something's gone wrong, but what?

Was the session publicized appealingly?
Was the session publicized enough?
Was the session in a time conflict with a popular activity?
Did girls realize they were particularly invited?
Aren't girls interested in computer graphics?
Do girls know what computer graphics means?
Are girls afraid they'll break the computer?
Do girls hate the teacher?

Program evaluation enables you to find the answer and correct the problem. You don't need multiple regressions, control groups, or a Ph.D. in statistical methodology. Instead, you use observations and conversations, simple recordkeeping, and short questionnaires to determine whether each of your strategies is working well enough to be worth your time and effort.

Tracking Student Computer Use

Since the point of a computer equity program is to increase girls' computer use, you need to find out if it's actually happening. The easiest way is to examine optional computer use: times at which girls use a computer when they don't have to.

Evaluating a Computer Equity Program   193

One kind of optional computer use is the drop-in type before, during, or after school when the computers aren't taken over by classes. Your basic all-purpose tool is the sign-up sheet. It can be posted on individual computers or at the computer room door. It can serve a dual purpose when it's a software checkout list as well. We've included several versions in Appendix A: choose or adapt one to suit your needs.

A sign-up sheet can tell you many things:

- By asking the date, you can find out the most popular days of the week: schedule strategy events then.
- By asking the time, you can find out the most popular time of day: make the computers available then.
- By asking which software they use, you can find out the most popular software: publicize what you have or get more of a similar type.
- By examining the time girls come to use the computer, you can find out which friends come together: target them as a group.
- By counting the computer users by sex, you have a general barometer of computer equity effectiveness.

The other kind of optional computer use is the elective course: mini-courses, after-school courses, or computer electives scheduled into the regular curriculum. Count kids by sex (and grade if you like) from the enrollment lists.

Required computer use is also important, of course. This means that teachers must require it, which in turn means that teachers must use computers themselves with their students. To find out whether this is indeed happening, ask teachers if and how they are using computers in class, or use the Faculty Pre/Post Questionnaire in Appendix A, Copyables.

Evaluating Individual Strategies

There are several easy but good ways to find out how individual strategies are working out. Here are a few:

Ask people. Ask girls what they think of Strategy A. Ask the teachers what effect they see from Strategy B. Ask parents at the PTA meeting whether they've heard about Strategy C from their daughters. Ask team members involved in implementing each strategy for their observations.

Check the sign-up sheets after computer equity events. If one strategy is for the science teacher to use a spreadsheet program in class experiments, is there an increase thereafter in girls' use of spreadsheet software?

Administer a questionnaire. In Appendix A there are several questionnaires you can use or adapt to assess student reaction to all the strategies you implement. There's also a questionnaire for parents. Or you can make up a quickie to suit a strategy, as in the computer graphics questionnaire reproduced here. When analyzing the questionnaire, take one question at a time. Analyze yes/no answers by sorting them manually into piles and then counting them. (It sounds primitive, but it's fast.) You have to copy fill-in answers, either on paper or with a word processing program. Analyze multiple-choice answers by making a cross-hatch tally for each answer and then counting the cross-hatch units. We actually find analyzing questionnaires full of suspense and a lot of fun.

COMPUTER GRAPHICS QUESTIONNAIRE

1. Are you a: _____ Girl _____ Boy

2. What is your grade? _____ Grade

3. Did you attend the after-school session on computer graphics?
   _____ Yes _____ No

   IF YES TO QUESTION 3:

4. What did you like MOST about the session? _____
   _____

5. What did you like LEAST about the session? _____
   _____

6. Would you like to attend another computer graphics session?
   _____ Yes _____ No

   IF NO TO QUESTION 3:

7. Why not? Check all that apply.
   ___ a. I didn't know about it.
   ___ b. I had something else to do then.
   ___ c. I've done computer graphics and I don't like it.
   ___ d. I haven't done computer graphics, but I don't think I'd like it.
   ___ e. My friends didn't go.
   ___ f. It didn't sound interesting.
   ___ g. Another reason: _____
   _____

If Your Strategy Isn't Working

Once you've identified the problem by means of one of the techniques above, the solution is usually obvious. Let's say you've asked several students who you thought would come to the computer graphics session why they didn't. You learn they didn't know it was being offered. You've now found out that your method of asking teachers to read an announcement in homeroom didn't work. Next time, you can make a more heartfelt plea to homeroom teachers to be sure to read the announcement, put up posters, announce the session over the loudspeaker or at an assembly, or all of the above. Then offer another session and see how many students come after you change your publicity method. If the problem is one you're not sure how to fix—what if the girls say they hate the teacher?—discuss it at the team's next followup meeting. Delicately.

ACCOUNTABILITY EVALUATION

The star of our field test was Alfred Nobel Junior High School in Los Angeles, California. Their sign-up sheets and mini-course enrollment records showed that girls' optional computer use increased from two girls in January to fifty-nine girls in May. This actually works out to an increase of 2,850 percent—when you start low, the results can be spectacular. The number of boys using computers also increased from twenty-nine to forty-two, or a tidy 45 percent.

The computer equity team was delighted. The girls gained new skills and had a lot of fun. The principal was proud. District officials used Nobel J.H.S. as the model when they expanded the computer equity program to other schools the following year. The school was featured in a cover story of a newsletter that went to all the schools in Los Angeles.

Now the acknowledged school experts in California on closing the computer gender gap, the computer equity team and the principal are visited by educators from schools across the country, get calls from newspaper reporters doing stories on the topic, and are invited to speak at professional meetings nationwide. *This is what accountability evaluation is for.*

Obtaining Accountability Data

If you're tracking students' computer use by means of sign-up sheets or enrollment records, you have half the accountability information you need. The other half is what you're comparing these results to, which you need in order to find out if you're making any progress.

Let's say ten girls have now signed up for the most advanced computer elective your school offers. That's very nice, but compared to what? How many enrolled in the course last year?

 0 girls: Triumph!
10 girls: Back to the drawing board.
20 girls: We'd rather not think about this possibility.

In other words you need baseline data, or information on what the computer use situation is before beginning to implement any strategies designed to improve it. If you took the Computer Neutrality Self-Test, you already have it. The sex ratio figures for after-school sessions, electives, and free-access computer time during the day constitute your baseline information.

If you don't have a month's worth of baseline information, get it *before* you implement any strategies. This is so important that it's worth delaying your computer equity program for it. The greater the difference between the before and after numbers, the better you'll look.

You can do accountability evaluation on a bigger scale than simple before/after numbers if you'd like to. Here are some ways to obtain wonderful public relations material to dramatize your success:

Pre- and Post-Questionnaires. Appendix A has the questionnaires we used in the Computer Equity Training Project field test schools to measure change in computer attitude and behavior on the part of students and faculty.

Student Essays. You can ask girls who have learned to love the computer to write about the experience—using a computer, naturally. This makes fine copy for an article about your program.

Photographic Record. Before and after pictures of the computer room make a strong impression. You can take photos of a nearly all-male computer room, then photos of girls grinning at the monitor, boys and girls huddled around a computer (but be sure a girl is actually at the computer, not just watching), girls' computer graphics work or word-processed school reports, and more. The pictures can be displayed in school and can be used to accompany articles in newsletters and newspapers.

Using Accountability Evaluation Results

You use accountability evaluation results to blow the school's horn, and consequently yours. This is very important! When you come up with solid evidence of your effectiveness, tell your principal. Then let the district office know. They ought to use you as a model for computer equity innovation among other schools in the district. Invite your local newspaper to write an article on your newsworthy program.

Aside from these intangible but very important public relations considerations, you can use accountability evaluation results to get cold cash. Your district office is more likely to increase your budget for computer hardware and software if you've given evidence of making such good use of the resources you have. Community service groups, clubs, associations, or companies are more likely to contribute money for hardware and software for the same reason. And with good accountability results, you're in an excellent position to submit a proposal for funding to your district or state education agency for expanded computer equity efforts.

All this money can be used for staff training, faculty stipends for time spent in planning and implementing computer equity strategies (which you're now donating for free), hardware or software, student field trips to local computer companies, and other purposes. You won't have much trouble thinking of good ways to use it.

Just as important as these outcomes is the satisfaction success gives you. You chose to be an educator because you wanted to help children become adults who participate fully and productively in our society, and because you wanted to help them stretch to the top of their ability. A successful computer equity program produces young women who are able to earn a good living doing work they enjoy. You deserve the credit.

AND FOR NEXT YEAR . . .

One of our pilot test schools decided to conduct a little experiment. After a spring term's computer equity program during which they doubled girls' computer use, the faculty deliberately carried out no computer equity strategies at all the following fall because they wanted to see what would happen. When the computer elective enrollments were examined late in the fall term, it was found that boys outnumbered girls two to one—the same ratio that had existed before their successful computer equity program the previous spring.

This really shouldn't be too surprising. A computer equity program is needed in the first place because girls enter school believing that computers are for boys. Without the counter-message provided by a computer equity program—computers are for girls, too!—it's entirely natural for girls to revert to their original notion. After all, they continue to see boys in the video arcade and the computer room, and men in the computer ads.

Because society won't stop sending the male message, you can't stop sending the female message. Next year, repeat the most successful computer equity strategies and try out a couple of new ones, using the same planning and evaluation procedures you used this year. In time, you'll find you won't need to spend nearly as much time and effort on computer equity as you do now. A few years' worth of computer equity success will make enthusiastic computer use a part of the school atmosphere. Older girls who have become computer converts will insist that younger girls try it. All you'll need to do is echo their urging by issuing personal invitations to the younger ones to come to the computer room.

About five years ago, Shallow Junior High School in Brooklyn, New York, got its first computers. Faculty noticed the usual gender gap. However, they were fortunate in having a principal who was convinced that computers are powerful educational tools and was devoted to the ideal of equal educational opportunity for both sexes. He insisted that all faculty members become computer-literate, that they all use computers with their students, and that they close the computer gender gap. The principal regularly mentioned the gender gap at faculty meetings, put copies of articles on the topic in teachers' mailboxes, and praised teachers who actively encouraged girls to use computers. He flooded the school with new computers and software purchased with money raised by faculty and students in all sorts of innovative ways.

Within a few years, Shallow Junior High had over a hundred computers and even a robot, and had earned the reputation as the showcase for what could be done with computers in a school. Teachers found that as children were drawn into the school's computer culture, they learned better and more enthusiastically. And after several years of deliberately targeting girls to share in the computer culture, the faculty no longer saw a computer gender gap past September of each school year.

You can do it too.

A Copyables

Menu

	GOTO PAGE
Forms	201
1. Computer Equity Strategy Planning Form	202
2. Student Computer Sign-up Forms	203
3. Software Sex Bias Evaluation Form	207
4. Software Evaluation Forms	208
Questionnaires	211
1. Computer Neutrality Self-Test	212
2. Student Pre/Post Questionnaire	214
3. Faculty Pre/Post Questionnaire	221
4. Sample Computer Equity Program Evaluation and Strategy Questions for Students	226
5. Home Computer Questionnaire for Students	233
6. Student Software Evaluation Questionnaire	234
7. Parent Questionnaire	235

FORMS

COMPUTER EQUITY STRATEGY PLANNING FORM

STRATEGY: _____   GOAL: _____ GIRLS REACHED   COORDINATOR _____

ACTIVITIES	DATE	WHAT ?	RESOURCES NEEDED WHEN ?	HOW ?	PERSON RESPONSIBLE

EVALUATION: HOW, WHEN, WHO?

Forms   203

COMPUTER SIGN-UP SHEET   Version 1

LAST   FIRST   MIDDLE
NAME _____   NAME _____   INITIAL _____   SCHOOL _____

Find today's date. In the blank, show how much time you spent on the computer by using this code:

    1 = Less than 15 minutes
    2 = Between 15 and 30 minutes
    3 = Between 31 and 45 minutes
    4 = Between 46 and 60 minutes
    5 = More than one hour

On the days you don't use the computer at all, leave the space blank.

At the end of the month, please add up all the numbers in the column and put this number in the TOTAL box at the bottom.

DECEMBER	JANUARY	FEBRUARY	MARCH	APRIL	MAY	JUNE
3 ___	2 ___	1 ___	1 ___	1 ___	1 ___	3 ___
4 ___	3 ___			2 ___	2 ___	4 ___
5 ___	4 ___	4 ___	4 ___	3 ___	3 ___	5 ___
6 ___		5 ___	5 ___	4 ___		6 ___
7 ___	7 ___	6 ___	6 ___	5 ___	6 ___	7 ___
	8 ___	7 ___	7 ___		7 ___	
10 ___	9 ___	8 ___	8 ___	8 ___	8 ___	10 ___
11 ___	10 ___			9 ___	9 ___	11 ___
12 ___	11 ___	11 ___	11 ___	10 ___	10 ___	12 ___
13 ___		12 ___	12 ___	11 ___		13 ___
14 ___	14 ___	13 ___	13 ___	12 ___	13 ___	14 ___
	15 ___	14 ___	14 ___		14 ___	
17 ___	16 ___	15 ___	15 ___	15 ___	15 ___	17 ___
18 ___	17 ___			16 ___	16 ___	18 ___
19 ___	18 ___	18 ___	18 ___	17 ___	17 ___	19 ___
20 ___		19 ___	19 ___	18 ___		20 ___
21 ___	21 ___	20 ___	20 ___	19 ___	20 ___	21 ___
	22 ___	21 ___	21 ___		21 ___	
	23 ___	22 ___	22 ___	22 ___	22 ___	24 ___
	24 ___			23 ___	23 ___	25 ___
	25 ___	25 ___	25 ___	24 ___	24 ___	26 ___
		26 ___	26 ___	25 ___		27 ___
	28 ___	27 ___	27 ___	26 ___	27 ___	28 ___
	29 ___	28 ___	28 ___		28 ___	
	30 ___		29 ___	29 ___	29 ___	
	31 ___			30 ___	30 ___	

| December | January | February | March | April | May | June |
| TOTAL | TOTAL | TOTAL | TOTAL | TOTAL | TOTAL | TOTAL |

204 THE NEUTER COMPUTER

COMPUTER SIGN-UP SHEET   Version 2

LAST NAME _____ FIRST NAME _____ GRADE _____

MONTH _____   YEAR _____

Put a check mark next to each day you use a computer during your free time.

1 _____	16 _____
2 _____	17 _____
3 _____	18 _____
4 _____	19 _____
5 _____	20 _____
6 _____	21 _____
7 _____	22 _____
8 _____	23 _____
9 _____	24 _____
10 _____	25 _____
11 _____	26 _____
12 _____	27 _____
13 _____	28 _____
14 _____	29 _____
15 _____	30 _____
	31 _____

VERSION 3

COMPUTER SIGN-UP SHEET

LAST NAME _____ FIRST NAME _____ GRADE _____

MONTH _____ YEAR _____

What did you do at the computer today? Find today's date. On that line, check all the computer activities you did.

COMPUTER ACTIVITIES

For Yourself

Date	Homework	Math or Spelling Practice	Word Processing	Data Base	Spread-sheet	Graphics	Programming	Games	Other: What?
1									
2									
3									
4									
5									
6									
7									
8									
9									
10									
11									
12									
13									
14									
15									
16									
17									
18									
19									
20									
21									
22									
23									
24									
25									
26									
27									
28									
29									
30									
31									

206 THE NEUTER COMPUTER

VERSION 4

COMPUTER SIGN-UP SHEET

DATE _____

Write your name below. On the same line, put a check mark below each of the computer activities you did today.

COMPUTER ACTIVITIES

For   Yourself

NAME	Homework	Math or Spelling Practice	Word Processing	Data Base	Spreadsheet	Graphics	Programming	Games	Other: what?

SOFTWARE SEX BIAS EVALUATION FORM *

                                            BIAS SCALE

	HIGH	MED	LOW	NONE

SUBJECT OR THEME

The subject matter or theme appeals to all students, regardless of gender, race, or ethnicity.

OVERALL STYLE OF ACTION

The style of action is likely to appeal to all students. The program is not dominated by aggressive, violent, or antisocial behavior. Sound and graphics are used appropriately to enhance the presentation of the subject.

SYMBOLS

The symbols (sprites, tokens, icons, prompts) are free of stereotypes. Masculine and feminine symbols are presented in an accurate, appropriate, and balanced way.

REINFORCEMENTS

Reinforcements or rewards are likely to motivate all students effectively. For example, rewards with both words and graphics are included.

ROLE REPRESENTATIONS

The program is free of role stereotyping. Girls and minorities as well as white males are shown in positions of action, leadership, status, and authority.

LANGUAGE USAGE

The program is free of sexist or racist language. For example, job titles do not refer to gender (police officer, not policeman); non-human objects such as a Logo turtle or a robot are not assumed to be male.

GENDER REPRESENTATION

Girls and boys are equally represented in the program.

* This form was developed by the Center for Educational Equity, American Institutes for Research, Palo Alto, California.

208 THE NEUTER COMPUTER

SOFTWARE EVALUATION CHECKLIST

PROGRAM NAME: _____ SOURCE: _____ COST: _____
SUBJECT AREA: _____ REVIEWER'S NAME: _____ DATE: _____

1. INSTRUCTIONAL RANGE
   _____ grade level(s)
   _____ ability level(s)

2. INSTRUCTIONAL GROUPING FOR PROGRAM USE
   _____ individual
   _____ small group (size: ___)
   _____ large group (size: ___)

3. EXECUTION TIME
   _____ minutes (estimated) for average use

4. PROGRAM USE(S)
   _____ drill or practice
   _____ tutorial
   _____ simulation
   _____ instructional gaming
   _____ problem solving
   _____ informational
   _____ other (_____)

5. USER ORIENTATION: INSTRUCTOR'S POINT OF VIEW
   low   high
   . . . . . .   flexibility
   . . . . . .   freedom from need to
                 intervene or assist

6. USER ORIENTATION: STUDENT'S POINT OF VIEW
   low   high
   . . . . . .   quality of directions (clarity)
   . . . . . .   quality of output (content & tone)
   . . . . . .   quality of screen formatting
   . . . . . .   freedom from need for external
                 information
   . . . . . .   freedom from disruption by system
                 errors
   . . . . . .   simplicity of user input

7. CONTENT
   low   high
   . . . . . .   instructional locus
   . . . . . .   soundness or validity
   . . . . . .   compatibility with other materials used

8. MOTIVATION AND INSTRUCTIONAL STYLE
   passive   active
   . . . . . .   type of student involvement
   low   high
   . . . . . .   degree of student control
   none poor   good
   . . . . . .   use of game format
   . . . . . .   use of still graphics
   . . . . . .   use of animation
   . . . . . .   use of color
   . . . . . .   use of voice input and output
   . . . . . .   use of nonvoice audio
   . . . . . .   use of light pen
   . . . . . .   use of anciliary materials

9. SOCIAL CHARACTERISTICS
   present and   not   present and
   negative   present   positive
   _____   _____   _____   competition
   _____   _____   _____   cooperation
   _____   _____   _____   humanizing of computer
   _____   _____   _____   moral issues or value judgments
   _____   _____   _____   summary of student performance

From: Heck, W.P., Johnson, J. and Kansky R.J. Guidelines for Evaluating Computerized Instructional Materials.
       National Council of Teachers of Mathematics, 1906 Association Dr., Reston, VA 22091
       $3.75

COURSEWARE EVALUATION FORM

Name of Program _____

Manufacturer's or Distributor's Name _____

Address _____

Cost _____ Copyright/Date _____

Available for what Microcomputers (Model and Memory) _____

Peripherals Needed _____

Reviewer's Name _____ Date _____

Description of Program _____
_____
_____

Appropriate grade level: primary   inter.   jr. high   sr. high   college

Type of computer application(s)   (check one or more)

    _____ simulation   _____ remediation
    _____ tutorial   _____ enrichment
    _____ drill and practice   _____ management (only)
    _____ game   _____ diagnostic/prescriptive
    _____ problem solving   _____ other _____

Kinds of courses for which this program is appropriate
_____

Prerequisite skills or courses needed
_____

ANALYSIS   (check yes, no or not applicable)

		YES	NO	NA
a.	Content has clear instructional objectives.	___	___	___
b.	Content is accurate.	___	___	___
c.	Content has educational value.	___	___	___
d.	Content is free of stereotypes.	___	___	___
e.	Content expresses positive human values.	___	___	___
f.	Program is appropriate for targeted audience.	___	___	___
g.	Computer branches to appropriate difficulty.	___	___	___
h.	Graphics/sound/color have instructional value.	___	___	___
i.	Frame display is effective.	___	___	___
j.	Students can use program easily.	___	___	___
k.	Teachers can utilize the program easily.	___	___	___
l.	Documentation is comprehensive.	___	___	___
m.	Computer is an appropriate tool for activity.	___	___	___
n.	User can control rate/sequence/directions.	___	___	___
o.	Feedback used is effective and appropriate.	___	___	___

RECOMMEND for purchase? ___ yes   ___ no   ___ conditional on:

Permission to reproduce for classroom use by Microcomputer Resource Center, Teachers College, Columbia University, New York, New York.

QUESTIONNAIRES

COMPUTER NEUTRALITY SELF-TEST

DIRECTIONS: Answer the questions, then choose [A] or [B] for each one.

1. Does your school make the computers available to students on a free-time basis before, during, or after school? If so, make a quick count of the students you see taking advantage of the opportunity:

   _____ Number of girls   _____ Number of boys

   A. _____ **Number of girls is higher.**
   B. _____ **Number of boys is higher.**

2. Who teaches the computer courses in your school?

   A. _____ **Mostly women.**
   B. _____ **Mostly men.**

3. Does your school have a computer elective course? If so, ask the person who teaches it for these figures:

   _____ Total enrollment   _____ Number of girls   _____ Number of boys

   A. _____ **Number of girls is higher.**
   B. _____ **Number of boys is higher.**

   If your school offers several computer electives, ask for the figures for the most advanced course.

4. Ask your students for a show of hands about how many of them have ever used a computer when they didn't have to for a class:

   _____ Number of girls   _____ Number of boys

   A. _____ **Number of girls is higher.**
   B. _____ **Number of boys is higher.**

5. Ask your students for a show of hands about how many of their mothers and fathers know how to use a computer:

   _____ Number of mothers   _____ Number of fathers

   A. _____ **Number of mothers is higher.**
   B. _____ **Number of fathers is higher.**

6. Ask for a show of hands about how many of your students have a computer at home:

   _____ Number of girls   _____ Number of boys

   A. _____ Number of girls is higher.
   B. _____ Number of boys is higher.

7. Ask the computer owners for a show of hands about who uses it most at home:

   _____ Number saying girls or women use it most.
   _____ Number saying boys or men use it most.

   A. _____ Number of girls or women is higher.
   B. _____ Number of boys or men is higher.

8. Who do you see in the video arcades?

   A. _____ Mostly girls.
   B. _____ Mostly boys.

9. Who do you see in computer ads on TV and in newspapers and magazines?

   A. _____ Mostly women or girls.
   B. _____ Mostly men or boys.

SCORING: Give yourself one point for each [B] answer, and 0 points for each [A] answer.

SCORE: _____   (Maximum score: 9)

THE NEUTER COMPUTER

STUDENT PRE/POST QUESTIONNAIRE

1. What grade are you in?

    (a) 7th grade
    (b) 8th grade
    (c) Other grade

2. Are you a girl or a boy?

    (a) Girl
    (b) Boy

3. What is your group identity?

    (a) Black, or Afro-American
    (b) Mexican-American, or Chicano, or Puerto Rican, or Hispanic
    (c) Oriental, or Asian-American
    (d) Native-American or American Indian
    (e) White, Caucasian
    (f) Mixed identity, or other

4. How long have you been using a computer?

    (a) I started using a computer for the first time this school year (that is, since September)
    (b) I have used a computer for about two years.
    (c) I have used a computer for about three years.
    (d) I have used a computer for more than three years.
    (e) I have never used a computer.

5. Would you be more likely to use a computer if your mother uses it?

    (a) Yes
    (b) No

6. Would you be more likely to use a computer if your father uses it?

    (a) Yes
    (b) No

7. Do you use a computer at home?

    (a) I have a computer at home, and I use it.
    (b) I have a computer at home, and I don't use it.
    (c) I don't have a computer at home.

8. Is there a computer that is <u>not</u> in school and <u>not</u> at home that you can use, such as at a friend's house, in a library, or in an office?

    (a) Yes
    (b) No

9. Have you ever had a computer class outside of school, such as at a camp or at an after-school center?

    (a) Yes
    (b) No

THE NEXT 9 QUESTIONS ASK ABOUT USING A COMPUTER IN YOUR CLASSES IN SCHOOL.

10. Have you used a computer in English (Language Arts) class? (a) Yes (b) No
11. Have you used a computer in math class? (a) Yes (b) No
12. Have you used a computer in social studies (history) class? (a) Yes (b) No
13. Have you used a computer in science class? (a) Yes (b) No
14. Have you used a computer in foreign language class? (a) Yes (b) No
15. Have you used a computer in art class? (a) Yes (b) No
16. Have you used a computer in music class? (a) Yes (b) No
17. Have you used a computer in computer class? (a) Yes (b) No
18. Have you used a computer in any other class in school? (a) Yes (b) No

THE NEXT 9 QUESTIONS ASK ABOUT THE ACTIVITIES YOU, YOURSELF, HAVE PERFORMED WITH A COMPUTER.

19. Have you loaded a program into memory? (a) Yes (b) No
20. Have you saved a program on a disk or tape? (a) Yes (b) No
21. Have you named or renamed a program file? (a) Yes (b) No
22. Have you made a copy of a program or file? (a) Yes (b) No
23. Have you deleted a program from a disk or tape? (a) Yes (b) No
24. Have you accessed a catalog or menu of saved programs? (a) Yes (b) No
25. Have you tested and debugged a program? (a) Yes (b) No
26. Have you used a printer? (a) Yes (b) No
27. Have you written a program? (a) Yes (b) No

28. How good are you at computers?

    (a) I'm very good at computers.
    (b) I'm okay at computers.
    (c) I'm not so sure how good I am at computers.
    (d) I'm not so hot at computers.
    (e) I'm terrible at computers.

29. How comfortable do you feel around computers?

    (a) I feel very comfortable around computers.
    (b) I feel sort of comfortable around computers.
    (c) I'm not sure how I feel around computers.
    (d) I feel a little uncomfortable around computers.
    (e) I feel very uncomfortable around computers.

30. Which way do you like to use a computer the most?

    (a) I like to play around with it just to see what I can do with it.
    (b) I like to use it to get something done that I need to do.
    (c) I never used a computer.

31. Do you like other people around you when you use a compter?

    (a) I like to be alone when I use a computer.
    (b) I like to have a computer to myself in the same room where other kids are using their computers, too.
    (c) I like it when another student and I use the same computer.
    (d) I like to be part of a group using the same computer.
    (e) I don't use a computer.

32. Would you be more likely to use a computer if girls you like use it?

    (a) Yes
    (b) No

33. Would you be more likely to use a computer if boys you like use it?

    (a) Yes
    (b) No

34. Would you be more likely to use a computer if teachers of your own sex used it?

    (a) Yes
    (b) No

35. Do you like arcade-type computer games?

   (a) I love this kind of game.
   (b) I like this kind of game.
   (c) I don't know, or I have never seen this kind of game.
   (d) I don't like this kind of game.
   (e) I hate this kind of game.

36. Who do you think likes computers more?

   (a) Only boys like computers.
   (b) Mostly boys and some girls like computers.
   (c) Boys and girls like computers equally.
   (d) Mostly girls and some boys like computers.
   (e) Only girls like computers.

37. If you want to see a certain movie but your friends don't want to see it, what would you decide to do?

   (a) I'd probably see the movie.
   (b) I probably wouldn't see the movie.

THE NEXT 5 QUESTIONS ASK ABOUT YOUR SCHOOL SUBJECTS.

	(a) I love it.	(b) I like it.	(c) So-So.	(d) I don't like it.	(e) I hate it.
38. How much do you like writing, such as compositions or reports?	(a)	(b)	(c)	(d)	(e)
39. How much do you like math?	(a)	(b)	(c)	(d)	(e)
40. How much do you like science?	(a)	(b)	(c)	(d)	(e)
41. How much do you like art?	(a)	(b)	(c)	(d)	(e)
42. How much do you like gym?	(a)	(b)	(c)	(d)	(e)

218 THE NEUTER COMPUTER

THE NEXT 8 QUESTIONS ASK ABOUT WHAT YOU USUALLY DO WITH YOUR TIME WHEN YOU ARE NOT IN CLASS.

		(a) No time at all.	(b) Very little time	(c) Some time.	(d) A lot of time.
43.	How much time do you usually spend doing homework?	(a)	(b)	(c)	(d)
44.	How much time do you usually spend with your friends?	(a)	(b)	(c)	(d)
45.	How much time do you usually spend doing chores or a job?	(a)	(b)	(c)	(d)
46.	How much time do you usually spend watching television?	(a)	(b)	(c)	(d)
47.	How much time do you usually spend doing sports?	(a)	(b)	(c)	(d)
48.	How much time do you usually spend reading (for yourself, not homework)?	(a)	(b)	(c)	(d)
49.	How much time do you usually spend using a computer?	(a)	(b)	(c)	(d)
50.	How much time do you usually spend in club or group activities?	(a)	(b)	(c)	(d)

THE NEXT 5 QUESTIONS ASK ABOUT HOW YOU SEE COMPUTERS IN YOUR FUTURE.

51. Do you plan to take computer courses in high school?

       (a) Yes
       (b) No
       (c) Not sure.

52. Do you plan to take a course in programming languages in high school (for example, in BASIC FORTRAN or PASCAL)?

       (a) Yes
       (b) No
       (c) Not sure

53. Do you plan to take a course in word processing in high school?

       (a) Yes
       (b) No
       (c) Not sure

54. Do you think that knowing how to use a computer will be important for you in the future?

       (a) Yes
       (b) No
       (c) Not sure

55. When you are an adult, how do you think you will use the computer?

       (a) Mostly for fun and entertainment.
       (b) Mostly for home uses such as budgeting and record-keeping.
       (c) Mostly for work purposes.
       (d) For fun, home, and work purposes equally.
       (e) I don't think I'll use a computer when I'm an adult.

220 THE NEUTER COMPUTER

ANSWER SHEET

STUDENT QUESTIONNAIRE

LAST   FIRST   MIDDLE
NAME _____   NAME _____   INITIAL _____

          SCHOOL _____   DATE _____

Read each question carefully. Find the ONE answer that you think is best for the question. When you have chosen your answer, write the letter of the answer in the blank space next to the question number. Do not write on the questionnaire. All answers belong on this answer sheet.

1. _____   19. _____   37. _____
2. _____   20. _____   38. _____
3. _____   21. _____   39. _____
4. _____   22. _____   40. _____
5. _____   23. _____   41. _____
6. _____   24. _____   42. _____
7. _____   25. _____   43. _____
8. _____   26. _____   44. _____
9. _____   27. _____   45. _____
10. _____   28. _____   46. _____
11. _____   29. _____   47. _____
12. _____   30. _____   48. _____
13. _____   31. _____   49. _____
14. _____   32. _____   50. _____
15. _____   33. _____   51. _____
16. _____   34. _____   52. _____
17. _____   35. _____   53. _____
18. _____   36. _____   54. _____
                                          55. _____

FACULTY PRE/POST QUESTIONNAIRE

1. What is your <u>primary</u> job?

      (a) Classroom teacher
      (b) Department head
      (c) Administrator
      (d) Counselor
      (e) Librarian (books)
      (f) Media center
      (g) Computer lab
      (h) Teacher aide
      (i) Other

Which of the following subjects do you teach or supervise? Choose one of the following answers for each question:

      (a) Yes
      (b) No

2. Art/graphic arts

3. Career education

4. Computer studies

5. English/language arts

6. Foreign languages

7. Guidance

8. Health

9. Home economics

10. Industrial arts

11. Mathematics

12. Music

13. Performing arts

14. Physical education/gym

15. Science

16. Social Studies/history

17. Are you female of male?

      (a) Female
      (b) Male

18. How many years have you worked in a school?

      (a) This is my first year.
      (b) Two to four years.
      (c) Five to ten years.
      (d) Eleven to twenty years.
      (e) Twenty-one or more years.

19. What is your age?

        (a) Between 20 and 29 years old.
        (b) Between 30 and 39 years old.
        (c) Between 40 and 49 years old.
        (d) Between 50 and 59 years old.
        (e) 60 years old or more.

20. What is your group identity?

        (a) Black, or Afro-American
        (b) Mexican-American, or Chicano, or Puerto Rican, or Hispanic
        (c) Oriental, or Asian-American
        (d) White, or Caucasian
        (e) Native-American, or American Indian
        (f) Mixed identity, or other

21. Have you used a computer to help you with administrative tasks in school, such as writing exams, calculating grades, maintaining class lists, etc.?

        (a) Yes
        (b) No

THE NEXT 9 QUESTIONS ASK ABOUT THE KINDS OF COMPUTER PROGRAMS OR ACTIVITIES YOU USE WITH YOUR STUDENTS. Choose one of the following answers for each question:

        (a) Yes
        (b) No

22. Have you used <u>data base management</u> programs with your students?

23. Have you used <u>spreadsheet</u> programs with your students?

24. Have you used <u>word processing</u> programs with your students?

25. Have you used <u>graphics</u> programs with your students?

26. Have you used <u>graph-making</u> programs with your students?

27. Have you used <u>CAI (drill and practice)</u> programs with your students?

28. Have you used <u>simulations</u> with your students?

29. Have you used <u>commercial data base services</u> (e.g., CompuServe) with your students?

30. Have you used <u>programming languages</u> with your students?

THE NEXT 9 QUESTIONS ASK ABOUT THE ACTIVITIES YOU, YOURSELF, HAVE PERFORMED
WITH A COMPUTER. Choose one of the following answers for each question:

    (a) Yes
    (b) No

31. Have you loaded a program into memory?

32. Have you saved a program on a disk or tape?

33. Have you named or renamed a program file?

34. Have you made a copy of a program file?

35. Have you deleted a program from a disk or tape?

36. Have you accessed a catalog or menu of saved programs?

37. Have you tested and debugged a program?

38. Have you used a printer?

39. Have you written a program?

40. Violence in children's software is a controversial topic among educators. Which one of the following statements best reflects your own opinion?

    (a) Children's software does have a lot of violence, but I don't see any harm in that.

    (b) I wish the software weren't so violent, but it seems necessary to maintain children's interest.

    (c) I am opposed to the violence in children's software because I think it harms children.

    (d) I don't think children's software is particularly violent.

    (e) I don't know enough about children's software to have an opinion on it.

224 THE NEUTER COMPUTER

Educators have suggested a number of ways in which boys and girls may have different feelings about computers, or may use them differently. For each of the next 11 questions, choose an answer according to the following diagram, based on your own observations of children.

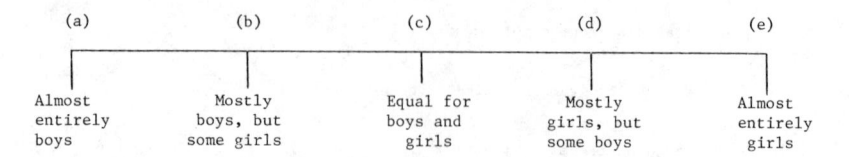

```
        (a)              (b)             (c)             (d)             (e)
         |                |               |               |               |
      Almost           Mostly          Equal for        Mostly          Almost
     entirely         boys, but        boys and        girls, but      entirely
       boys          some girls         girls         some boys         girls
```

41. Who uses the computer in an exploratory manner, just to see what can be done with it?

42. Who uses the computer in a goal-oriented manner, to get something done?

43. Who uses the computer for word processing?

44. Who uses the computer for math?

45. Who uses the computer for graphics or music?

46. Who uses the computer for programming?

47. Who uses arcade-type computer games?

48. Who seems afraid to let their computer ignorance show?

49. Who seems happy to work alone at a computer, with no friends nearby?

50. Who uses the computer intensely: often and for long periods of time?

51. Who enjoys using the computer?

ANSWER SHEET

FACULTY QUESTIONNAIRE

LAST NAME _____ FIRST NAME _____ MIDDLE INITIAL _____

SCHOOL _____ DATE _____

Please read each question carefully. Choose only <u>one</u> answer for each question, and write it in the space provided. Please do not write on the questionnaire.

1. _____	18. _____	35. _____
2. _____	19. _____	36. _____
3. _____	20. _____	37. _____
4. _____	21. _____	38. _____
5. _____	22. _____	39. _____
6. _____	23. _____	40. _____
7. _____	24. _____	41. _____
8. _____	25. _____	42. _____
9. _____	26. _____	43. _____
10. _____	27. _____	44. _____
11. _____	28. _____	45. _____
12. _____	29. _____	46. _____
13. _____	30. _____	47. _____
14. _____	31. _____	48. _____
15. _____	32. _____	49. _____
16. _____	33. _____	50. _____
17. _____	34. _____	51. _____

SAMPLE COMPUTER EQUITY
PROGRAM AND STRATEGY EVALUATION QUESTIONS FOR STUDENTS

Below are a number of questions you can use for a survey of your students to guage the effectiveness of your computer equity program. You can copy them, adapt them, or invent others to wind up with the most appropriate questions for your particular computer equity program and school circumstances.

Assuming your questionnaire is to be filled out by computer-using students as well as those who don't use computers, you need a "branching" question to avoid asking computer-use questions to students who can't answer them because they haven't used computers. There are two ways to do this.

1) Put the questions everyone can answer up front, followed by questions that only apply to the computer users. Separate the two groups of questions this way:

Did you use a computer at school this term?   Yes _____   No _____

    IF YOU ANSWERED "NO," STOP HERE.
    IF YOU ANSWERED "YES," KEEP GOING.

2) Put some questions everyone can answer up front, then questions for computer users only, followed by attitude-type questions everyone can answer. Your branching mechanism becomes:

Did you use a computer at school this term?   Yes _____   No _____

    IF YOU ANSWERED "YES," KEEP GOING.

    IF YOU ANSWERED "NO," SKIP TO QUESTION #23.

You can make up a separate answer sheet, or you can have students write their answers on the questionnaire itself. If you choose the latter, leave a lot of blank space between questions when you type the questionnaire to help kids write their answers on the right lines.

<u>Analysis</u>. If you are doing this manually, first separate the pile of completed questionnaires into two groups by sex, or into more groups if you are analyzing by grade as well -- for example, 7F, 7M, 8F, 8M, 9F, 9M. (If you aren't analyzing by grade, don't bother to ask for grade.) Count each group.

Second, manually separate each group into a subgroup for those who have used computers this term and another for those who haven't. Count each subgroup. If the non-computer users have not answered any other questions, set those aside.

Third, proceed subgroup by subgroup to record answers for each question in cross-hatch fashion. Make a count for each item and for each subgroup. If you don't have a huge number of students, you can record the responses on a blank questionnaire. When the responses have been recorded, calculate percentages for each one -- for example, "48 percent of the female 7th grade computer users said they preferred to share a computer with a friend."

Fourth, examine the results. Which were your most effective strategies? Should you improve the others or drop them? Which computer-use preferences can you accomodate and reinforce? Are there any problem areas you need to work on?

Or, you can use a computer for the analysis. Manually separate the groups and subgroups as in steps 1 and 2, and then use a data base program or a spreadsheet to enter the responses. If you analyze the questionnaire by computer, you must consult in advance with the person who will be doing the data entry to find out if the answers can be processed in the form they are supplied. If not, you'll need to rephrase or reformat the question or the answer.

BASIC IDENTIFYING QUESTIONS

Are you a girl or a boy?   A girl _____   A boy _____

What is your grade?   Grade _____

SAMPLE STRATEGY-RELATED QUESTIONS

Was there a special effort in school this term   Yes _____
to encourage girls to use a computer?   No _____
                                               I don't know _____

How have the following things changed your computer use?

        1   This made me use computers more.
        2   This made me use computers less.
        3   This had no effect on my computer use.
        4   This didn't happen.

a. Parent workshop   _____
b. Girls' Computer Lunch   _____
c. The computer art contest   _____
d. The computer bulletin board   _____
e. The Computer Career Fair   _____
f. Teachers asked me to.   _____
g. My friends are using them more.   _____

Which of the following things encouraged you to use a school computer this term? Write "1" for the most important, "2" for the next most important, and so on. Write "0" for those that didn't have any effect on you at all.

_Write here the strategies you carried out._____   _____
_____   _____
_____   _____
_____   _____
_____   _____

How many times did you attend the "girls only"   More than 10 times _____
computer sessions this term?   5 to 9 times _____
                                                     2 to 4 times _____
                                                          1 time _____
                                                        No times _____

Did your teachers use computers in class more
this term than they did before?   Yes _____   No _____

How many times this term did you look at the   More than 5 times _____
computer bulletin board?   3 to 5 times _____
                                                   Once or twice _____
                                                        No times _____

Which arrangement of the computers in the computer room do you prefer?

    a. The way it is now.   _____
    b. The way it was before.   _____
    c. It doesn't matter.   _____

Did your parents mention any of the following to you?

    a. Articles about computer equity   Yes _____ No _____
    b. The computer equity table at the PTA meeting Yes _____ No _____
    c. The computer equity meeting for parents   Yes _____ No _____
    d. The computer workshops for parents   Yes _____ No _____

Was there any change in how much your parents talked with you about computers this term?

    a. Yes, they talked to me about computers more than before.   _____
    b. Yes, they talked to me about computers less than before.   _____
    c. No, there was no change.   _____

SAMPLE QUESTIONS ON STUDENTS' COMPUTER USE AND PREFERENCES

How much did you use a computer this year, compared to last year?

    a. I used it more this year. _____
    b. I used it more last year. _____
    c. About the same both years. _____
    d. Didn't use it either year. _____

When did you use a school computer this year? Check all that apply.

    a. In the computer literacy class _____
    b. In a computer elective class _____
    c. In another class (such as science) _____
    d. In my free time _____

Are you more likely to use computers when girls you like use them?   Yes _____ No _____

Are you more likely to use computers when boys you like use them?   Yes _____ No _____

If you studied programming in both BASIC and Logo, which did you like better?   BASIC _____   Logo _____

Which of the following best describes the way you like to work with computers? Choose one.

    a. Alone, with nobody else around. _____
    b. A computer to myself, but other people can be there, too. _____
    c. A computer to myself, but a friend at the next computer. _____
    d. Share a computer with a friend. _____
    e. Part of a group at one computer. _____

Below is a list of things you can do on a computer. Which do you like best? Write "1" for best, "2" for next best, and so on.

    a. Graphics _____
    b. Word processing _____
    c. Composing music _____
    d. Using a data base program _____
    e. Using a spreadsheet program _____
    f. Programming in Logo _____
    g. Programming in BASIC _____
    h. Using educational games _____
    i. Using a graphing program _____
    j. Games _____
    k. Telecommunications _____

What do you use a computer for? Write "1" for most, "2" for next most, etc.

   a. Homework
   b. Extra help with my subjects
   c. Educational software
   d. Games
   e. Personal uses

Which one of these sentences best describes how you feel about using a computer?

   a. I like to use it to get something done that I have to do or I want to do, but I don't much care about all the other things it can do.

   b. I like to use it for the fun of seeing all the things I can make it do, whether or not they're useful to me.

            a _____ b _____

SAMPLE QUESTIONS ABOUT STUDENTS' COMPUTER ATTITUDES

Do your parents want you to learn how to use a computer?

   a. They want me to very much.
   b. They feel it's my decision.
   c. They don't think I should.
   d. They don't care about it.

Does it matter to you whether a computer teacher is a man or a woman?

   a. Yes, I prefer a male computer teacher.
   b. Yes, I prefer a female computer teacher.
   c. No, it doesn't matter.

If a girl isn't interested in computers, why is that? Check all the reasons that apply.

   a. Computers are boring.
   b. Computers are too hard to learn.
   c. There's nothing useful you can do with a computer.
   d. Her friends don't use computers.
   e. She has too many other things to do.
   f. There are too many boys in the computer room.
   g. She thinks she'll break the computer.
   h. You get too lonely using a computer.
   i. The boys in the computer room make her feel unwelcome.
   j. The computer teacher makes her feel unwelcome.
   k. She's afraid of the computer.
   l. Her parents don't let her stay after school to use it.

232   THE NEUTER COMPUTER

How do you feel about computers?   I love them.   _____
                                    I like them.   _____
                                    I don't care.   _____
                                    I don't like them. _____
                                    I hate them.   _____

Do you think your attitude about computers has changed this term?

    a. Yes, I like them more.
    b. Yes, I don't like them as much.   _____
    c. No, my attitude hasn't changed.

Do most of your friends use computers?   Yes _____   No _____

Do you think it will be important for Americans ten years from now to know how to use computers?

		MEN				WOMEN		
a.	For school	Yes	___	No	___	Yes	___	No	___
b.	For work	Yes	___	No	___	Yes	___	No	___
c.	For home	Yes	___	No	___	Yes	___	No	___
d.	For fun	Yes	___	No	___	Yes	___	No	___

How important do you think computers will be for YOU PEPRSONALLY in ten years?

    1 Absolutely essential   For school? _____
    2 Important   For work?   _____
    3 Don't know   For home?   _____
    4 Not very important   For fun?   _____
    5 Absolutely useless

HOME COMPUTER QUESTIONNAIRE FOR STUDENTS

1. What grade are you in?   Grade _____

2. Are you a girl or a boy?   Girl _____   Boy _____

3. How many people live in your house?   Number of men _____
                                                                Number of women _____
                                                                Number of boys _____
                                                                Number of girls _____

4. Do you have a computer at home?   Yes _____   No _____

     If you answered NO, stop here.
     If you answered YES, keep going.

5. How many men use the computer in your house?   Number of men _____

6. How many women use the computer in your house?   Number of women _____

7. How many boys use the computer in your house?   Number of boys _____

8. How many girls use the computer in your house?   Number of girls _____

9. Do you use the computer in your house?   Yes _____   No _____

10. Who uses the computer the most at home? Check one.   Man _____
                                                                                              Woman _____
                                                                                                 Boy _____
                                                                                                 Girl _____

STUDENT SOFTWARE EVALUATION QUESTIONNAIRE

_____
            Name of Program

1. Are you: A girl _____   A boy _____

2. What grade are you in?   Grade _____

            GRADES   A   Excellent
                      B   Good
                      C   Fair
                      D   Poor
                      E   Failing

3. Give this program a grade for the fun and enjoyment you had.   3. _____

4. Give this program a grade for how much it held your interest.   4. _____

5. Give this program a grade for the way it looked on the screen. 5. _____

6. Give this program a grade for its sound effects.   6. _____

7. Give this program a grade for how much it helped you learn.   7. _____

8. One important thing about this program is that it _____
   _____

        How do you feel about this?   I love it.   _____
                                                     I like it.   _____
                                                     I don't care.   _____
                                                     I don't like it. _____
                                                     I hate it.   _____

9. Would you like to play this program again?   Yes _____   No _____

PARENT QUESTIONNAIRE

PART A - ABOUT YOUR FAMILY

1. What are the sexes and ages of your children? Please check those who know how to use a computer.

NAME	M/F	AGE	KNOWS COMPUTERS
_____	___	___	___
_____	___	___	___
_____	___	___	___
_____	___	___	___
_____	___	___	___

2. What is your occupation?

   Mother: _____
   Father: _____

3. Do you know how to use a computer?

   Mother: YES   NO
   Father: YES   NO

4. Do you have a computer at home?   YES   NO

5. If you have a computer at home, who uses it and for what purpose (for example, letters, games, budgeting, business, etc.)? Please indicate how much family members use the computer by writing "1" for the person who uses it most, "2" for the person who uses it nearly as much, and so forth.

RELATIONSHIP	SEX	AGE	PRIMARY PURPOSE	USE LEVEL
Mother	F	---	_____	_____
Father	M	---	_____	_____
_____	__	__	_____	_____
_____	__	__	_____	_____
_____	__	__	_____	_____
_____	__	__	_____	_____
_____	__	__	_____	_____

6. Which of the following things have taken place in your family? Please check those that apply to your son(s) and daughter(s) who are 8 or older.

	SON(S)	DAUGHTER(S)
a. Child has talked to parent about computer class in school.	_____	_____
b. Child has talked to parent about extra-curricular computer use in school.	_____	_____
c. Parent has used a computer with a child.	_____	_____
d. Parent has talked about computer careers with a child.	_____	_____

7. What is your impression of your children's feelings about computers? For each statement below, please write YES, NO, or DON'T KNOW as they apply to your son(s) and daughter(s) who are 8 or older.

	SONS(S)	DAUGHTER(S)
a. My children think computers are fun.	_____	_____
b. My children think computers are useful.	_____	_____
c. My children have considered computer-related careers for themselves.	_____	_____
d. My children expect to use computers when they grow up.	_____	_____

8. How important do YOU think it is for your son(s) and daughter(s) to know how to use a computer in the years to come? Please use the following code numbers as they apply to your children who are 8 or older.

```
            1 = Absolutely essential
            2 = Important
            3 = So-so
            4 = Not very important
            5 = Absolutely useless
```

	SON(S)	DAUGHTER(S)
a. Important for school	_____	_____
b. Important for work	_____	_____
c. Important for home	_____	_____
d. Important for recreation	_____	_____

WE WELCOME ANY COMMENTS YOU MAY HAVE. PLEASE WRITE THEM ON THE OTHER SIDE OF THIS PAGE.

THANK YOU VERY MUCH FOR FILLING OUT THIS QUESTIONNAIRE. WE'LL LET YOU KNOW THE RESULTS AS SOON AS POSSIBLE.

PART B - AFTER A COMPUTER EQUITY WORKSHOP

1. Before you came here tonight, how aware were you of the gender gap in computer use among children? Please check one.

	MOTHER	FATHER
I didn't know anything about it.	_____	_____
I had heard a little about it.	_____	_____
I knew a lot about it.	_____	_____

2. How much effort do you think teachers should be putting into encouraging girls to use computers more? Please check one.

	MOTHER	FATHER
A lot of effort: this is a very important problem.	_____	_____
Some effort: this is a problem, but others are more important.	_____	_____
No effort: this is not a problem at all.	_____	_____

3. Now that you have learned about computer equity, which of the following do you think you might do with your daughter(s) at home? Please write YES or NO for each.

	MOTHER	FATHER

FOR HOME COMPUTER OWNERS:

	MOTHER	FATHER
a. Learn how to use a computer myself.	_____	_____
b. Spend more time at a computer with my daughter(s).	_____	_____
c. Encourage her to use a computer more.	_____	_____
d. Talk more with her about computer-related careers.	_____	_____
e. Enroll her in an after-school or summer computer workshop or camp.	_____	_____
f. Limit my son(s)'s time at a computer.	_____	_____
g. Mothers only: spend more time at a computer myself when she can see me doing it.	_____	
h. I won't do anything differently.	_____	_____

FOR NON-HOME COMPUTER OWNERS:

	MOTHER	FATHER
a. Buy a home computer.	_____	_____
b. Learn how to use a computer myself.	_____	_____
c. Encourage my daughter(s) to use a computer more.	_____	_____
d. Talk more with her about computer-related careers.	_____	_____
e. Enroll her in an after-school or summer computer workshop or camp.	_____	_____
f. I won't do anything differently.	_____	_____

B Resources

Menu

	GOTO PAGE
Computer Equity	239
1. Computer Equity Bibliography	239
2. Computer Equity Audios and Visuals	244
3. Computer Equity Experts and Programs	245
4. Women and Computing Associations	247
Computer Education	248
1. Books on Computers in Education	248
2. Computer Magazines	248
3. Computer Education Associations, Organizations, and Conferences	249
Sex Equity	251
1. Books on Sex Equity	251
2. Sex Equity Associations, Organizations, and Conferences	251
Other Resources	253
1. Technology Careers Resources	253
2. Teacher Training Sources	254

See also the resources at the end of Chapters 1 through 7.

COMPUTER EQUITY

1. Computer Equity Bibliography

SPECIAL ISSUES ON COMPUTER EQUITY: *Equal Play*, Spring/Fall 1983; *The Computing Teacher*, April 1984; and *Sex Roles: A Journal of Research*, August 1985.

Adams, R. and Zimmerman, J. "Women in Computing," *Interface*, December 1983, pp. 78–88.

Anderson, Ronald E., Welch, Wayne W., and Harris, Linda J. "Computer Inequities in Opportunities for Computer Literacy," National Science Foundation, Washington, D.C., Project Report, September 1983.

Bakke, Thomas et al. "Ideas for Equitable Computer Learning," American Institutes for Research, Palo Alto, Calif., 1985.

Bakon, C., Nielsen, A., and McKenzie, J. "Computer Fear," *Educational Leadership*, September 1983, p. 27.

Becker, Henry Jay. "School Uses of Microcomputers: Reports from a National Survey." April 1983–November 1984, Nos. 1–6, Center for Social Organization of Schools, Johns Hopkins University, Baltimore.

———. "Men and Women As Computer-Using Teachers," *Sex Roles*, August 1985, pp. 137–48.

Beyers, Charlotte. "Bridging the Gender Gap," *Family Computing*, August 1984, pp. 38–41.

Boss, J. A. "Sexism Among the Micros," *The Computing Teacher*, January 1982, pp. 55–57.

Brady, Holly, and Slesnick, Twila. "Girls Don't Like Fluffware Either," *Classroom Computer Learning*, April/May 1985, pp. 22–28.

Bumgarner, M. A. "Software for Girls: More than Sugar and Spice," *Family Computing*, August 1984, pp. 42–46.

Callan, Mary Ann. "An Equality in Computer Aptitude: New Test Indicates that Women Do as Well as Men," *Los Angeles Times*, January 6, 1985.

Campbell, Patricia. "Computers and Children: Eliminating Discrimination Before It Takes Hold," *Equal Play*, Women's Action Alliance, New York City, Spring/Fall 1983 (computer equity issue), pp. 4–7.

Campbell, Patricia and Russell, Susan Jo. "Microcomputers and Women's Educational Equity," *Hands On!*, Technical Education Research Centers, Cambridge, Mass., Spring 1984, pp. 16–17.

Caplan, Paula. "Do Sex Differences in Spatial Abilities Exist?" *Equal Play*, Women's Action Alliance, New York City, Spring/Fall 1983 (computer equity issue), pp. 15–16.

Chen, M. "Sex Differences in Computer Use: The Relationship Between Computer Experiences and Attitudes," research prospectus, Department of Communications, Stanford University, Palo Alto, Calif. March 1984.

Cherry, Susan Spaeth. " 'Friendly' Approach Pushes Girls On Line," *Chicago Tribune*, May 5, 1985.

Clarke, Valerie A. "Computing in a Social Context," *Proceedings of the 4th World Conference on Computers in Education*, Vol. 2, 1985, pp. 833–38.

Collis, Betty. "Sex Differences in Secondary School Students' Attitudes Toward Computers," *The Computing Teacher*, April 1985, pp. 33–6.

——————. "Psychological Implications of Sex Differences in Attitudes Toward Computers: Results of a Survey," *International Journal of Women's Studies*, Vol. 8, No. 3, May/June 1985, pp. 207–13.

"Computer Education: Terminal Inequity?" *Graduate Woman*, American Association of University Women, April 1985, pp. 1 ff.

"Computer Learning: 'Boy' Software, 'Girl' Software," *Curriculum Product Review*, March 1984, p. 8.

Edwards, Carol. "Achieving Equity," *The Computing Teacher*, April 1984, pp. 62–63.

Emery, C. Eugene. "Study Finds Women Have Innate Ability at Computer," *Boston Globe*, June 9, 1985.

Erickson, Kenneth. *Off and Running*, Computer EQUALS, Berkeley, Calif., 1986.

Fetler, Mark. "Sex Differences on the California Statewide Assessment of Computer Literacy," *Sex Roles*, August 1985, pp. 181–92.

Fisher, Glenn. "Access to Computers," *The Computing Teacher*, April 1984, pp. 24–7.

——————. *Sex Equity in Computer Education: A Bibliography*. Educational Product Information Exchange Institute (EPIE), July 1984.

——————. "The Social Effects of Computers in Education," *Electronic Learning*, March 1984, pp. 26–28.

Frank, Shirley. "Are Girls Better at Computer Details, Too?" *Equal Play*, Women's Action Alliance, New York City, Spring/Fall 1983 (computer equity issue), pp. 11–14.

Gilliland, Kay. "EQUALS in Computer Technology," *The Computing Teacher*, April 1984, pp. 42–44.

Golden, Gayle. "Texas Women Learn to Hone High-Tech Talent," *Dallas Morning News*, April 22, 1985.

Gray, Lovett S. "Schools that Overcome Girls' Computer Shyness," *The New York Times*, November 12, 1984.

Gutek, Barbara and Bikson, Tora. "Differential Experiences of Men and Women in Computerized Offices," *Sex Roles*, August 1985, pp. 123–36.

Halcrow, A. "The First Lady of Computing," *Interface Age*, December 1983, p. 86.

Hall, Paula Quick. "Inventing Solutions: Getting Girls into Science and Engineering," *Equal Play*, Women's Action Alliance, New York City, Fall 1984 (career education issue), pp. 13–14.

Hawkins, Jan. "Computers and Girls: Rethinking the Issues," *Sex Roles*, August 1985, pp. 165–80.

Hawkins, Jan, Scheingold, K., Gearhart, M., and Berger, C. "Microcomputers in Schools: Impact on the Social Life of Elementary Classrooms," *Journal of Applied Developmental Psychology*, 3, 1982, pp. 361–73.

Hess, Robert and Miura, Irene. "Gender Differences in Computer Camps and Classes," *Sex Roles*, August 1985, pp. 193–204.

"High School Girls Shown Superior at Computer Programming," *Education Daily*, June 3, 1985.

Jaye, E. "She Built Her Own Computer," *Digit*, August–September 1984, pp. 28–29.

Kerr, Cathy Davidson. "The Computer Room at Some Schools Is in Danger of Being a Boys' Domain," *Philadelphia Inquirer*, June 16, 1985.

Kiesler, Sara, Sproul, Lee, and Eccles, Jacquelynne E. "Second Class Citizens?" *Psychology Today*, March 1983, pp. 40–48.

Knapp, L. R. "Women and Computers," *San Francisco Focus*, October 1983, pp. 8–15.

Kolata, Gina. "Equal Time for Women," *Discover*, January 1984, pp. 24–27.

Kotlowitz, Alex. "The Computer-Generated Gap," *Wall Street Journal*, September 16, 1985, p. 48C.

Kreinberg, Nancy, and Stage, Elizabeth K. "EQUALS in Computer Technology," in *The Technological Woman: Interfacing with Technology*, New York: Praeger, 1982, pp. 251–59.

Linn, Marcia. "Fostering Equitable Consequences from Computer Learning Environments," *Sex Roles*, August 1985, pp. 229–40.

Lockheed, Marlaine. "Determinants of Microcomputer Literacy in High School Students," *Educational Computing Research*, Vol. 1, No. 1, 1985, pp. 81–96.

──────. "Determinants of Student Computer Use: An Analysis of Data from the 1984 National Assessment of Educational Progress," Educational Testing Service, Princeton, N.J., November 1985.

──────. "Women, Girls, and Computers: A First Look at the Evidence," *Sex Roles*. August 1985, pp. 115–23.

Lockheed, Marlaine, Nielsen, Antonia, and Stone, Meredith. "Sex Differences in Microcomputer Literacy," paper presented at the National Educational Computer Conference, Baltimore, Md., June 1983.

Lockheed, Marlaine, and Frakt, Steven. "Sex Equity: Increasing Girls' Use of Computers," *The Computing Teacher*, April 1984, pp. 16–18.

McClain, Ellen Jaffe. "Do Girls Resist Computers?" *Popular Computing*, January 1983, pp. 66–78.

McKenzie, Jamieson. "The Computer Gender Gap: A Princeton Up-Date (1985)," unpublished paper, Princeton Public Schools, N.J.

Mandinach, Ellen, and Corno, Lyn. "Cognitive Engagement Variations Among Students of Different Ability Level and Sex in a Computer Problem Solving Game," *Sex Roles*, August 1985, pp. 241–52.

Marrapodi, Maryann. "Females and Computers? Absolutely!" *The Computing Teacher*, April 1984, pp. 57–58.

Martin-McCormick et al. "Programming Equity into Computer Education: Today's Guide to Schools of the Future," Project on Equal Education Rights, Washington, D.C., 1985.

Microcomputer Usage in Schools, 1983–1984. Denver: Quality Education Data, 1984.

Miura, Irene T. and Hess, Robert T. "Sex Differences in Computer Access, Interest, and Usage," paper presented at the American Psychological Association, Anaheim, Calif., August 1983.

───────. "Enrollment Differences in Computer Camps and Summer Classes," *The Computing Teacher*, April 1984, pp. 28–30.

Parker, Janet, and Widmer, Constance. "Some Disturbing Data: Sex Differences in Computer Use," paper presented at the National Educational Computing Conference, 1984.

Podemski, R. S., Husk, S., and Jones, A. B. "Micros and the Disadvantaged," *Electronic Learning*, March 1983, pp. 20–22.

Revelle, G. et al. "Sex Differences in the Use of Computers," paper presented at the American Educational Research Association, New Orleans, April 1984.

Rix, Henri. "Girls and the New Technology Don't Compute," *Kansas City Star*, March 3, 1985.

Rose, Ray. "Equity Issues in the Use of Computers in School," New England Center for Equity Assistance, Andover, Mass., 1982.

───────. "Identifying Equitable Software," *The Computing Teacher*, April 1984, p. 51.

Sanders, Jo Shuchat. "The Computer Equity Training Project," *Equal Play*, Women's Action Alliance, New York City, Spring/Fall 1983 (computer equity issue), p. 17.

───────. "The Computer Gender Gap: Close It While There's Time," paper presented to the New York State Association for Educational Data Systems, Lake Kiamesha, N.Y., November 1985.

───────. "The Computer: Male, Female, or Androgynous?" *The Computing Teacher*, April 1984, pp. 31–34.

───────. "Here's How You Can Help Girls Take Greater Advantage of School Computers," *American School Board Journal*, April 1985, pp. 37–38.

───────. "Making the Computer Neuter," *The Computing Teacher*, April 1985, pp. 23–27.

───────. "Making Computers More Attractive to Girls," paper presented at the National Council of Teachers of Mathematics, San Antonio, April 1985.

───────. "Reflections from the Computer Equity Training Project," paper presented to the American Educational Research Association, Chicago, April 1985.

───────. "Update on the Computer Equity Training Project," *Equal Play*, Women's Action Alliance, New York City, Fall 1984 (career education issue), p. 24.

Sanders, Jo Shuchat and Stone, Antonia. *The Neuter Computer: Computers for Girls and Boys*. New York: Neal-Schuman Publishers, 1986.

Scheingold, Karen. "Issues Related to the Implementation of Computer Technology in Schools: A Cross-Sectional Study," paper presented at the National Institute of Education Conference on Issues Related to the Implementation of Computer Technology in Schools, Washington, D.C., February 1981.

Schubert, Jane G. and Bakke, Thomas. "Practical Solutions to Overcoming Equity in Computer Use," [sic] *The Computing Teacher*, April 1984, pp. 28–30.

Schubert, Jane G., Dubois, Phyllis, et al. "Ideas for Equitable Computer Learning," American Institutes for Research, Palo Alto, Calif., 1985.

Slesnick, Twila. "Software for Girls: A Sexist Solution?" *Proceedings of the 4th World Conference on Computers in Education*, Vol. 2, 1985, pp. 839–41.

Stage, E., Kreinberg, N., Eccles, J., and Becker, J. "Increasing Participation and Achievement of Girls and Women in Mathematics, Science, and Engineering," in S. Klein (ed.), *Handbook for Achieving Sex Equity Through Education*, Maryland: Johns Hopkins University Press, 1984, pp. 237–68.

Stasz, Cathleen, Shavelson, Richard, and Stasz, Clarice. "Teachers as Role Models: Are There Gender Differences in Microcomputer-Based Mathematics and Sciences Introduction?" *Sex Roles*, August 1985, pp. 149–64.

Steele, William. "Your Daughter and the Computer: Have Terminals Become the Boys' Turf?" *Working Mother*, February 1984, pp. 76ff.

Strausberg, Robin. "Leaving the Girls Behind," *Teaching, Learning, Computing*, February 1984, pp. 54–59.

_____. "Helping the Girls Catch Up," *Teaching, Learning, Computing*, March 1984, pp. 56–61.

Sturdivant, Patricia. "Access to Technology: The Equity Paradox," *The Computing Teacher*, April 1984, pp. 65–67.

Turkle, Sherry. *The Second Self: Computers and the Human Spirit*, New York: Simon and Schuster, 1984.

"Today's Problems, Tomorrow's Crises: A Report of the National Science Board commission on Precollege Education in Mathematics, Science, and Technology," National Science Board, National Science Foundation, Washington, D.C., October 1982.

Umrigar, Thrity. "The Gender Gap in Computers," *The Journal*, Lorain, Oh., August 4, 1985.

van Gelder, Lindsy. "Help for Technophobes," *Ms.*, January 1985, pp. 89–91.

Verheyden-Hilliard, Mary Ellen. "The Drops that Fill the Glass: Teachers and Students, One on One," *Equal Play*, Women's Action Alliance, New York City, Fall 1984 (career education issue), pp. 8–9.

Ware, Mary Catherine, and Stuck, Mary Frances. "Sex-Role Messages vis-a-vis Microcomputer Use: A Look at the Pictures," *Sex Roles*, August 1985, pp. 205–14.

Watt, Dan. "Bridging the Gender Gap," *Popular Computing*, September 1984, pp. 54–59.

Weld, Elizabeth New. "Women and Computers," *Boston Globe*, July 7, 1985.

White, Mary Alice. "Wanted: Parents Who Are not Technological Sheep," *Equal Play*, Spring/Fall 1983 (computer equity issue), pp. 7–9.

Wilder, Gita, Mackie, Diane, and Cooper, Joel. "Gender and Computers: Two Surveys of Computer-Related Attitudes," *Sex Roles*, August 1985, pp. 215–28.

Winkle, L. and Mathews, W. "Computing Equity Comes of Age," *Phi Delta Kappan*, January 1982, pp. 313–15.

Wrege, R. "High (Tech) Anxiety," *Popular Computing*, January 1982, pp. 46–52.

Zientara, M. "Five Powerful Women," *Infoworld*, May 21, 1984, pp. 57–61.

2. Computer Equity Audios and Visuals

WOMEN IN COMPUTER SCIENCE
Women in Science Videotape Series
B322 School of Dentistry
University of Michigan
Ann Arbor, MI 48109
(313) 763-3337
30 mins., color, computer graphics
3/4" U-matic, 1/2" VHS, 1/2" Beta
Rental or 10-day preview: $15
Purchase: $100
Women in computer careers, both professionals and students, discuss their work, career decisions, training, financing their education, and how they combine a professional life with family and personal time.

FUTURES UNLIMITED I:
EXPANDING YOUR HORIZONS IN MATHEMATICS AND SCIENCE
Futures Unlimited Videotape
Consortium for Educational Equity
Rutgers University
4090 Kilmer Campus
New Brunswick, NJ 08903
(201) 932-2071
29 mins., color
3/4" U-matic, 1/2" VHS
Rental: $20
Purchase: $125 prepaid; I and II together, $225
Demonstrates the connection between mathematics and careers as six women discuss their jobs, education, and training. One is a systems analyst, and another is a data processing director.

FUTURES UNLIMITED II:
EXPANDING YOUR HORIZONS IN TECHNICAL AND VOCATIONAL EDUCATION
Futures Unlimited Videotape
Consortium for Educational Equity
Rutgers University
4090 Kilmer Campus
New Brunswick, NJ 08903
(201) 932-2071
29 mins., color
3/4" U-matic, 1/2" VHS
Rental: $20
Purchase: $125 prepaid; I and II together, $225
Profiles five women working in high-paying trades and technologies who talk about their training, personal lives, and career goals.

FUTURES: FROM HIGH SCHOOL
TO HIGH TECH
Futures Unlimited Videotape
Consortium for Educational Equity
Rutgers University
4090 Kilmer Campus
New Brunswick, NJ 08903
(201) 932-2071

15 mins., color
3/4" U-matic
Accompanying booklet
Loan only

Creates an awareness of equity issues for teachers and counselors, and emphasizes the very different preparation needed by today's students to succeed in the high-tech world. On loan from the Consortium only to Consortium members; annual membership fee required.

THE COMPUTER WORLD—OPEN TO YOU
Technical Education Research Centers
1696 Massachusetts Ave.
Cambridge, MA 02138
(617) 547-0430

10 mins., color
Slide-tape

This slide-tape is part of a software package of games and tools prepared for fourth through seventh graders; the package emphasizes girls. Contact June Foster at TERC for access information.

TO GET HER ON LINE
Project S.E.E. (Sex Equity in Education)
Department of Education
721 Capitol Mall
Sacramento, CA 95814
(916) 322-7388

This free poster shows K–12 multi-ethnic children, especially girls, at the computer. Do you get the pun in the title?

WOMEN COMPUTE
Australian Computer Society
G.P.O. Box 2423
Adelaide 5001, Australia

Australia is a hotbed of computer equity activity. This poster emphasizes computer and other technological careers for women, and it's available at low or no cost. Write for information.

3. Computer Equity Experts and Programs

PATRICIA CAMPBELL
Campbell-Kibler Associates
Groton Ridge Heights
Groton, MA 01350
(617) 448-5402

Dr. Campbell has been combining her interests in computers and educational equity for twenty years in work that ranges from introducing computers to Head Start children to researching women's entry into engineering careers. She can help with training and developing programs, media products, and educational software.

CAROL EDWARDS
Southern Coalition for Educational

Equity, Inc.
75 Marietta St., N.W., Suite 308
Atlanta, GA 30303
(404) 522-5566

Carol Edwards is Director of Project MiCRO, a multi-state program that teaches computer literacy and analytical thinking skills to minority and economically disadvantaged girls and boys. They involve teachers, principals, and parents to increase life chances for youths at risk by means of computer education.

MARIAN FISH
Department of Educational Psychology
Graduate Center, City University of New York
33 W. 42 St.
New York, NY 10036
(212) 790-4462

Dr. Fish is an educational psychologist who specializes in the evaluation of computer equity programs.

KAY GILLILAND
Computer EQUALS
Lawrence Hall of Science
University of California
Berkeley, CA 94720
(415) 642-1823

Kay Gilliland directs Computer EQUALS, a program that provides computer training for teachers with an emphasis on computer equity.

MARLAINE LOCKHEED
Educational Testing Service
Division of Educational Research and Evaluation
Princeton, NJ 08541
(609) 734-5643

Dr. Lockheed is Senior Researcher and an educational sociologist who studies the factors affecting students' use of computers, with special attention to computer equity for girls.

JO SANDERS
Sex Equity in Education Program
Women's Action Alliance
370 Lexington Ave., Rm. 603
New York, NY 10017
(212) 532-8330

Ms. Sanders, a co-author of this book, specializes in the development and evaluation of computer equity programs in schools, and staff training in computer equity.

JANE SCHUBERT
PHYLLIS DUBOIS
Center for Educational Equity
American Institutes for Research
1791 Arastradero Rd.
Box 1113
Palo Alto, CA 94302
(800) 421-8800

Dr. Schubert and Ms. DuBois are research scientists and program developers in computer equity, offering workshops and seminars that emphasize practical ways to create equitable learning environments in the classroom and in extracurricular programs.

ANTONIA STONE
Playing to Win
106 E. 85 St.
New York, NY 10028
(212) 650-0229

Ms. Stone, a co-author of this book, directs Playing to Win, which provides consulting services on

increasing the access of
underserved populations to
computers.

JOY WALLACE
32 Pleasant Terrace
Lawrence, MA 01841
(617) 794-0662

Ms. Wallace is a specialist in
computer education with emphasis
on computer equity for girls.
Experienced in program
development and staff training, she
is Director of Northeast EQUALS,
and gives "EQUALS in
Technology" workshops to
educators.

LESLIE WOLFE
JENNIFER TUCKER
Project on Equal Education Rights
(PEER)
1413 K St., N.W., 9 Fl.
Washington, DC 20005
(202) 332-7337

Dr. Wolfe directs PEER and its
National Center for Computer
Equity, which provides consulting
services and publications on
computer equity for girls. Ms.
Tucker directs the National Center
for Computer Equity.

4. Women and Computing Associations

ASSOCIATION FOR WOMEN IN
COMPUTING
407 Hillmoor Dr.
Silver Spring, MD 20901

Publishes a newsletter, holds a
national conference, and has a
speakers bureau. Sixteen local
chapters hold monthly meetings.

NATIONAL ALLIANCE OF
WOMEN IN COMMUNICATIONS
INDUSTRIES
Box 33984
Washington, DC 20033
(202) 293-1927

Holds a national conference and
produces technology equity
materials.

WOMEN IN INFORMATION
PROCESSING
Lock Box 39173
Washington, DC 20016
(202) 328-6161

Offers networking opportunities
and membership benefits.
Publishes a quarterly newsletter
"ForumNet."

WOMEN IN INSTRUCTIONAL
TECHNOLOGY
New York Institute of Technology
French Chateau, Rm. 101
Old Westbury, NY 11568
(516) 686-7700

Publishes a newsletter and holds a
national conference.

COMPUTER EDUCATION

1. Books on Computers in Education

Hunter, Beverly. *My Students Use Computers*, Reston, Va.: Reston Publishers, 1983. Provides detailed lesson plans for using computers in a variety of subject areas for grades K–8.

Levy, Steven. *Hackers*, New York: Dell Books, 1985. If Sherry Turkle's book (see below) doesn't get you to understand why some girls avoid computers, this one will. A fascinating exposure to young men who trade everything for the chance to work with computers, and where it gets them.

Lias, Edward J. *Future Mind*, New York: Little, Brown, 1982. Discusses the effect of computers on individuals and society.

Naiman, Adeline. *Microcomputers in Education: An Introduction*, Cambridge, Mass.: TERC, 1982. Still one of the best guides to school computing around. See Organizational Resources for address and other information.

Papert, Seymour. *Mindstorms: Children, Computers, and Powerful Ideas*, New York: Basic Books, 1982. The "guru" of Logo explains his learning philosophy.

Paterson, Dale, ed. *The Intelligent Schoolhouse: Readings on Computers and Learning*, Reston, Va.: Reston Publishers, 1984. A collection of the computer experiences of teachers, children, and others.

Taylor, Robert P., ed. *The Computer in the School: Tutor, Tutee, Tool*. New York: Teachers College Press, 1980. A collection of essays on computer use, presented historically.

Turkle, Sherry. *The Second Self: Computers and the Human Spirit*, New York: Simon & Schuster, 1984. An exploration of how computers affect computer users, including a fascinating section on why so few hackers are female and on male/female approaches to computers.

2. Computer Magazines

Most computer magazines regularly publish reviews of software and sometimes of hardware. *Consumer Reports* also reviews products in the computer field. Listed below are selected magazines especially about educational computing. Another good source for titles is *Classroom Computer Learning*'s Directory of Educational Computing Resources, published in August.

Classroom Computer Learning
Pitman Learning, Inc.
19 Davis Dr.
Belmont, CA 94002

$22.50 for 9 issues/year.

The Computing Teacher
ICCE
University of Oregon
1787 Agate St.
Eugene, OR 97403

$21.50 for 9 issues/year.

Electronic Learning
Scholastic, Inc.
730 Broadway
New York, NY 10003

$19 for 8 issues/year.

Teaching and Computers
Scholastic, Inc.

730 Broadway
New York, NY 10003

$19 for 8 issues/year.

T.H.E. Journal
2955 S. Daimler St.
Santa Ana, CA 92705

Free for 8 issues/year to schools.

3. Computer Education Associations, Organizations, and Conferences

A number of national associations publish newsletters or journals that focus on classroom use of computers. Several of them host national and/or regional or state conferences. If you are conveniently located, attend; if not, send for the conference proceedings.

American Federation of
Information Processing Societies
(AFIPS)
1899 Preston White Dr.
Reston, VA 22091
(703) 620-8900

Co-sponsors National Computer Conference, publishes quarterly journal Annals of the History of Computing, and responds to requests for information.

American Society for Information Science (ASIS)
1010 Sixteenth St., N.W.
Washington, DC 20036
(202) 659-3644

A membership organization that holds national conferences and publishes a journal and bulletin.

Association for Computing Machinery (ACM)
11 W. 42 St.
New York, NY 10036
(212) 869-7440

Publishes a journal, articles, monographs. Co-sponsor of

National Education Computing Conference (NECC). Has special interest group on computer users in education.

Association for Educational Data Systems (AEDS)
1201 Sixteenth St.
Washington, DC 20036
(202) 822-7845

Publishes a journal and monographs. Has state chapters. Co-sponsor of NECC.

Black Data Processing Associates (BDPA)
2783 Roberts Ave.
Philadelphia, PA 19129
(215) 843-4120

Assists minorities to achieve upward mobility in DP, with thirteen chapters, monthly meetings, and an annual convention.

Educational Computer Consortium of Ohio (ECCO)
1123 S.O.M.

Cleveland, OH 44124
(216) 461-0800

Provides technical assistance, software evaluation, and a computer equity program.

International Council for Computers in Education (ICCE)
University of Oregon
1787 Agate St.
Eugene, OR 97403
(503) 686-4408

Publishes *The Computing Teacher*. Co-sponsor of NECC.

National Logo Exchange
Box 5341
Charlottsville, VA 22905

Publishes a newsletter, holds an annual conference, and sponsors a national user group.

Minnesota Educational Computing Consortium (MECC)
3490 Lexington Ave. N.
St. Paul, MN 55112
(612) 481-3500

Produces software and offers technical assistance.

National Council for the Social Studies (NCSS)
3501 Newark St., N.W.
Washington, DC 20016
(202) 966-7840

Publishes *Social Education* and software evaluation guidelines.

National Council of Teachers of Mathematics (NCTM)
1906 Association Dr.
Reston, VA 22091
(703) 620-9840

Publishes *The Arithmetic Teacher* and *The Mathematics Teacher*, both of which feature computers. Sponsors annual national and regional conferences.

National Science Teacher Association (NSTA)
1742 Connecticut Ave.
Washington, DC 20009
(202) 328-5800

Publishes a number of journals. Holds conferences.

Technical Education Research Centers (TERC)
1696 Massachusetts Ave.
Cambridge, MA 02138
(617) 547-0430

Publishes the newsletter *Hands On!*, and provides teacher training and technical assistance.

State Computer Coordinators. Most State Departments of Education have a computer coordinator. A list is not practical since the names are subject to change, but the position remains. You can write to the Computer Education Coordinator, Department of Education in your state capital.

Computer Education Resource Centers. Many state departments of education maintain, or are affiliated with, resource centers which provide computer instruction, software, software preview opportunities, and other educational computer-related services. Your state computer coordinator will know if there is such a center in your area.

User Groups. Computer users tend to band together to exchange information, software, problems, and solutions. They are usually organized by type of computer: Apple IIe, MacIntosh, IBM-PC, etc. Look for them in the "meeting notice" section of your newspaper or ask at computer stores.

SEX EQUITY

1. Books on Sex Equity

Cauley, Constance Drake. *Time for a Change: A Woman's Guide to Nontraditional Occupations*, Garrett Park Press, 1981. Discusses barriers to women in nontraditional occupations and how to overcome them. Provides descriptions of ten good jobs, including computer service technician.

Shapiro, June, Kramer, Sylvia, and Gunerberg, Catherine. *Equal Their Chances: Children's Activities for Non-Sexist Learning*, Englewood-Cliffs, N.J.: Prentice-Hall, 1981. Provides down-to-earth, realistic, and thoroughly teacher-tested activities in many subject areas for grades K–8. Includes a marvelous chapter on math and science.

Shuchat, Jo (Sanders), Guinier, Genii, and Douglas, Aileen. *The Nuts and Bolts of NTO (NonTraditional Occupations): Helping Women Enter Nontraditional Occupations, Second Edition*, Metuchen, N.J.: Scarecrow Press, 1986. The most comprehensive book on the subject. Stresses technological occupations. (Also available through ERIC.)

Skolnick, Joan, Langbort, Carol, and Day, Lucille. *How to Encourage Girls in Math and Science*, Englewood-Cliffs, N.J.: Prentice-Hall, 1982. The best book we know on the topic. Reviews early childhood factors that lead to "math and science divided by sex," and contains excellent activities for sex-fair learning. Focus is not on computers.

2. Sex Equity Associations, Organizations, and Conferences

AMERICAN EDUCATIONAL
RESEARCH ASSOCIATION
1230 Seventeenth St.
Washington, DC 20036
(202) 223-9485

Holds national and regional conferences and has a special interest group "Research on Women in Education."

EQUALS IN COMPUTER
TECHNOLOGY
Lawrence Hall of Science
University of California
Berkeley, CA 94720
(415) 642-1823

Provides teacher training and computer equity materials.

NATIONAL COALITION FOR SEX
EQUITY IN EDUCATION
Box 766
Madison, WI 53703

This is the foremost organization in sex equity in education. Publishes a newsletter and holds a national conference.

NATIONAL WOMEN'S STUDIES
ASSOCIATION
University of Maryland
College Park, MD 20742
(301) 454-3757

Publishes a newsletter and holds a national conference.

PROJECT ON EQUAL EDUCATION
RIGHTS (PEER)

1413 K St., N.W., 9 Fl.
Washington, DC 20005
(202) 332-7337

Computer equity projects and materials, other educational equity activities.

WOMEN'S ACTION ALLIANCE
Sex Equity in Education Program
370 Lexington Ave., Rm. 603
New York, NY 10017
(212) 532-8330

Provides staff development, technical assistance, and materials development for sex equity in education, including computer equity.

3. Sex Desegregation Assistance Centers.
The ten regional federally funded centers provide technical assistance and teacher training in sex equity in education at no cost to schools. Call or write for information to the center nearest you.

REGION I: MAINE, NEW
HAMPSHIRE, VERMONT,
MASSACHUSETTS,
CONNECTICUT, AND RHODE
ISLAND
Mr. John M. Giordano
Equity House, Inc.
New England Equal Education
Center
630 Oakwood Ave., Suite 226
West Hartford, CT 06110
(203) 522-7166

REGION II: NEW YORK, NEW
JERSEY, PUERTO RICO, AND
VIRGIN ISLANDS
Ms. Rebecca Lubetkin
Consortium for Educational Equity
Rutgers University, Kilmer Campus
New Brunswick, NJ 08903
(201) 932-2071

REGION III: PENNSYLVANIA,
DELAWARE, VIRGINIA, WEST
VIRGINIA, MARYLAND, AND
DISTRICT OF COLUMBIA
Dr. Joyce Kaser
Mid-Atlantic Center for Sex Equity
5010 Wisconsin Ave., N.W., Suite 310
Washington, DC 20016
(202) 885-8517

REGION IV: KENTUCKY,
TENNESSEE, NORTH CAROLINA,
SOUTH CAROLINA, GEORGIA,
ALABAMA, MISSISSIPPI, AND
FLORIDA

Dr. Gordon Foster
University of Miami
School of Education and Allied
Professions
Box 240065
Coral Gables, FL 33124
(305) 284-3213

REGION V: MINNESOTA,
WISCONSIN, MICHIGAN,
ILLINOIS, INDIANA, AND OHIO
Dr. Charles D. Moody, Sr.
University of Michigan
1046 School of Education Building
Ann Arbor, MI 48109
(313) 763-9910

REGION VI: NEW MEXICO,
OKLAHOMA, ARKANSAS,
TEXAS, AND LOUISIANA
Dr. Bennat C. Mullen
Stephen F. Austin State University
Box 6078
Nacogdoches, TX 75962
(409) 569-5307

REGION VII: NEBRASKA, IOWA,
KANSAS, MISSOURI
Mr. C. L. Hutchins
Mid-Continent Regional
Educational Laboratory
4709 Belleview
Kansas City, MO 64112
(816) 756-2401

REGION VIII: MONTANA, NORTH
DAKOTA, SOUTH DAKOTA,
WYOMING, UTAH, AND
COLORADO
Dr. Percy A. Morehouse, Jr.
Weber State College
Mountain West Sex Desegregation
Assistance Center
7350 Harrison Blvd.
Ogden, UT 84408
(801) 626-6650

REGION IX: CALIFORNIA,
NEVADA, AND ARIZONA
Dr. Jane Schubert
American Institutes for Research
Center for Educational Equity
Box 1113
1791 Arastradero Rd.
Palo Alto, CA 94302
(415) 493-3550

REGIONS X, XI AND XII:
WASHINGTON, OREGON, IDAHO,
ALASKA, HAWAII, GUAM,
AMERICAN SAMOA, TRUST
TERRITORIES, AND CANAL ZONE
Dr. Ethel Simon-McWilliams
Northwest Regional Educational
Laboratory
300 S.W. Sixth Ave.
Portland, OR 97204
(503) 295-0211

OTHER RESOURCES

1. Technology Careers Resources

"Careers in Science"
Association for Women in Science
1346 Connecticut Ave., N.W., Suite 1122
Washington, DC 20036
(202) 833-1998

This is an excellent bibliography of

resources for science careers, including computer science and engineering/technology. Also provides a list of women's groups offering career assistance.

"Dewar's Career Profile: Computer Professionals"
Schenley Imports Company
888 Seventh Ave.
New York, NY 10019
(212) 621-8000

With many quotes, describes a survey of computer professionals on aspirations and expectations, job environments and conditions, and more.

General Electric publications
General Electric Company
Educational Communications Programs
Fairfield, CT 06431

Publications include "What's It Like to Work with Computers?" "What's It Like to be an Engineer?" "What's It Like to be a Technician?" and "Take It from Us: You Can Be an Engineer." The latter booklet focuses exclusively on minority groups, and the first three show a mixture of men and women, whites and minority people.

"Minorities in Engineering"
National Action Council for Minorities in Engineering
3 W. 35 St.
New York, NY 10001
(212) 279-2626

Pamphlet describes engineering and related technical jobs, and opportunities for minority students.

The Computer Careers Handbook
By Connie Winkler
Arco Publishing Co.
200 Old Tappan Rd.
Old Tappan, NJ 07675
(201) 767-5000

Describes where the jobs and money are, where to get education and training. Includes job projections and a good chapter on opportunities for women and minorities.

"Women on the Job: Careers in the Electronic Media"
American Women in Radio and Television
Available from: The Women's Bureau
U.S. Department of Labor
200 Constitution Ave., N.W.
Washington, DC 20210

Describes job opportunities in the electronic media, including engineering and production.

2. Teacher Training Sources

COMPUTER PLACE
Boston Science Museum
Science Park
Boston, MA 02114

Offers free courses for teachers in educational computing, including programming languages. If you're not in the Boston area, call your nearest science museum to find out if it offers similar services.

EQUALS IN COMPUTER
TECHNOLOGY
Lawrence Hall of Science
University of California
Berkeley, CA 94720
(415) 642-1823

Offers a thirty-hour teacher training course in computer education with a focus on equitable computer opportunities for girls and minority students.

PLAYING TO WIN
106 E. 85 St.
New York, NY 10028
(212) 650-0229

A non-profit organization dedicated to promoting equity of computer access and education, PTW provides on-site workshops in computer applications with an equity emphasis.

TECHNICAL EDUCATION
RESEARCH CENTERS
1696 Massachusetts Ave.
Cambridge, MA 01238
(617) 547-0430

Offers workshops on-site or at TERC for schools or school districts. Also offers workshops on computer education for special needs students and on microcomputer-integrated science explorations.

WOMEN'S ACTION ALLIANCE
Sex Equity in Education Program
370 Lexington Ave., Rm. 603
New York, NY 10017
(212) 532-8330

On-site training for educators in sex equity in education, especially computer equity and nontraditional occupations.

WOMEN'S COMPUTER LITERACY
PROJECT
1195 Valencia St.
San Francisco, CA 94110
(415) 821-9276

Offers computer training designed for women in a "woman-centered environment," with courses given in locations across the United States.

C About the Computer Equity Training Project

	GOTO PAGE
Menu₊	
Introduction	257
Background and Goal	257
Advisory Committee	257
Literature Review	258
Pilot Test	258
Development of *The Neuter Computer*	262
Field Test	262
Public Education Component	266

INTRODUCTION

In October 1983, Women's Action Alliance was awarded a grant from the Women's Educational Equity Act Program, U.S. Department of Education, to conduct the Computer Equity Training Project. The grant number was G008302954, and the amount of the award was a total of $305,148 for the two-year project. Jo Shuchat Sanders was the Project Director and Antonia Stone the Computer Specialist. Denise Copper, Linda Lindsay, and Nikki Persley consecutively were the Administrative Assistant.

BACKGROUND AND GOAL

Even though far less was known about the computer gender gap in 1983 than now, evidence for its existence was beginning to surface. Sylvia Kramer, the Executive Director of the Alliance, saw that the gender gap tended to arise first at the junior high/middle school level. Realizing that girls would be handicapped educationally and occupationally if they avoided the computer in school, she decided to target the project at seventh and eighth grade girls. She also realized that computer equity became an issue when girls had a choice about whether or not to get involved with computers. So she decided to focus on optional computer use: before, during, and after school, and computer elective courses.

The goal of the project was to develop and test strategies to assist educators in closing the computer gender gap. To do this, we conducted a literature review, carried out a developmental pilot test, drafted and then field-tested *The Neuter Computer*, revised and found a publisher for the book, and engaged in a variety of public education activities about computer equity.

ADVISORY COMMITTEE

An Advisory Committee met formally twice during the project. Individual members provided help and assistance many more times than that. They were: *Beryl Banfield*, Director for Women's Equity, Metropolitan Center for Educational Research, Development, and Training, New York University, New York City; *Bonnie Brownstein*, President, Institute for Schools of the Future, City College School of Education, City University of New York, New York City; *Pat Camp-*

bell, Director, Campbell-Kibler Associates, Groton, Massachusetts; *Walteen Grady*, Sex Equity Coordinator, New York City Public Schools, New York City; *Mario Guzman*, Program Officer, New York Community Trust, New York City; *Herb Kohl*, Director, Coastal Ridge Research and Educational Center, Point Arena, California; *Ann Lewin*, Executive Director, National Learning Center, Washington, D.C.; *Marlaine Lockheed*, Director of Educational Research and Evaluation, Educational Testing Service, Princeton, New Jersey; *Becky Lubetkin*, Executive Director, Consortium for Educational Equity, Rutgers University, New Brunswick, New Jersey; *Carole Morning*, Vice President, National Action Council for Minorities in Engineering, New York City; *Adeline Naiman*, Director of Software, HRM Software, Cambridge, Massachusetts; *Linda Roberts*, Senior Policy Analyst, Office of Technology Assessment, Congress of the United States, Washington D.C.; *Guy Watson*, Director, Learning Materials Laboratory, College of Education, University of New Mexico, Albuquerque; and *Mary Alice White*, Director, Electronic Learning Laboratory, Teachers College, Columbia University, New York City.

LITERATURE REVIEW

In the fall of 1983 we reviewed the available literature for information on the evidence for a computer gender gap in all spheres—school, home, camp, the workforce, and the media. We also looked for documentation on the causes of the gap.

We found a fair amount of hard evidence and issued a Research Summary in November 1983. But, we found little information about what causes the computer gender gap. Augmenting our research by contacts with educators in a position to observe the situation firsthand, we compiled a list of suspected or alleged factors responsible for the imbalance between girls' and boys' computer use, and published it in an article in *The Computing Teacher*, in April 1984.

PILOT TEST

In the fall of 1983 we selected three schools to serve as developmental pilot test schools during the spring term of 1984.

Site Selection

We contacted sex equity specialists and computer coordinators across the country and asked them to recommend junior high or middle schools that met the following criteria:

1. The schools have sufficient number of computers relative to its student body with at least 64K of memory.
2. Students have voluntary access to computers before, during, and/or after school.
3. Relevant school staff has observed that there is a sex discrepancy in optional computer use, with boys outnumbering girls significantly.
4. School is willing to carry out the pilot test responsibilities: meet twice with project staff, devise and implement computer equity strategies, administer pre- and post-tests to students and faculty, and maintain computer use records.

We also considered balance in terms of location in the United States, ethnic/racial composition of the student body, and population density. Based on all these considerations and after discussion with the principals, we chose the following schools to participate in the pilot test:

Franklin Junior High School, Whitewater, Wisconsin. This is a small university town with a primarily white population.

Mount Hebron Middle School, Upper Montclair, New Jersey. This is a New York metropolitan suburban town. The student population is 52 percent minority, most of whom are black.

Waldport Junior High School, Waldport, Oregon. This is a fishing and logging village on the coast with a primarily white population.

Computer Equity Strategies

A committee of five to fifteen educators and a couple of parents at each school met with project staff in January 1984, the day after we gave an in-service session to the entire faculty on computer equity. In response to the list of alleged causes of the computer gender gap, the committees developed the computer equity strategies described below.

Project staff telephoned a liaison person at each school every

260 THE NEUTER COMPUTER

two weeks for a progress report, and visited each school one final time at the end of the term for feedback and recommendations for the book we would soon write.

Franklin Junior High School. The committee chose six strategies, only one of which they did not actually carry out.

- *Girls' computer lunch:* reserve computers one day per week for girls only.
- *Parent workshop series:* six workshops on computers and computer equity.
- *Physical arrangement of hardware:* alter the arrangement of the computer furniture to promote sociability of use.
- *Bulletin board:* on computer developments, with an emphasis on women.
- *Computer week:* speakers, demonstrations, etc. (This did not take place.)
- *Software acquisition:* to make computer use more pervasive in the curriculum.

Mount Hebron Middle School. Due to unavoidable delays, Mt. Hebron did not actually start its computer equity project until March. As a result, they were not able to carry out their more ambitious strategies during the term.

- *Girls' day:* reserve one day per week for girls only.
- *Computer career day:* occupational representatives, demonstrations, etc. (This did not take place.)
- *Girls' leadership:* invite the most popular girls in the seventh and eighth grades to participate in the project.
- *Parent involvement:* Saturday morning workshop with well-known keynote speaker, equity presentation, student demonstrations of computers, questions and answers. (This did not take place.)
- *Community awareness:* local media coverage of project. (Partial implementation occurred.)

Waldport Junior High School. The committee chose five strategies to follow, totally different from the other two schools.

- *Intramural license:* reserve one period per week for girls only to earn computer competency licenses.

- *Computer graphics:* train art teacher to use Koala Pad in art class.
- *Staff training:* in-service session on computer equity and computers.
- *Logo:* switch from BASIC to Logo in the introductory computer course.
- *Parent information:* inform parents about computer equity via newsletter; have a computer equity table at parent/teacher meeting night.

Results

Although recordkeeping techniques varied from school to school, girls' voluntary computer use increased at all three pilot test schools.

Franklin Junior High School. Optional computer use was recorded by date and sex of student. Computer teachers were a white man and two white women. The month before the pilot test, girls logged in 221 times; during the final month they logged in 313 times—an increase of 42 percent. A computer elective was offered to students during the pilot test, and it proved to be the most popular elective option for girls and boys alike.

Boys' computer use increased even more than girls': from 492 times per month before the pilot test to 828 times at the end—a 68 percent increase. The project was apparently responsible.

The year after the pilot test, Franklin Junior High School decided not to carry out any computer equity strategies. Girls' enrollment in the computer elective dropped from half the class at the end of the pilot test to a third of it a year later. This is the same ratio that had existed before the pilot test began.

Mount Hebron Middle School. The computer teacher noted the students who came regularly to use the computers in their free time. Before the pilot test, two girls and ten boys were regular computer users, while at the end there were fifteen girls and ten boys. According to the teacher, a black woman, the computer attracted both white and black female students.

Waldport Junior High School. The computer teacher, a white man, also counted regular computer users. The figures increased from two girls and twenty boys to nine girls and twenty boys. The pre- and post-tests from the Wisconsin and Oregon schools were analyzed by Dr. Marlaine Lockheed of the Educational Testing Service in Princeton, New Jersey. (A post-test administration problem at the New Jersey school made their data unusable.) She found that while all students increased in computer competence over the course of the term, girls' competence levels increased more than boys'. Gains were larger at the Oregon school, perhaps because these girls' initial computer measures were much lower than those of the Wisconsin girls. She found significant pre-/post-results for teachers only in Oregon, where they reported greater computer use and knowledge of their school's computer resources at the end of the pilot-test period.

Finally, each school administered its own questionnaire to girls at the end of the term on the effectiveness of the strategies it had implemented. At Franklin Junior High School, girls cited "seeing my friends use computers" as the most influential factor (51 percent) in increasing their own computer use, with the girls' computer lunch coming in second (30 percent). Mount Hebron Middle School and Waldport Junior High School had similar results, with 56 percent and 65 percent of the girls in these schools respectively saying they are more likely to use computer if "girls you like use them."

The end-term questionnaires indicate that it is not so much the presence of boys as the absence of girls' friends—likely at this age to be other girls—that discourages girls from using computers.

DEVELOPMENT OF *THE NEUTER COMPUTER*

The next six months were spent drafting *The Neuter Computer* based on the pilot test experience as well as additional information-gathering from the literature and knowledgeable people across the country. We also selected field test sites during this time.

FIELD TEST

Using similar criteria, we chose five schools for the field test in the spring term of 1985.

Site Selection

Three schools were designated experimental sites. At each of the three, project staff met with the computer equity faculty committee at the beginning of the term as they selected and planned their strategies from *The Neuter Computer*. We called them every two weeks for progress reports and visited again at the end of the term for feedback and book revision recommendations.

To isolate the effect of participating in a major national project, one school was designated an attention control site. The Project Director gave a one-hour in-service session on computer equity to the entire faculty, and project staff called every two weeks for progress reports. But the faculty did not receive a copy of *The Neuter Computer* to work with. The fifth school served as the pure control site, with no intervention of any kind.

All five schools kept standardized daily records on students' optional computer use. All five administered pre- and post-tests to seventh and eighth grade students and to the faculty. We selected three experimental schools: *Alfred Nobel Junior High School*, Northridge, California. Located in the city of Los Angeles, this is a basic-skills magnet school with a 45 percent minority student body, most of whom are black and some Hispanic. The primary computer teacher was a white woman. *Gering Junior High School*, Gering, Nebraska. The school is in a very small town in an agricultural area, with 15 percent minority students (most Hispanic, some black and Native American). Many of the white students are of German descent. The computer teacher was a white male. *Camel's Hump Middle School*, Richmond, Vermont. Richmond is a small town in northern Vermont with a primarily white population. The computer teacher was a white male.

The attention control school chosen was: *Cumberland Middle School*, Cumberland, Rhode Island. This is a medium-sized town with 25 percent minority students, most of whom are Portuguese. And the control school chosen was: *Lamar at Trenton Middle School*, McAllen, Texas. This small city is on the Mexican border, and has 95 percent Mexican-American students.

Computer Equity Strategies

The three experimental schools chose to implement a number of strategies over the course of the term. The Nobel Junior High School implemented

- *Computer graphics:* offer a five-week afternoon minicourse with special recruitment of girls.
- *Word processing:* teach word processing to Language Arts teachers, who will then teach students, with special recruitment of girls. (By the end of the term, only the first half of this strategy had taken

place, although a teacher did use some Language Arts software with students.)
- *Logo minicourse:* offer an afternoon minicourse in Logo with special recruitment of girls.
- *Girls' committee:* invite popular girls with leadership ability to join a girls' computer committee; develop computer-related projects.
- *Write proposal:* submit a proposal to the State Education Department for computer equity funding. (This strategy did not take place.)

Gering Junior High School implemented

- *Computer equity awareness:* hold an in-service session for faculty, distribute computer equity materials, hold informal conversations, publicize the project in the school newsletter.
- *Girls' days and boys' days:* offer after-school computer times reserved for girls and boys separately.
- *Student computer supervisors:* recruit students, especially girls, to supervise the computer room.
- *Parent open house:* Hold an evening session for parents to inform them about computer equity and have students demonstrate computers.
- *Daytime computer access:* Allow students to go to the computer room during required reading periods, with special encouragement of girls.

The six strategies implemented by Camel's Hump Middle School were

- *Promote software use:* compile an information manual on school's software to promote more widespread use of computers.
- *In-service session on computer equity:* for entire staff, taught in part by state's sex equity coordinator.
- *Parent workshops:* four sessions on computer equity and computers.
- *Parent volunteers:* recruit parents, particularly mothers, to supervise the computer room.
- *Daytime computer access:* open computer room during intramural period to all students at first, then recruit girls particularly if low response.
- *School newspaper:* students write for the new school newspaper on a word processor.

Results

As measured by daily records, girls' computer use increased an average of 144 percent in the three experimental schools, from a total of sixty-three girls using the computer during the first month of the project to a total of 154 girls in the last month. Boys' computer use held steady on the average over the term.

The greatest gain was recorded by Nobel Junior High School, with Gering Junior High in second place. School variations appear to correspond to the number of computer equity strategies targeted directly at girls (as opposed to intermediaries such as teachers or parents) implemented at the schools.

The attention control school reported an increase of 14 percent in girls' computer use, from fourteen girls at the beginning to sixteen at the end. The pure control school actually recorded a small decrease from four to three girls. Boys' computer use increased slightly at both schools during the term.

Girls' enrollment in an elective computer course increased at Gering Junior High School during the field test term. The previous year, twenty-eight boys and twelve girls had enrolled; girls were 30 percent of the class. The field-test year, sixty-six boys and forty-eight girls enrolled; girls were 42 percent of the class.

As in the pilot test, an end-term questionnaire was administered at the three experimental schools to gauge the effect of the various strategies that had been implemented. According to girls, the most effective strategy at the California school was the graphics minicourse (30 percent), with the girls' committee a close second (28 percent). In the Nebraska school, access to the computer room during reading period was rated most highly at 59 percent, while the separate boy/girl days was second at 39 percent. In the Vermont school, parents' encouragement was cited by 21 percent of the girls as most effective in encouraging them to use computers.

The pre-/post-tests administered to students and faculty were analyzed by Drs. Marian Fish and Alan Gross, from the Department of Educational Psychology, City University of New York Graduate Center. We quote the central finding from their report:

> The most important result in the present evaluation is the evidence that with intervention girls used the computer significantly more than the boys in the experimental schools, the reverse being true in the control schools. In the control schools when students are "left on their own," boys use the computers more than girls. However, when teachers are sensitized to equity issues and specific strategies are provided

as in *The Neuter Computer*, girls show even greater usage of computers than boys. This is the first empirical evidence that direct intervention targeted at girls can increase voluntary computer usage.

The evaluators also found that both boys and girls in the experimental schools reported a greater increase in computer usage and knowledge than the control school students did: "Thus, intervention, though it was female directed, appeared to benefit the male students' perception of usage and knowledge as well."

Unlike students' computer behavior, no statistically significant differences were found between the pre-test and the post-test results of the experimental girls and boys on computer-related attitudes. The evaluators suggest that while five months may be sufficient to induce changed behavior, a longer time period may be necessary to induce changed attitudes.

Drs. Fish and Gross did not find any evidence that minority girls responded any differently to computer equity strategies than white girls did. They did find, however, that control school teachers were somewhat more computer-competent than those in the experimental schools, ruling out the possibility that the experimental school results were caused by greater computer ability on the part of their teachers.

PUBLIC EDUCATION COMPONENT

Throughout the Computer Equity Training Project, we publicized computer equity by means of articles, television and radio interviews, workshops, and speeches. Since many educators and parents are unaware of the computer gender gap, we felt it was important to bring the issue to their attention as much as possible.

Appendix B, Resources, lists the articles and papers published by the project staff. In 1984, Women's Action Alliance published a special issue on computer equity in its journal on sex equity in education, *Equal Play*. We assisted reporters from many newspapers in the United States and several national magazines to prepare articles on computer equity. We gave dozens of workshops and speeches to sex equity and computer education specialists and to classroom teachers at conferences and meetings across America, and were interviewed a number of times on national and local television and radio programs.

We also have been in contact with hundreds of educators, policy

About the Computer Equity Training Project 267

makers, researchers, and advocates in the United States and even abroad, providing information and suggestions on computer equity and learning from them in exchange.

We plan to continue our computer equity work in the future, and would greatly appreciate hearing from you with suggestions for improving this book or new ways we can get the word out that girls and computers do, indeed, go together.

Index

ADA, 103
Administrators
   and computer equity, 133, 140–42, 186
   district strategies for, 141–44
   school strategies for, 111, 133–41
   state and national strategies for, 144–45
Adult education workshops, 155
Advanced placement computer credit, 61
ADVENTURE CONSTRUCTION SET, 107
Advertisements, gender bias in, 7–8, 103–104, 105, 151–52
After-school projects, and database programs, 47
American Association of University Women, 129
American Educational Research Association, 251
American Federation of Information Processing Societies, 249
American Society for Information Science, 249
Analytical abilities, 31, 74
Animated graphics, 32, 34
Antisocial values. See Violence.
Apple, 50
Arcade games. See also Violence.
   attraction of, 16, 18
   barred from schools, 28, 75
ARCADE MACHINE, 149
Arithmetic. See Math classes.
Art classes, software for, 31, 48
Art museums, classes at, 159

Art shows, and graphics software, 33
Artificial intelligence, 62
Association for Computing Machinery, 249
Association for Educational Data Systems, 249
Association for Women in Computing, 247
Association for Women in Science, 253
Audiovisuals, 32, 74, 122
Authors, as guest speakers, 41

Banners, 32, 168
BASIC, 61, 66
   interactive computer conversations with, 63
   learned through graphics, 34, 61–62
   teachers' courses for, 67
Baud rate, 86
Bell (telephone) standards, 86
Black Data Processing Associates, 249
Boys. See also Arcade games; Gender.
   approach to computer use, 6, 16, 25–26
   monopolizing computers, 5, 15, 101
Budgets, by students with spreadsheets, 56
Bulletin boards, 102–103, 112–13

Business classes, and telecommunications, 84
Businesses, field trips to, 48–49, 157, 171–72, 174

CAI, 70
Career choice
  and gender, 8, 9–13
  and math avoidance, 17–18
Career education, and databases, 48
Career fairs, 121–23, 129
Cataloging. See Database software.
Center for Educational Equity, 246
Charts, 38, 57
  of computer use, 113, 119, 136, 163–64
Citizens' action, and computer literacy, 12
Citizens Advisory Committee on Sex Equity in Education, 129
Class notes, 40, 106–107
Classroom management programs, 49, 137, 168
Classwide learning projects, software for, 74
Clerical computer jobs. See also Student computer jobs.
  gender and salaries in, 8, 10–11
COBOL, 66, 103
College Entrance Examination Board, 61
Color monitors. See Monitors.
Color printer/plotter, 33
Commercial art studios, field trips to, 32–33
Commercial databases, 49, 81
  charges for, 83, 86, 87
  demonstrated by parents, 150
  for student reports, 83–84
Commission on the Status of Women, 129
Commodore 64 BASIC, 34
Commodore 64 Logo, 62–63, 64

Communications software, evaluation of, 87
Community. See also Fund raising.
  computer room used by, 125, 139
  role models from, 120–21, 126, 129
  special events for, 121–25, 126–27
Community bulletin boards, 84, 87–88
Community organizations, computer courses in, 158, 175
CompuServe, 49, 81, 83, 84, 87, 150
Computathon, 128, 140, 176–77
Computer access. See Hardware; Scheduling.
Computer applications. See also Graphics; Word Processing.
  preferred by girls, 5, 16, 25–26, 94–95, 110, 111, 115–16, 142
Computer art, 113, 114–15
Computer-assisted instruction, 70
Computer avoidance, 6, 9, 12, 16–18
Computer Awareness Day, 117–18
Computer camps
  directories of, 159
  enrollments in, 6
  for girls, 129–30
Computer career choices, 8, 9–13, 17–18
Computer career fairs, 121–23, 129
Computer clubs, 66, 81, 163
Computer courses, 5, 141. See also Computer applications.
  girls' and boys' approach to, 6, 16, 25–26
  segregation of, 110, 120
Computer dating, 169
Computer education resource centers, 250
Computer electives, scheduling of, 95
Computer EQUALS, 246

Computer equity. *See also* Boys; Girls; Role models.
  and administrators, 133–45
  classroom strategies for, 94–96, 100–108
  community strategies for, 120–30, 157–59
  conferences on, 126–27
  district-level strategies for, 141–45
  girls' strategies for, 162–77
  home strategies for, 170–73
  parents task force and, 153–54
  program evaluation and continuity of, 140–41, 190, 192–98
  publicity for, 143–44, 154
  schoolwide strategies for, 94–96, 108–20, 184–85
  state and national strategies for, 144–45
  teachers' strategies for, 184–90
  and women's organizations, 129
Computer Equity Evening, 123–25
Computer Equity Training Project, viii, 257–67
  field test, xiv–xv, 262–66
  pilot test, xiii–xiv, 258–62
  strategies in, 110, 112, 133, 259–61
  surveys by, 4, 109, 113, 261
Computer graphics. *See* Graphics software.
Computer hardware. *See* Hardware.
Computer lessons, 125, 138, 140, 158
Computer literacy
  and career options, 9–10
  and political consequences, 12
Computer magazines. *See also* Advertisements.
  male slant of, 6, 7, 103–104, 105, 151–52
Computer Neutrality Self-Test, 2–3
Computer Place, 254

Computer professionals, as speakers, 127, 186
Computer room. *See also* Boys; Girls; Scheduling.
  arrangement of, 102, 113–14
  opened after hours, 125, 139
  supervised by girls, 112, 137, 139, 166
Computer shows, 121, 157–58, 175
Computer stores
  assistance from, 28–29, 159
  examining products in, 157
  lending hardware, 27, 115, 122
  and publicity, 143–44, 175
Computer time. *See also* Scheduling; Sign-up sheets.
  monopolized by boys, 5, 15, 101
Computer training
  careers and, 12–13
  for teachers, 136–37, 138
Conferences, 126–27, 129, 144
Contests, 115–16
Cooperative computer use
  class notes and, 106–107
  and furniture arrangement, 113–14
  and girls' motivation, 19, 38, 71, 94, 166–67
  and simulation projects, 72, 74
  and software evaluation, 74, 77, 107–108
  writing and, 38, 167
Costs
  budgeting of, 77, 118–19, 140
  of modems, 86
  of telecommunications, 81, 83, 86, 87–88
Creative writing, and word processing, 37–38, 40, 116, 167
Credit, for computer-room supervision, 166
Cross-referencing, and databases, 46
Curriculum. *See also* Software.
  equity policy and, 142–43

Curriculum (*continued*)
  integration of computers in, 31, 48, 71, 100–101

Daisy wheel printers, 41
Database software. *See also* Commercial databases; CompuServe; The Source.
  contests and recreation with, 116, 169
  curriculum applications for, 47–48, 49, 150
  hardware for, 49–50
  for hobbies, 47, 167
  home uses for, 149, 170
  selection criteria for, 50
  terminology for, 46–47
Demographic data, in social studies, 55–56
Demonstrations
  at career fairs, 122
  by girls, 102, 111–12, 124, 154–55, 172
  at special events, 117
Disabled students
  and electronic mail, 82, 85
  and software, 34
Displays, 123, 174–75. *See also* Bulletin boards.
District computer coordinator, 137
District meetings, 141
District publications, 142
Dot matrix printers, 41, 57
DREAM HOUSE, 107
Drill and practice exercises
  programmed by students, 39, 63–64, 71
  software for, 70, 71, 77

Ecology, and simulations, 72
Educational Computer Consortium of Ohio, 249

Educational software. *See also* Software.
  gender bias in, 76, 96, 105
  and violence, 18–19
EDUCATIONAL SOFTWARE EVALUATION CONSORTIUM (ICCE), 79
Efficiency, and computers, 8–9
Electronic bulletin boards. *See* Electronic mail.
Electronic mail. *See also* Commercial databases.
  for home-bound students, 82, 85
  on home computers, 84, 149
  as interschool project, 82–83
  organized by students, 65–66, 169–70
Emotional development, and violent software, 18–19
ENIAC, 103
Enrollments. *See* Charts; Gender.
EPIE (Educational Product Information Exchange), 79
EQUALS, 4
Equals in Computer Technology, 251
Essays, and word processing, 38, 167–68
Ethics, and computer issues, 117
Evaluation services, 77
Experiments
  in computer-based labs, 70, 73–74
  on spreadsheets, 56, 57

Family computer projects, 149
Family Computing, 149
Federation of Business and Professional Women, 129
Field trips. *See also* Speakers; Special events.
  to businesses, 48–49, 157, 171–72, 174

to computer shows, 121, 157–58, 175
with parents, 157–58, 171–72
to print shops and newspapers, 32–33, 40
Formatting commands, 38, 42
FORTRAN, 66
Forms, 202–209
Free periods, computer use in, 4, 5
Fund raising
  activities, 118–19, 128, 139–40, 169
  by administrators and parents, 128, 139–40, 143, 155, 197

Game paddles, 78
Games, 149
Gender. See also Advertisements; Computer magazines.
  and approach to computer use, 15, 25–26
  of computer owners, 105–106
  in computer-related occupations, 8–13
  and frequency of computer use, 4–5, 195–96
  and mathematical ability, 6, 14, 16–18
  and software marketing, 19–20, 104
  and violence in programs, 18–19
Gender bias
  in parents, 6, 15, 148, 151
  in teachers, 15, 17, 95
Geography, and databases, 48
GEOLOGY SEARCH, 74
Geometry, and Logo, 65
GERTRUDE'S PUZZLE, 149
Girl Scouts, 129
Girls. See also Peer encouragement; Peer pressure.
  attitudinal obstacles to computers in, 94–96, 142–43

and computer applications, 16, 25–26, 142
computer equity strategies for, 162–77
demonstrating computers, 102, 124, 154–55, 172
enrollment of, in computer courses, 4–5, 130, 163–64
parental restrictions on, 148, 151
software evaluation and, 75–77
as teachers, 111–12, 125, 137, 168, 170, 175
Girls' computer committee, 110–11, 121, 162–63
Grades, calculated by computer, 55
Grammar drills, 39
Grants, 140
Graph-drawing programs, 38, 53–54, 57, 58
Graphics software
  contests with, 116
  evaluation of, 33–34
  hardware for, 33–34, 66
  and illustrated writing, 31, 39, 40, 150
  improvements in, 70
  posters with, 32, 168
  and programming languages, 34, 61–62
  and publicity, 32, 164, 166, 167
Graphics tablet, 33
Graphics utility programs, 34
Greeting cards, with computer graphics, 32, 167
Group activities. See Cooperative computer use.

Hackers, gender of, 118
Handicapped students. See Disabled students.
Hard copy. See Printers.
Hardware. See also Monitors; Printers.

274　INDEX

Hardware (continued)
　borrowed from computer stores, 27, 106, 115, 122
　borrowed from schools, 129–30, 138, 139
　for computer graphics, 33
　for database software, 49–50
　for educational software, 78
　fund raising for, 139–40
　for labs and simulations, 78
　for number programs, 57
　placement of, 102, 113–14
　for programming languages, 66–67
　purchased by parents, 106, 153
　for word processing, 41–42
Health classes, 48, 73
Hobbies, and database software, 47, 167
Holidays, and computer activities, 32
Home computers
　gender of users, 5–6, 105–106, 170
　equity strategies with, 149–50
　uses for, 47, 167, 170–71
Home responsibilities, and computer time, 15, 148, 151
Homework, 150, 166–68
　hardware access and, 106, 138–39
Hopper, Grace, 103, 168
Hospitals, field trips to, 49

Illustration, with computer graphics, 31, 39, 40, 150
Inhouse trainer, 137
In-service sessions, 133–35, 185–86
Individualized instruction, 39
Information management, and databases, 46–47
Instructional software, improvements in, 70

Instructional time, and girls teaching, 112
Integrated software, 50
Interactive computer conversations, 62–63
Interactive software. See Cooperative computer use.
International Council for Computers in Education, 250
Interschool computer clubs, 66, 163
Interschool electronic mail, 82
Interschool simulations, 84–85
Invitations, with computer graphics, 32, 167

Joysticks, 33–34, 66, 78
Junior League, 129

Keyboarding. See Typing skills
KOALA PAD, 33, 34
KRELL, 62–63, 64

Labor force, women in, 11
Labs, computer-based, 73–74, 78
League of Women Voters, 129
Legal offices, field trips to, 48–49
Letters, and word processing, 39
LEXIS, 48
Libraries, field trips to, 49
Lightpens, 33–34
Literary magazines, 40, 116
Literature, and databases, 48
Logo
　and graphics, 34, 61–62
　programmed by students, 61, 64, 65
　software for, 66, 95
　teachers' courses for, 67
Lovelace, Countess Ada Byron, 103, 168

INDEX 275

Macintosh, 34
MacPAINT, 34
Male characters, in educational software, 76, 96, 105
Male identification
 in computer media, 76, 103–104
 of math and machines, 14
Math avoidance
 and career choice, 17–18
 linked to computer avoidance, 6, 14, 16–18
Math classes
 and music software, 73
 problems for, 39, 48, 65, 71, 84
 spreadsheets in, 56–57
Measurement sensors, 78
Media coverage, of computer equity events, 127, 143
Memorization. See Drill and practice exercises.
MICROSIFT, 79
Minnesota Educational Computing Consortium, 250
Modems, 66, 81, 84, 85
 connection of, 86–87
 evaluation of, 85–86
Monitors
 for computer graphics, 33
 for database software, 49
 for educational software, 78
 for number programs, 57
 for programming, 66
 for telecommunications, 87
 for word processing, 41–42
Monochrome monitors. See Monitors.
Mouse, 33–34, 78
Movies, with computer graphics, 32, 158
Music classes, software for, 73

National Alliance of Women in Communications Industries, 8, 247
National Assessment of Educational Process in Science, 4
National Coalition for Sex Equity in Education, 252
National Council for Social Studies, 79, 250
National Council of Teachers of Mathematics, 79, 250
National Federation of Women Business Owners, 129
National Logo Exchange, 66
National Organization for Women, 129
National Science Teacher Association, 250
National Women's Studies Association, 252
The Neuter Computer, development of, viii–ix, 262
Newsletters
 to parents, 126, 136, 154, 196
 for students, 164–65
 to teachers, 136, 141, 142
Nonassertiveness, and computer access, 15
Number processing
 applications for, 55–57
 preparation requirements for, 58
 software for, 53–55

Online databases, 49, 83, 87–88
Optional computer use. See also Scheduling.
 gender of students, 4, 5, 192–93
 segregation of, 109–10
THE OTHER SIDE, 84–85

Packaging, of software for girls and women, 7, 19–20
Paddles, 66
PAINT, 34

276 INDEX

Parental encouragement, and gender, 6, 15
Parental restrictions, on girls, 15, 148, 151
Parents
  awareness of inequity and, 111, 125–26, 151–52, 172–73
  computer lessons for, 125, 139
  group strategies for, 126, 153–55
  pressuring administrators, 156
  as role models, 148, 149, 152, 166
  special events for, 123–25
  subscribing to magazines, 152, 170–71
Parties, 107, 150
Pascal, 61, 66
Peer encouragement
  and girls' computer committee, 110–11
  and group work, 94, 108, 165–66
  and segregation in scheduling, 109–10
Peer pressure, against computer use, 13–14, 16, 17, 148
PFS FILE, 50
Physical education, 73–74, 168
PINBALL CONSTRUCTION SET, 107, 149
Pilot equity programs, 144–45
Playing to Win, 158, 246, 255
Poems, 38
Posters, 32, 168
Preparation requirements
  for educational software, 78
  for numbers programs, 58
  for programming languages, 67
  for word processing, 42–43
PRESIDENT ELECT, 171
Principals. See Administrators.
PRINT SHOP, 32, 111, 164, 167
Print shops, field trips to, 32–33
Printers
  for computer graphics, 33
  for database software, 49–50
  for educational software, 78
  for number programs, 57
  for programming, 66–67
  for telecommunications, 87
  for word processing, 41
Programming
  boys interest in, 115
  gender of students and, 4, 5, 115
  learned through graphics, 61–62
  teachers' preparation for, 67
Programming languages
  applications for, 62–66
  and computer graphics, 34
  selection of, 61–62
  software for, 66
Project on Equal Education Rights (PEER), 4, 247, 252
PTA, 140, 153, 154
Public domain communications programs, 87
Public information databases, 49
Publicity campaigns, 143–44, 163–64, 173–75
Punctuation drills, 39

Questionnaires, 2–3, 135–36, 194, 212–37

Raffles, 118–19
Reading comprehension drills, 39
Reading lists, and database programs, 48
Recreational programs, and violence, 18–19
Reports, 38, 167–68
  and databases, 48, 83
Required computer courses, 5, 142
Ride, Sally, 103, 121
ROBOT ODYSSEY, 171
ROCKY'S BOOTS, 149

INDEX 277

Role models. See also Advertising; Computer magazines.
  parents as, 148, 149, 152
  peers as, 14
  women as, 105, 120–21
Rural schools, 85, 87

Salaries, and computer literacy, 8, 10–11
Scheduling. See also Computer time; Sign-up sheets; Supervisors.
  after-school time, 15, 158
  announcements, 164
  class computer-time, 71, 101, 106
  nonschool hardware, 27, 115, 122
  optional computer time, 95, 108–110
  simulations, 72
School-board meetings, 142
School message-center, 169–70
School newspapers
  announcements in, 164, 166
  software for, 40, 116
Science classes, software for, 48, 56, 57, 72
Science museums, 158
Segregation, and computer equity, 109–10, 120
Sex Desegregation Assistance Centers, 134
Sex Equity in Education Program, 246, 255
Sex-role norms, computer use and, 13–15, 17, 19–20
Sex-stereotyped characters, 76, 103–105
Sign-up sheets, 101, 108, 193–94
Silk screening, 33
Simulations, 70, 72
  interschool, 84–85
  preparation time for, 78

programmed by students, 65
software evaluation, 77, 88
Social studies
  and computer-based labs, 73–74
  computerized statistics in, 55–56
  field trips for, 48–49
  and simulations, 72, 84–85
  and UPI, 83
Software
  compatibility of, 50, 53, 58
  for classwide learning projects, 74
  for homework, 150, 171
  for modems, 87
  improvements in instructional, 70
  packaging of, 7, 19–20
  review committee, 138
  sex-stereotypes in, 7, 15, 103–105, 151
  for student writing, 37–38, 40, 116, 167
Software evaluation, 27–28, 138
  and appeal to girls, 19–20, 75–77
  of communications programs, 87
  for gender bias, 95, 104–105
  of number programs, 57–58
  by students, 72
  of programming languages, 66
  of word processing, 41–42
Software manuals, 28–29, 95
Sound synthesizers, 73
The Source, 49, 81, 83, 87, 150
Southern Coalition for Educational Equity, Inc., 245
Speakers. See also Field trips; Special events.
  at conferences, 122, 127, 144, 195
  for in-service sessions, 134–35
  honoraria for, 143
  as role models, 41, 120–22, 163
Special education, software for, 37, 74

Special events. See also Field trips; Speakers.
  career fairs, 121–23
  conferences, 117–18, 126–27
  for parents, 123–25
Spelling checkers, 42
Spelling drills, 39, 71
Spreadsheets
  chart computer use, 53–55, 116
  for physical education, 168
  in math and science classes, 56–57, 194
  selection criteria for, 57–58
State computer coordinator, 137–38, 250
State sex equity specialists, 134
Statistics, in social studies, 55–56
Stock market information, 84
Student activities, budgets for, 56
Student computer jobs, 159, 177
Student computer use, charts of, 113, 136
Student message center, 65–66
Student software evaluation, 72
Student surveys, of home computer use, 105–106
Summer computer courses, 119–20
Supervisors
  girls as, 112, 137, 139, 166, 175
  parents as, 156
  recruitment of, 139, 166

Teachers. See also Classroom management programs; Preparation requirements.
  after-school computer use by, 138
  and computer equity plans, 184–90
  effect of assumptions of, 15, 16, 100, 136
  in-service training for, 28, 136–37

  invited to computer room, 135
  and programming, 67
Technical Education Research Centers, 250, 255
Technology, fear of, 12, 136
Telecommunications, 81–82
  and online databases, 49, 83, 87–88
  and rural schools, 85, 87
Telecourses, 85
Television sets, as monitors, 41
TERRAPIN, 62–63, 64
Title IV, 134
Title IX, 134–35, 143, 186
Trainer, for teachers, 137–38
True BASIC, 34
Typing skills, 37, 71

UPI DATA NEWS, 83
U.S. Department of Labor statistics, 9–10, 11
User's goups, 143, 159, 177, 251

Valentine's Day, 169
VCRs, 78
Video games. See Arcade games.
Violence
  in arcade games, 18–19, 28, 75, 96
  negative to girls, 76
  in software, 18–19, 104–105
Vocabulary expansion, 38
Volunteers, 139, 156, 166, 175
THE VOYAGE OF THE MIMI, 74

Women. See also Advertisements; Computer magazines.
  in computer history, 103, 123, 168
  as role models, 105, 120–21